Self-Knowledge

OXFORD **PHILOSOPHICAL** CONCEPTS

OXFORD PHILOSOPHICAL CONCEPTS

Christia Mercer, Columbia University
Series Editor

PUBLISHED IN THE OXFORD PHILOSOPHICAL CONCEPTS SERIES

Efficient Causation
Edited by Tad Schmaltz

Moral Motivation
Edited by Iakovos Vasiliou

Sympathy
Edited by Eric Schliesser

Eternity
Edited by Yitzhak Melamed

The Faculties
Edited by Dominik Perler

Self-Knowledge
Edited by Ursula Renz

Memory
Edited by Dmitri Nikulin

FORTHCOMING IN THE OXFORD PHILOSOPHICAL CONCEPTS SERIES

Health
Edited by Peter Adamson

Space
Edited by Andrew Janiak

Evil
Edited by Andrew Chignell

Persons
Edited by Antonia LoLordo

Dignity
Edited by Remy Debes

Embodiment
Edited by Justin E. H. Smith

Animals
Edited by G. Fay Edwards and
Peter Adamson

Pleasure
Edited by Lisa Shapiro

OXFORD **PHILOSOPHICAL** CONCEPTS

Self-Knowledge

A HISTORY

Edited by Ursula Renz

OXFORD
UNIVERSITY PRESS

OXFORD

UNIVERSITY PRESS

Oxford University Press is a department of the University of Oxford. It furthers
the University's objective of excellence in research, scholarship, and education
by publishing worldwide. Oxford is a registered trade mark of Oxford University
Press in the UK and certain other countries.

Published in the United States of America by Oxford University Press
198 Madison Avenue, New York, NY 10016, United States of America.

Library of Congress Cataloging-in-Publication Data
Names: Renz, Ursula, editor.
Title: Self-knowledge : a history / edited by Ursula Renz.
Description: New York : Oxford University Press, 2016. |
Series: Oxford philosophical concepts
Identifiers: LCCN 2016012172 (print) | LCCN 2016034011 (ebook) |
ISBN 9780190226428 (pbk. : alk. paper) | ISBN 9780190226411 (hardcover : alk. paper) |
ISBN 9780190226435 (updf) | ISBN 9780190630553 (epub)
Subjects: LCSH: Self (Philosophy)—History. | Self-knowledge, Theory of—History.
Classification: LCC BD438.5 .S44155 2016 (print) | LCC BD438.5 (ebook) |
DDC 126—dc23
LC record available at https://lccn.loc.gov/2016012172

1 3 5 7 9 8 6 4 2
Paperback printed by WebCom, Inc., Canada
Hardback printed by Bridgeport National Bindery, Inc., United States of America

Contents

Reflection IV   Self-Portraiture

Series Editor's Foreword

Oxford Philosophical Concepts (OPC) offers an innovative approach to philosophy's past and its relation to other disciplines. As a series, it is unique in exploring the transformations of central philosophical concepts from their ancient sources to their modern use.

OPC has several goals: to make it easier for historians to contextualize key concepts in the history of philosophy, to render that history accessible to a wide audience, and to enliven contemporary discussions by displaying the rich and varied sources of philosophical concepts still in use today. The means to these goals are simple enough: eminent scholars come together to rethink a central concept in philosophy's past. The point of this rethinking is not to offer a broad overview, but to identify problems the concept was originally supposed to solve, and to investigate how approaches to them shifted over time, sometimes radically.

Recent scholarship has made evident the benefits of reexamining the standard narratives about western philosophy. OPC's editors look beyond the canon and explore their concepts over a wide philosophical landscape. Each volume traces a notion from its inception as a solution to specific problems through its historical transformations to its modern use, all the while acknowledging its historical context. Each OPC volume is *a history* of its concept in that it tells a story about changing solutions to its well-defined problem. Many editors have found it appropriate to include long-ignored writings drawn from the Islamic and Jewish traditions and the philosophical contributions of women. Volumes also explore ideas drawn from Buddhist, Chinese, Indian, and other philosophical cultures when doing so adds an especially helpful new perspective. By combining scholarly innovation with focused and astute analysis, OPC encourages a deeper understanding of our philosophical past and present.

One of the most innovative features of OPC is its recognition that philosophy bears a rich relation to art, music, literature, religion, science, and other cultural practices. The series speaks to the need for informed interdisciplinary exchanges. Its editors assume that the most difficult and profound philosophical ideas can be made comprehensible to a large audience and that materials not strictly philosophical often bear a significant relevance to philosophy. To this end, each OPC volume includes Reflections. These are short stand-alone essays written by specialists in art, music, literature, theology, science, or cultural studies that *reflect on* the concept from their own disciplinary perspectives. The goal of these essays is to enliven, enrich, and exemplify the volume's concept and reconsider the boundary between philosophical and extraphilosophical materials. OPC's Reflections display the benefits of using philosophical concepts and distinctions in areas that are not strictly philosophical, and encourage philosophers to move beyond the borders of their discipline as presently conceived.

The volumes of OPC arrive at an auspicious moment. Many philosophers are keen to invigorate the discipline. OPC aims to provoke philosophical imaginations by uncovering the brilliant twists and unforeseen turns of philosophy's past.

Christia Mercer
Gustave M. Berne Professor of Philosophy
Columbia University in the City of New York
June 2015

Acknowledgments

This book would never have seen the light of the day without the support of many people and institutions. I am particularly thankful to all the authors for their commitment during the whole process. Without their enthusiasm, inspiration, and willingness to revise their views and chapters, this volume would never have become what it now is. During my stay at Harvard, I received continual encouragement from Richard Moran, Matt Boyle, and Allison Simmons. Many thanks to Christia Mercer for both her invitation to edit this volume and her persistent advice and help in the course of materializing it. Discussions with Amelie Rorty and Robert Schnepf were, from the very beginning, a constant source of inspiration and insight. Special thanks go to Dina Emundts, who, besides sharing an interest in this topic through many discussions, co-organized the conference "The Ideal of Self-Knowledge" at the University of Konstanz, where versions of the main chapters were first discussed. Thanks to the *Deutsche Forschungsgemeinschaft*, the Alexander von Humboldt Foundation, and the University of Konstanz for the funding of this event. Finally, I would like to thank the University of Klagenfurt for providing the funds needed for the preparation of the final manuscript, and Johann Stefan Tschemernjak and Sebastian Kletzl for their help with it.

Klagenfurt/Zürich, January 2016

Contributors

MARCEL VAN ACKEREN is Visiting Professor for Philosophy in Berne (Switzerland). He has worked on ancient philosophy, especially Heraclitus, Plato, and Marcus Aurelius. He has published a two-volume monograph on Marcus Aurelius and edited Blackwell's *Companion to Marcus Aurelius*. He also works on moral demandingness and coedited *The Limits of Moral Obligation* for Routledge. He also is interested in the relation of historical and systematic perspective in philosophy and will edit *Philosophy and the Historical Perspective* (Proceedings of the British Academy) for Oxford University Press.

JOHANNES BRACHTENDORF is Professor of Philosophy in the Department of Catholic Theology (University of Tübingen), and has held several visiting appointments in the United States, Austria, and Chile. In 2002 he held of the Augustinian Endowed Chair in the Thought of Augustine at Villanova University in the United States. He is author of *Fichtes Lehre vom Sein: Eine kritische Darstellung der Wissenschaftslehren von 1794, 1798/99 und 1812* (1995), *Die Struktur des menschlichen Geistes nach Augustinus: Selbstreflexion und Erkenntis Gottes in "De Trinitate"* (2000), and *Augustins Confessiones* (2005). He has published translations of Augustine's *De libero arbitrio* (2006) and of Thomas Aquinas' *On happiness* (*Summa Theologiae* I-II q. 1–5) (2012). He is the editor of the Latin-German edition of Augustine's complete works and coeditor of the *Oxford Guide to the Historical Reception of Augustine*.

DINA EMUNDTS is Professor of Philosophy at the University of Konstanz, Germany. She is author of *Kant's Übergangskonzeption im Opus postumum* (2004) and of *Erfahren und Erkennen: Hegels Theorie der Wirklichkeit* (2012).

She edited *Self, World, Art: Metaphysical Topics in Kant and Hegel* (2013) and is the editor (together with Sally Sedgwick) of the *International Yearbook of German Idealism.*

YASMINE ESPERT is an art history doctoral candidate at Columbia University and an alumna of the Fulbright US Student program. Her research interests include the cinematic medium, the Caribbean, and diaspora. She is the Graduate Fellow for the Digital Black Atlantic Project, a working group supported by the Center for the Study of Social Difference at Columbia University.

AARON GARRETT is Associate Professor of Philosophy at Boston University. He specializes in early modern and modern moral and political philosophy. He is author of many articles on modern philosophy, *Meaning in Spinoza's Method* (2003), and *Berkeley's Three Dialogues* (2008), and editor of numerous works, including critical editions of Francis Hutcheson and John Millar, the *Routledge Companion to Eighteenth Century Philosophy, Scottish Philosophy in the Eighteenth Century* (with James Harris), and the forthcoming *Oxford Handbook of the Philosophy of the Enlightenment* (with James Schmidt).

CHARLES GUIGNON did his graduate work at Heidelberg and Berkeley and has published *Heidegger and the Problem of Knowledge* (1983), "What Is Hermeneutics?" (1999, in *Re-envisioning Psychology*), the collection *The Good Life* (1999), *On Being Authentic* (2004), together with books and essays on existentialism, Dostoevsky, Bernard Williams, Charles Taylor, and others. He is currently professor at the University of South Florida.

RACHANA KAMTEKAR is Associate Professor of Philosophy at the University of Arizona. Her specialization is in ancient Greek and Roman philosophy, especially ancient ethics, politics, and moral psychology. Most of her published articles are on Plato, but she has also published on Aristotle, the Stoics, and virtue ethics, both ancient and contemporary. She is currently writing a book entitled *Desire and the Good: An Essay on Plato's Moral Psychology.*

JOHN LIPPITT is Professor of Ethics and Philosophy of Religion at the University of Hertfordshire. His publications include *Humour and Irony in Kierkegaard's Thought* (2000); the *Routledge Philosophy Guidebook to Kierkegaard and Fear and Trembling* (2003; second edition under contract); and *Kierkegaard and the Problem of Self-Love* (2013). He is coeditor, with George Pattison, of *The Oxford*

Handbook of Kierkegaard (2013). Other interests include the virtues; the philosophy of love and friendship; the relationship between philosophy and theology; and the relevance of philosophy to psychotherapy.

DERMOT MORAN is Professor of Philosophy at University College Dublin and a member of the Royal Irish Academy. He has published widely on medieval philosophy (especially Christian Platonism) and contemporary European philosophy (especially phenomenology). His books include *Introduction to Phenomenology* (2000), *Edmund Husserl: Founder of Phenomenology* (2005), *Husserl's Crisis of the European Sciences: An Introduction* (2012), and, coauthored with Joseph Cohen, *The Husserl Dictionary* (2012). He has edited Husserl's *Logical Investigations*, 2 vols. (2001), and *The Routledge Companion to Twentieth Century Philosophy* (2008). In 2012 he was awarded the Royal Irish Academy Gold Medal in the Humanities.

TOBIAS MYERS is Assistant Professor of Classics at Connecticut College. His research has focused on narrative strategy in Greek poetry, particularly Theocritus and Homer. He is finishing a book-length analysis of the *Iliad*'s gods in their role as observers of the poem's action.

DOMINIK PERLER is Professor of Philosophy at Humboldt-Universität zu Berlin. His current research focuses on theories of mind in late medieval and early modern philosophy. His books include *Ancient and Medieval Theories of Intentionality* (ed., 2001), *Theorien der Intentionalität im Mittelalter* (2002), *Zweifel und Gewissheit: Skeptische Debatten im Mittelalter* (2006), *Transformationen der Gefühle: Philosophische Emotionstheorien 1270–1670* (2011), and *The Faculties: A History* (ed., 2015).

LAURA QUINNEY teaches English and Comparative Literature at Brandeis University. She is the author of *Literary Power and the Criteria of Truth, William Blake on Self* and *Soul,* and *The Poetics of Disappointment: Wordsworth to Ashbery.*

BERNARD REGINSTER is Professor and Chair in the Department of Philosophy at Brown University. He has published extensively on nineteenth-century philosophy, particularly in ethics and moral psychology. He is the author of *The Affirmation of Life* (2006) and is currently completing another book on Nietzsche's critique of morality, *The Will to Nothingness.* He also has a substantial interest in philosophical issues arising from psychoanalysis, and he has begun to publish on recent psychoanalytic theories of intersubjectivity. He is the director of the program for Ethical Inquiry at Brown University, and a member of the Council of Scholars of the Erikson Institute at the Austen Riggs Center in Massachusetts.

PAULIINA REMES is Professor in Theoretical Philosophy, especially the history of philosophy, in Uppsala University. She is the author of *Plotinus on Self: The Philosophy of the "We"* (2007) and *Neoplatonism* (2008), as well as the editor, together with Svetla-Slaveva Griffin, of *The Routledge Handbook of Neoplatonism* (2014). Remes has also published articles on Plato.

URSULA RENZ is Professor of Philosophy at the University of Klagenfurt, Austria. She is author of *Die Rationalität der Kultur: Kulturphilosophie und ihre transzendentale Begründung bei Cohen, Natorp und Cassirer* (2002), *Die Erklärbarkeit der Erfahrung: Realismus und Subjektivität in Spinozas Theorie des menschlichen Geistes* (2010), and coeditor of the *Handbuch Klassische Emotionstheorien* (2008, second edition 2012) and *Baruch de Spinoza: Ethica more geometrico demonstrata. A Collective Commentary.* Her book *Die Erklärbarkeit der Erfahrung* has been awarded the Journal of the History of Philosophy Book Prize 2011.

SEBASTIAN RÖDL is Professor of Philosophy at the Universität Leipzig. He previously served as Associate Professor at the University of Pittsburgh and as Ordinarius für Philosophie at the University Basel. Among his publications are *Categories of the Temporal* (2012) and *Self-Consciousness* (2007).

CHRISTOPHER SHIELDS is the George N. Shuster Professor of Philosophy and Concurrent Professor of Classics at the University of Notre Dame. He is an Honorary Research Fellow and formerly Tutor of Lady Margaret Hall and Professor of Classical Philosophy in the University of Oxford. He is the author *Aristotle's De Anima, Translated with Introduction and Notes* (2015), *Order in Multiplicity: Homonymy in the Philosophy of Aristotle* (1999), *Classical Philosophy: A Contemporary Introduction* (2003; revised and expanded as *Ancient Philosophy: A Contemporary Introduction* (2012)), and, with Robert Pasnau, *The Philosophy of Thomas Aquinas* (second edition 2015). He is the editor of *The Blackwell Guide to Ancient Philosophy* (2002) and *The Oxford Handbook of Aristotle* (2013).

CHRISTINA VAN DYKE received her PhD from Cornell University in 2000 and is professor in the Department of Philosophy at Calvin College. She has published widely on medieval philosophy and is currently working on a book on Aquinas on happiness, in connection with her new translation and commentary on Aquinas' *Treatise on Happiness* (with Thomas Williams). She is also editing a four-volume Major Works in Medieval Philosophy for Routledge.

CHRISTOPHER S. WOOD is Professor and Chair in the Department of German, New York University. Before coming to NYU, he held appointments at Yale University, the University of California, Berkeley, Vassar College, and the Hebrew University, Jerusalem, and has been awarded several fellowships (American Academy in Rome, American Academy in Berlin, Institute for Advanced Study, Princeton, Internationales Forschungszentrum für Kulturwissenschaften, Vienna; the Kolleg-Forschergruppe BildEvidenz at the Freie Universität Berlin; and the John Simon Guggenheim Foundation). Wood is the author of *Albrecht Altdorfer and the Origins of Landscape* (1993, reissued with new afterword, 2014); *Forgery, Replica, Fiction: Temporalities of German Renaissance Art* (2008) (awarded the Susanne M. Glasscock Humanities Book Prize for Interdisciplinary Scholarship); and *Anachronic Renaissance* (with Alexander Nagel) (2010). He is the editor of *The Vienna School Reader: Politics and Art Historical Method in the 1930s* (2000).

Introduction

Ursula Renz

I.1. THE TWOFOLD IMPORTANCE OF THE CONCEPT OF SELF-KNOWLEDGE

The concept of self-knowledge is often regarded as crucial in two respects. First, it is assumed that for a thing to be an agent or epistemic subject requires that it be epistemically acquainted with some of its properties or states in a way that others are not.[1] It is expected, in other words, that if we lacked the kind epistemic self-intimacy that we in fact have, we would not be the kind of beings that we are. Second, following a frequent and long-standing view, some sort of

---

1 This view is widely held by theorists on self-knowledge; cf. Brie Gertler, *Self-Knowledge* (New York: Routledge, 2011), 2–4; Gertler, "Self-Knowledge," in *The Stanford Encyclopedia of Philosophy*, ed. Edward N. Zalta, Summer 2015 ed., http://plato.stanford.edu/archives/sum2015/entries/self-knowledge/.

self-knowledge is required for wisdom.[2] It is, on this presumption, by coming to know oneself better or by understanding oneself in light of some knowledge about human nature that people mature. These two convictions are not abstract ideals advocated only by philosophers; they are intuitions that are rooted in our folk-psychological concepts. We may not think about it very often in everyday life, but we take for granted that our being a person or mental subject depends in a constitutive way on some form of epistemic self-intimacy.[3] And we are also used to thinking that what qualifies someone as a wise person is, among other things, the unusual extent or depth of his or her self-knowledge.[4]

In recent debate, self-knowledge has predominantly been examined from the perspective of its constitutive role for human mentality. In particular, discussions in analytic philosophy have focused almost exclusively on those properties of self-knowledge that are associated with the alleged epistemic privilege or authoritative relation of human subjects with regard to knowledge of their own mental states, and thus on features relating to the problem of human subjectivity.[5] Certainly, some sort of epistemically privileged position with regard to one's own mental states may be taken as constitutive for human subjectivity. To provide an understanding, therefore, of what precisely this privilege

---

2 This point is regularly mentioned in literature about the concept of wisdom and the epistemology of psychoanalysis; see John Kekes, "Wisdom," *American Philosophical Quarterly* 20 (1983), 277–83, 280; Valerie Tiberius, *The Reflective Life: Living Wisely with Our Limits* (Oxford: Oxford University Press, 2008), 111–20; Jonathan Lear, "Wisdom Won from Illness: The Psychoanalytic Grasp of Human Being," *International Journal of Psychoanalysis* 95 (2014), 677–93.

3 This is obvious from thought experiments with zombies in philosophy of mind. These would not be comprehensible if we did not share the intuition that people differ from zombies in having some primitive form of self-knowledge.

4 For recent psychological research on laypeople's conceptions of wisdom, cf. J. Glück and S. Bluck, "Laypeople's Conceptions of Wisdom and Its Development: Cognitive and Integrative Views," *Journal of Gerontology: Psychological Sciences 66B* (2011), 321–24.

5 A recent exception is Quassim Cassam, *Self-Knowledge for Humans* (Oxford: Oxford University Press, 2014).

may be taken to consist in is an important task of philosophy.[6] But the flip side of this focus is that those aspects of self-knowledge that may help to account for its moral impact or, more specifically, the role it plays in the acquisition of wisdom have hardly been examined in recent philosophy.

Considering the larger history, the importance assigned to the concept was just as often derived from the role self-knowledge presumably plays in the achievement of wisdom. Some philosophers even claimed that the acquisition of self-knowledge is the very end of philosophical inquiry; to engage in philosophy, they thought, is to explore and thereby to ennoble the self. In contrast to many contemporary accounts, their concern with self-knowledge was immediately practical. Not only is self-knowledge constitutive of the kind of things we are, but it crucially matters for the individual persons we are or want to become. Or so they thought. Notwithstanding this emphasis on self-knowledge's ennobling effects, however, they usually considered it an ideal that is only seldom reached.

One might regret that this second, moral or wisdom-related aspect of self-knowledge, which was quite important for the history of the concept, is largely absent in contemporary discussion. One reason for this shift in emphasis is obviously that philosophy has become an academic discipline hosted at research institutions. In antiquity, in contrast, philosophy was practiced at schools that conceived of it as a way of life.[7] And it was as a way of life that philosophy was also regarded in the monastic culture of the early Middle Ages, where self-knowledge was often discussed in connection with the question of our distinction from and relation to God.[8]

---

6 For a survey of possible accounts on this, cf. still William Alston, "Varieties of Privileged Access," *American Philosophical Quarterly* 8 (1971), 223–41.

7 See Pierre Hadot, *Philosophy as a Way of Life*, ed. Arnold I. Davidson, trans. Michael Chase (Oxford: Blackwell, 1995), 264–76.

8 See Pierre Courcelle, *Connais-toi toi-même de Socrate à Saint Bernard* (Paris: Études Augustiniennes, 3 vols. 1974–75), who points this out in the chapter on the monastic culture, 1:232–91. The case is different for philosophical discourse at medieval universities; cf. Hadot, *Philosophy as a Way*, 270f.

But recent concern with the epistemic relation of subjects to their own mental states has its merits. Consider for a moment what reasons there might be behind the unusually wide scope of the concept. What could be the rationale for invoking the notion of "self-knowledge" in both ways, to denote a self-relation constituting our being mental subjects and to promote insights taken to contribute to our personal or moral perfection? At first, one is tempted to think that there is no good reason for this twofold usage of the term and that it is simply a matter of equivocation. Indeed, my awareness of my being captured by present thoughts is different from Socrates' insight into the grounds of his having the reputation of being the wisest of the Athenians. But this is not to say that these are two completely different philosophical phenomena lacking any deeper relationship. On the contrary, many philosophers, when addressing the question of how self-knowledge can yield wisdom, engage in inquiries into structural features of human self-awareness that appear also in discussions about the privileged access of the first person to her mental life. So, for instance, as the first two chapters of this volume show, both Plato and Aristotle display a striking interest in the reason why self-knowledge can both be knowledge itself and be about knowledge.

Indeed, a closer view of the two aforementioned senses of self-knowledge shows that they share a feature emphasis on which is crucial for any discussion of the concept of self-knowledge. In both cases, self-knowledge is not merely a matter of knowing a certain object. To put it in philosophical terms: it is not to be reduced to the *de re* knowledge that a certain fact obtains. Consider my awareness of my being captured by the present thought: to count as an instance of self-knowledge, it is not sufficient for me to believe that "Ursula Renz is captured by some thought p"; rather, I must know that the property of "being captured by thought p" *applies to me* right now. Likewise, Socrates did not know himself to be the wisest of the Athenians simply by adopting the view enunciated by the oracle of Delphi saying, "Socrates is the wisest of all Athenians." Rather, before he could even ask himself whether this sentence was true or not, Socrates had to understand it as referring to *himself.* This suggests that *self-reference* on the part of the subject holding a belief p is a necessary requirement for p to qualify as an instance of self-knowledge.[9] In technical terms, self-knowledge is essentially *de se* knowledge.[10] And while it is an open question how this feature is to be accounted for in detail, its being necessary does explain, to a certain extent, why philosophers used to address quite different beliefs as instances of self-knowledge.

Yet, as Socrates' story illustrates, there are additional requirements for that kind of self-knowledge whose acquisition is expected to yield wisdom. I can know that I am captured by my actual thoughts simply *by having* these thoughts. But the case of Socrates is different. Before he could even decide whether the sentence enunciated by the oracle at Delphi was true or not, he had to inquire into the pretentions of wisdom of a couple of other Athenians. This shows that some instances of self-knowledge, while referring to the epistemic subject in a way that is transparent to herself, still require a special effort. It is arguably due to this special effort that these instances of knowledge are considered a moral achievement and a prerequisite for wisdom.

As we shall see, this presumption raises several interesting philosophical questions. Before elaborating on them, however, let me clarify the terminology used henceforth. To distinguish the kind of

---

9 For the role of self-reference, see famously Sidney Shoemaker, "Self-Reference and Self-Awareness," *Journal of Philosophy* 65 (1968), 555–67; Hector-Neri Castañeda, "'He': A Study of the Logic of Self-Consciousness," *Ratio* 8 (1966), 130–57; Elisabeth Anscombe, "The First Person," in *Collected Papers*, vol. 2: *Metaphysics and the Philosophy of Mind* (Minneapolis: University of Minnesota Press 1981), 21–36; and chapter 7 of Gareth Evans, *The Varieties of Reference*, ed. John McDowell (Oxford: Oxford University Press, 1982), 205–66. For a more recent discussion that connects the issue of self-reference with the problem of self-knowledge, cf. Lucy O'Brien, *Self-Knowing Agents* (Oxford: Oxford University Press, 2007), 49–73.

10 In using this terminology, I do not take a stance with regard to David Lewis' thesis that attitudes *de se* are primary to attitudes *de dicto*, which are only propositional; cf. his "Attitudes *De Dicto* and *De Se*," *Philosophical Review* 88 (1979), 513–43. Nor do I commit myself to Lewis' view that all *de re* knowledge is a species of *de se* knowledge. My point is merely that to count as self-knowledge, a (justified true) belief must be thought by the person holding it as applying to herself. Cf. also François Recanati, "De Re and De Se," *Dialectica* 63 (2009), 249–69.

self-knowledge which is considered an achievement and a prerequisite for wisdom from the trivial self-knowledge we display in daily life, I will refer to the former by the phrase "Socratic self-knowledge." In using this terminology, however, I do not want to commit myself to the view that these are two completely different issues. Rather, the phenomena subsumed under the notion self-knowledge share some family resemblances; to get a clearer grasp of them, I think, is highly relevant for many concerns.

I.2. Toward a Folk Psychology of Socratic Self-Knowledge: A Primer

Some cynically tempered minds might wonder whether the ideal of Socratic self-knowledge is not a myth. Does Socratic self-knowledge describe a real option to be achieved in principle by humans? Is it not mere illusion? Are we not, as both ancient and early modern skeptics claimed, the more inclined to fall prey to self-deception the more we aspire to achieve Socratic self-knowledge? Indeed, as several chapters and reflections of the present volume show, the possibility of self-knowledge is frequently questioned in philosophy and literature.[11]

These are serious objections to the promotion of Socratic self-knowledge. However, in order to address them properly, more needs to be said about what we expect to be at stake in the acquisition of Socratic self-knowledge. For the sake of argument, therefore, suppose that Socratic self-knowledge can be achieved by human subjects. What, then, is the person whom we think to have achieved it assumed to know? In other words, what are the epistemological requirements for Socratic self-knowledge?

Let us consider Socrates' story again. To begin with, note that Socrates knows more than what contemporary debate on self-knowledge would

---

11 In this volume, cf. chapter 5 for Pyrrhonian skepticism; chapter 9 for early modern moralist writing; and Reflection II for Romantic poetry.

assume. Recent analysis has taken it for granted that in usual circumstances we have self-knowledge of both our actual mental states and our standing mental attitudes. Certainly, this was never meant to rule out situations where this is not so, but it was merely taken to describe the ordinary condition of human minds. In fact, I can be quite hungry, but only notice it when my colleague asks me if I want to join him for lunch. Likewise, it may happen that we, hidden to ourselves, foster a desire to simply disappear, while at the same time avoiding becoming aware of this desire. Even occurrent mental states can be subconscious; whereas knowledge of our attitudes can be oppressed. Still, there is the presumption that failures in one's knowing one's actual states or standing attitudes must be explained against the background of the notion that generally self-knowledge of these items comes for free.

The picture changes when it comes to Socratic self-knowledge. What Socrates came to know were neither his actual mental states nor his standing attitudes. On the contrary, when he initially heard what the oracle was saying about him, he might have felt it to be in a certain tension with his immediate self-awareness. Rather than viewing himself as a wise person, he perceived himself as ignorant of almost everything that the Athenians valued. But then he realized that it is the very acceptance of his own ignorance with regard to so many things that distinguished him from all those Athenians who claimed to know things without really knowing them.

Now, one might say, this is not really *self*-knowledge: it is not knowledge Socrates had of *himself* or some of *his* properties. Rather it is knowledge of the other Athenians' epistemic failures, and this is why the story is just as much satirizing the pretensions of the Athenians as it is meant to describe Socrates' learning process. Moreover, arguably, Socrates' knowledge of his own ignorance is deeply ironic.[12] Yet, while this is certainly true, there is more to be said about the state of mind he

---

12 Jonathan Lear, *A Case for Irony* (Cambridge, MA: Harvard University Press, 2011), 22–24.

finally acquires. Consider for a moment what makes us (or made Plato) think of Socrates as being wiser than the other Athenians. Presumably, this thought depends on a twofold idea: First, it is assumed that their failures were not completely accidental, but were lapses into real pitfalls. Second, Socrates is regarded as having a certain grasp of these pitfalls; he understood the causes that prompted the Athenians to fail. Socrates' wisdom essentially relates to the twofold notion that to claim to know something is not actually to know it and that people who claim to know things are disposed to think that they know them. And this only adds to his self-perception of being ignorant of many things and to the insight that being a human being himself, he is not safe from falling prey to the observed disposition to overrate one's own knowledge.

Thus, Socrates' wisdom entails at least four epistemic accomplishments. Socrates must

(i)   grasp the conceptual distinction between belief and knowledge,

(ii) know the anthropological fact that people, when thinking of their own convictions, tend not always to draw the aforementioned distinction properly,

(iii) hold that he himself is not particularly knowledgeable, and

(iv) notice that he himself can easily fall prey to the aforementioned human disposition to take his beliefs to constitute knowledge.

Certainly, this analysis can be further elaborated. So, one might ask, what does the anthropological tenet of man's disposition to overrate the extent of his knowledge ultimately amount to? And what is involved, psychologically speaking, in the acknowledgment of one's own falling under this (or like) conditions? Moreover, one might question whether these are really distinct requirements or whether, for instance, knowledge of some anthropological fact does not necessarily, and perhaps even trivially, involve acknowledgment of one's own being subject to it. Finally, skeptics might object that this analysis misses the irony of the story that must be captured in order to see the real difficulty of the matter at stake here. Be that as it may, given this analysis, we can assume that there is some instance of *self*-knowledge involved in Socratic wisdom. He does not have knowledge of external facts or objects merely.

I.3. Some More Folk Psychology: Four Types of Self-Knowledge and Their Relations

In the first section, I characterized what could be called the overarching genus of self-knowledge by the following condition: for a justified true belief p to qualify as self-knowledge it is required that it be *de se* about the subject who holds p. As this condition purportedly applies to knowledge of a whole bunch of phenomena, it might be helpful to introduce some kind of prima facie classification. Considering the historical material, I suggest in particular distinguishing the following four types of self-knowledge:

1. *Self-knowledge of one's actual states.* This first type of self-knowledge is usually taken to involve knowledge, or awareness, of one's occurrent mental states such as one's sensations, impressions, perceptions, afterimages, or passing thoughts. Note that the emphasis on *mental* states is not meant to preclude that we know bodily states in the very same way. On the contrary, this kind of self-knowledge includes knowledge of pain states, tickles, states of sleepiness or fatigue, hunger and thirst, as well as knowledge of the position of one's limbs, and so on. Thus, whether the properties to be known apply to the body or the mind is irrelevant here. What is essential, instead, are two other features: (1) Self-knowledge of one's actual states is taken to consist in a special epistemic relation; that is, it is assumed that we are acquainted with these states in an irreducibly first-personal way that is not available from other stances; (2) as self-knowledge of this first type is about occurrent

states, which are momentary in kind and may likely disappear, when the circumstances change, what we underline by self-attributing these properties is often *that* they obtain of us in a given moment.

2. *Self-knowledge of one's standing attitudes.* A second type of self-knowledge relates the subject to her standing attitudes.[13] Most importantly, this involves knowledge of one's beliefs and other propositional attitudes, but it also encompasses knowledge of one's values and the ends one aims at, as well as of all kinds of preferences, desires, and intentions. *How* these properties are known by the person who has them is a matter of controversy.[14] However, it is uncontroversial that, just as with the first type of self-knowledge, there is the presumption that these features are subject to some sort of epistemic privilege bound up with the first-person perspective. But unlike the case of the first type of self-knowledge, self-knowledge of one's standing attitudes is not necessarily a matter of a person's actual awareness; I can, but need not, be aware of my being convinced that my mother is well these days. Rather, I come to know of my attitudes when I reflect on my mind and pay attention to its content, whatever "reflection" or "attention" precisely mean here. Note, also, that attitudinal properties are distinct from the objects of the first type of self-knowledge in that they usually obtain of a person for a longer period of time. Perhaps this is also the reason why self-knowledge of one's attitudes is often taken to constitute a continuous self-relation which may be crucial for the person one is.

---

13 See Richard Moran, *Authority and Estrangement: An Essay on Self-Knowledge* (Princeton: Princeton University Press, 2001), xxxiii, where the distinction between the first two kinds of self-knowledge was first noticed; as well as Matthew Boyle, "Two Kinds of Self-Knowledge," *Philosophy and Phenomenological Research* 78 (2009), 133–64.

14 Besides the approach by Moran, *Authority and Estrangement*, cf. Sidney Shoemaker, "Self-Knowledge and 'Inner Sense,'" *Philosophy and Phenomenological Research* 54 (1994), 249–314; Tyler Burge, "Our Entitlement to Self-Knowledge," *Proceedings of the Aristotelian Society* 96 (1996), 91–116; Akeel Bilgrami, *Self-Knowledge and Resentment* (Cambridge, MA: Harvard University Press, 2006); and O'Brien's *Self-Knowing Agents.*

3. *Self-knowledge of one's dispositional properties.* A third type of self-knowledge consists in the subject's knowledge of her dispositions such as character traits, patterns of behavior, capacities, and limitations, including certain features deriving from cultural or biographical influences. One might wonder why this constitutes a separate type of knowledge. In fact, in ordinary thought, these properties are often mixed with the aforementioned attitudes. Moreover, both are considered crucial aspects of the personality of the subject, and rightly so, I think. A person's standing conviction that life is exciting can just as much be a characteristic of her as her disposition to always run out of time. Yet there is an important epistemological difference regarding the way in which we know of these properties: While one can know of one's conviction that life is exciting simply by considering one's views about life, one cannot know one's disposition to run out of time simply by considering one's plans and preferences; we more likely learn about these things by reflecting on external sources of information, such as other people's observations, or historical or biographical information.[15] This indicates that I am in no principally privileged epistemic position with regard to the knowledge of my dispositional properties; indeed, they may be completely hidden to me. Thus the distinction of this third kind of self-knowledge relies on the assumption that we can come to know ourselves better by noticing our having certain properties that, while they are perhaps essential to our personality, are not subject to some epistemic privilege of the first person.

4. *Self-knowledge of one's being subject to the human condition.* As a fourth type of self-knowledge, we may distinguish insights related to one's acceptance of the human condition. As already mentioned, this kind of self-knowledge is not to be reduced to the defense

---

15 Cf. Crispin Wright, "Self-Knowledge: The Wittgensteinian Legacy," in *Knowing Our Own Minds*, ed. Crispin Wright, Barry C. Smith, and Cynthia Macdonald (Oxford: Clarendon Press, 1998), 13–45, 14.

of anthropological doctrines. Rather, it requires the subject's acceptance of their holding *de se*. How explicitly they must be stated as holding *de se* is not clear. In any case, it is not a matter of mere implication; to qualify as an instance of self-knowledge, the affirmation of anthropological tenets must involve my awareness that they apply to me too. However, notwithstanding this requirement, being about specific features of humankind, broadly speaking, empirical sources play a crucial role for this type of self-knowledge. What kind of experience is involved is not determined: it can be scientific knowledge,[16] but it can also be derived from life experience, from reading novels and biographies, or from contemplating history. Thus, given this fourth kind of self-knowledge, there must be a way of learning about oneself from applying general ideas about mankind to one's own case.

Having these four types in view, several questions might arise. Generally, there is the worry concerning whether these are really distinct types of self-knowledge, or whether they do not merely separate out the contents relating to our self-conception. I don't think so, and this is at least not what the previous classification is meant to show, its rationale being rather the assumption that different types of contents constituting different types of objects of self-knowledge go along with different kinds of epistemic self-relation people may have to themselves. Thus, the distinction of types of contents may serve as a heuristic for the detection of a more fundamental difference between types of self-relation that all may be, and in fact have been, considered as constituting self-knowledge.

There is a second concern. Suppose these four types of self-knowledge exist. Would we, as philosophers, not have to dig deeper and try to establish some grounding relation between these types to the effect that one of them can be advocated as the very basis of all epistemic

---

16 This has been pointed out in Peter Carruthers' review on Cassam's *Self-Knowledge for Humans*, in *Notre Dame Philosophical Reviews* 2015.04.16.

self-relations? Does not philosophical analysis only begin where this last task is taken seriously? Perhaps this is indeed so.[17] As a matter of fact, philosophers of all times have tended to address this concern, yet—and this is significant—with quite different results. Considering the history of the concept, there have been several shifts regarding the answer to the question on which phenomena people ought to focus in their striving for self-knowledge. When reflecting, for instance, on the ancient imperative to know oneself, philosophers for a long time invoked self-knowledge of the fourth kind. Note that this is how the Delphic injunction was originally intended to be read. When the inscription "Gnōthi seauton" was fixed at the temple of Apollo, it was meant to remind the reader, who was about to enter the temple dedicated to one of the most sublime gods, of his belonging to the category of merely mortal beings.[18] In contrast, philosophers inspired by Plato's *Alcibiades I* were appealing to the ideal of self-knowledge in order to emphasize the eternal part of human soul.[19] Yet another ancient tradition, which considered self-knowledge as a means for the cultivation of the self, emphasized the importance of human nature and its role in the constitution of our moral and epistemic dispositions.[20] Thus even within those approaches concerned with Socratic self-knowledge there is great variety.

---

17 Cf. Boyle, "Two Kinds of Self-Knowledge." Boyle convincingly argues that we should abstain from positing only one singular way in which people know their own minds (142f.), but nonetheless asks what self-relation self-knowledge requires. He further maintains that in answering this question, self-knowledge of one's attitudes "must find a fundamental place in any satisfactory account of self-knowledge" (147).

18 Walter Burkert, *Griechische Religion der archaischen und klassischen Epoche* (Stuttgart: Kohlammer, 2011), 30, points out that the Delphic injunction demanded the acknowledgment of some general facts about mankind. Quoting from an earlier version of Burkert's book, F. P. Hager, "Selbsterkenntnis," in *Historisches Wörterbuch der Philosophie*, ed. Joachim Ritter and Karlfried Gründer, vol. 9 (Basel: Schwabe, 1995), 406–13, 406, notes that the original wording of the precept of Delphi was either "Know, O man, that you are not a God!" or "Know thyself, man, as a mortal being, in your mortality!"

19 Hager, "Selbsterkenntnis," 407 and 410f., but cf. chapter 1 in this volume for an alternative reading of Plato's *Alcibiades*.

20 See Hadot, *Philosophy as a Way*, 206f., and chapter 3 in this volume.

It is also wrong to assume that the interest in the epistemology of self-knowledge, and in connection with that an increased emphasis on the first two kinds of self-knowledge mentioned above, is the result of modern philosophy.[21] Many modern philosophers have been interested in the moral aspects of self-knowledge, whereas the epistemology of self-knowledge of actual states and attitudes attracted philosophers of all times. What distinguishes their approach from the contemporary concern with the first person is that they often employed the analysis of epistemological issues to defend views related with the third and fourth types of self-knowledge. Indeed, several chapters of this volume show that structural analysis of features related to the first person can be found already in Plato, Aristotle, and Augustine; but it also turns out that the concern with the moral impact of self-knowledge is quite present in modern philosophy.[22]

What is remarkable about the history of the concept of self-knowledge is thus not primarily the wide scope of the concept, but rather the almost *exclusive* interest of contemporary analytical philosophy in the first two types of self-knowledge. From a historical perspective, therefore, we should resist the temptation to reduce these four types of self-knowledge to one basic self-relation. Perhaps there is such a basic self-relation, but no conclusive argument has been provided for it so far.

I.4. PROBLEMS AND QUESTIONS

As documented by this volume, historical discussion on the concept of self-knowledge addressed a whole range of interconnected issues.

1. *Structural features of self-knowledge.* Several structural features are discussed in relation to the conception of self-knowledge.

---

21 Such a misconception of the history of the concept is fatally promulgated in the otherwise accurate book by Gertler, *Self-Knowledge*, 28f.

22 Cf. on the one hand chapters 1, 2, and 5, and on the other chapters 12, 13, and 14 of the present volume.

Is self-knowledge a form of higher-order knowledge, or is it a
feature belonging to the same level as its very objects?[23] Does self-
knowledge require knowledge to consist in a reflexive relation,
or does knowledge rather, like seeing, preclude application to
itself?[24] What is self-knowledge considered as a process? Does
it require that we go through particular phases, following a
determinate order? Or is self-knowledge only defined in terms
of its result or some epistemic state we might achieve in many
different ways?

Some of these questions are well known from contemporary debate.
Yet in historical texts, they are often addressed against the background
of some specific understanding of the Delphic imperative, "Gnōthi
seauton." In consequence, they were often discussed in connection
with issues related to Socratic self-knowledge, such as these:

2. *The moral impact of self-knowledge.* Following the Delphic
   injunction, self-knowledge is assumed to have an influence on
   our moral actions and attitudes, or to ennoble the self. But what
   does this impact eventually consist in? Is it simply a matter of
   providing agents with anthropological knowledge that allows
   them to act in accordance with their aims, or is it meant to
   increase the very morality of persons achieving it? If so, how can
   we account for this ennobling effect? Is it the result of improved
   self-control or rather of people's more deliberately embracing
   who they are?[25] And is self-knowledge really necessary, or would
   any deliberately chosen self-conception do this job? Finally, is it
   not just as conceivable that self-knowledge makes people more
   cunning or even evil?

---

23 This is a crucial issue in the medieval scholastics; cf. chapter 6 of the present volume.

24 Both Plato and Aristotle were concerned with this problem; cf. chapters 1 and 2 in this volume.

25 See chapter 12 in this volume for a discussion of this question with regard to Schopenhauer
and Freud.

3. *The contents of Socratic self-knowledge.* Which contents are the typical objects of Socratic self-knowledge? One might be tempted to
conceive of Socratic self-knowledge mostly in terms of the third
kind of self-knowledge distinguished above, and this mostly in relation with dispositions constituting one's personal weaknesses or
vices. However, quite as often Socratic self-knowledge was assumed
to consist in knowledge of one's being subject to the human condition. Moreover, in describing the human condition, some appealed
to structural features of the human mind,[26] whereas others pointed
to the importance of our being embodied persons.[27] More recently,
the notion of biographical and historical influences upon one's life
has also been taken into consideration,[28] a concern that is also present in modern literature and arts.[29]

4. *The second- and third-personal perspectives on the self.* In many cases
mere reflection on, or attendance to, one's mental life is not sufficient in order to acquire Socratic self-knowledge. We often depend
on external sources of knowledge. This raises the question of what
kind of external knowledge we may rely on. Can scientific insights
help us with knowing ourselves better? What is the role of visual
techniques? Can, for example, selfies be considered as a source of
self-knowledge?[30] What is the role of friends? What contribution is
made by reflection on the life of others, and what is the role of historical understanding of the cultural values shaping our communities?
How do certain methods practiced by philosophers, such as cross-
examination or self-dialogue, employ instances of the second-person

---

26 This is discussed in the present volume with relation to Plotinus in chapter 4, Augustine in
chapter 5, Husserl in chapter 13, and the debate about the first person in analytic philosophy in
chapter 15.

27 As discussed in chapter 7, this was an important concern of female medieval mystics.

28 That is a major concern of the hermeneutic tradition; cf. chapter 14 in this volume.

29 See Reflection III for exemplary analysis.

30 For an affirmative answer cf. Reflection IV.

perspective?[31] And how can we get from third-personal evidence to *de se* knowledge?[32] Considering religious approaches, finally, the question arises of how our relating to God in a second-personal manner is assumed contribute to self-knowledge.[33]

5. *The possibility of Socratic self-knowledge.* The demand to acquire self-knowledge confronts us with several epistemological and psychological challenges. Naturally, there is the danger of error; we often conceive of ourselves in wrong terms. Sometimes, for example when objective knowledge is lacking, we cannot possibly do better. But there is also a widespread tendency to resist full *de se* acknowledgment of some property as applying to oneself, in particular where this would involve embracing a disenchanting view of oneself. These difficulties have led philosophers to question the notion that Socratic self-knowledge is a possible achievement for humans. Moreover, some have even denied self-knowledge's necessarily being a valuable end. Striving for self-knowledge, they claimed, makes people more self-concerned, or estranged from their original human stance.[34]

Certainly, this list of issues only hints at some of the concerns addressed in the history of the concept of self-knowledge, and much more could be said about each independent question raised here. Considering this list, however, it is obvious that the concept of self-knowledge has an extremely rich history that surpasses, if not in precision, then at least in extension, the range of problems addressed in contemporary philosophy.

---

31 In the present volume, this is discussed in relation to Marcus Aurelius' *Meditations* in chapter 3 and Shaftesbury's *Soliloquy* in chapter 8.

32 See, e.g., the discussion of Descartes and Hobbes in chapter 8 in this volume.

33 This is an important point of Kierkegaard's later views about Christianity; cf. chapter 11 in this volume.

34 Skeptical views on self-knowledge were widespread in French and English moralistic writing; cf. chapter 9 in this volume.

I.5. Aims of This Volume

It is the declared aim of this volume to draw attention to both the pre-history of features of self-knowledge actively debated and issues that are often neglected nowadays. Therefore, authors were asked not to focus exclusively, or even primarily, on epistemological and cognitive psychological features of trivial self-knowledge, but to pay attention to aspects that relate, or may be interpreted as relating to, Socratic self-knowledge as well. In particular, it turned out that the Delphic injunction, while it was quite differently interpreted, was a common inspiration of many philosophers as well as of artists and poets. Moreover, among the aims of the volume are to provide a historical grasp of the background behind contemporary discussion, and to juxtapose different strands of contemporary philosophy. Altogether, we hope to inspire a new way of looking at the problem of self-knowledge and the impact this concept has upon our discipline and culture.

Reflection I

DOES HOMER'S ODYSSEUS KNOW HIMSELF?

Tobias Myers

Ten years after Troy's fall, a stranger appears alone on the Phaeacians' shore. They are impressed by his manner and bearing, but do not know, as we do, that he is Odysseus, still trying to get home from Troy. At a banquet held in the stranger's honor, the court bard, Demodocus, performs a song of the Trojan War, one "whose fame (*kleos*) at that time reached heaven," namely "the quarrel of Odysseus and Peleus' son, Achilles" (νεῖκος Ὀδυσσῆος καὶ Πηλεΐδεω Ἀχιλῆος, 8.75).[1] Odysseus begins to sob, quietly; King Alcinous notices and tactfully calls for a change of entertainment. Later that day, Odysseus praises Demodocus for performing that earlier song so convincingly, "as though present yourself, or having heard from another." He then requests another Trojan War lay: "Sing of the design of the wooden horse" (ἵππου κόσμον ἄεισον / δουρατέου, 8.492–93), says Odysseus, "which Odysseus once filled with men and led into the citadel as a deception (*dolos*), and they laid waste to Troy" (ὅν ποτ᾽ ἐς ἀκρόπολιν δόλον ἤγαγε δῖος Ὀδυσσεὺς / ἀνδρῶν ἐμπλήσας οἵ ῥ᾽ Ἴλιον ἐξαλάπαξαν, 8.494–95).[2]

---

1 Translations in this reflection are my own; references to Homer's text are to the edition by Thomas W. Allen, *Homeri Opera* (Oxford: Clarendon, 1949–51).

2 An otherwise unknown episode from the Trojan War, which reads very like a variation on the *Iliad* proem.

When Demodocus obliges, Odysseus again begins to sob quietly.
This time, Alcinous sees fit to publicly ask his guest to declare who
he is, to tell his story—and to explain his tears. "I am Odysseus,"
Odysseus declares to the stunned Phaeacian court, "Laertes' son, a
concern to all men because of my deceptions (*doloi*)—and my fame
(*kleos*) reaches heaven!" But albeit his narration takes all night, and
four books of the *Odyssey*, he never directly answers the question of
why he weeps.

Certainly, the pain of recalling past hardships is a recurring trope
in the *Odyssey*. Yet the last song, which Odysseus himself requests,
is that of his own great victory in war—the quintessence of the
kleos for which a Homeric hero strives. Why does Odysseus weep *at
this song*? Homer describes Odysseus' reaction using a remarkable
extended simile:

ταῦτ᾽ ἄρ᾽ ἀοιδὸς ἄειδε περικλυτός: αὐτὰρ Ὀδυσσεὺς
τήκετο, δάκρυ δ᾽ ἔδευεν ὑπὸ βλεφάροισι παρειάς.
ὡς δὲ γυνὴ κλαίῃσι φίλον πόσιν ἀμφιπεσοῦσα,
ὅς τε ἑῆς πρόσθεν πόλιος λαῶν τε πέσῃσιν,
ἄστεϊ καὶ τεκέεσσιν ἀμύνων νηλεὲς ἦμαρ:
ἡ μὲν τὸν θνήσκοντα καὶ ἀσπαίροντα ἰδοῦσα
ἀμφ᾽ αὐτῷ χυμένη λίγα κωκύει: οἱ δέ τ᾽ ὄπισθε
κόπτοντες δούρεσσι μετάφρενον ἠδὲ καὶ ὤμους
εἴρερον εἰσανάγουσι, πόνον τ᾽ ἐχέμεν καὶ ὀιζύν:
τῆς δ᾽ ἐλεεινοτάτῳ ἄχεϊ φθινύθουσι παρειαί:
ὡς Ὀδυσεὺς ἐλεεινὸν ὑπ᾽ ὀφρύσι δάκρυον εἶβεν.
(Od. 8.514–31)

This, then, sang the famous bard; but Odysseus was
melting, and tears wet his cheeks below his eyelashes.
As a woman cries, falling upon her dear husband,
who has fallen in front of his city and people,
warding off from his town and children the cruel day—

she sees him dying and panting,
and pouring over him piercingly wails; but from behind
they strike her back and shoulders with spears
and lead her into slavery, to toil and grief;
and her cheeks are wasted by most piteous suffering—
so Odysseus under his brows wept piteous tears.

The point of comparison is as striking as the imagery is
vivid: Odysseus, hearing recounted his own central role in the
sacking of a city, weeps like a woman whose city is being sacked.
Yet the narrator is silent about the workings of Odysseus' mental
"organs," the *thymos, noos*, and so on, which so often feature in
Homeric scenes of powerful emotion. There is no space here to
consider the many interpretations scholars have proposed for
this scene and the charged simile.[3] For my part, I believe that
the function of the scene is precisely to tempt audiences with
multiple possibilities, without ever guiding us to one particular
understanding of Odysseus' thoughts. This is indeed how one
depicts psychological depth in literature—by gesturing, without
revealing a bottom.[4]

Rather than reveal Odysseus' thoughts, the scene does invite us to
consider the kind of mental experience that generates his response.
One might describe the effect in this way: Homer is depicting for
us the image of a man, Odysseus, in the act of gazing into a mirror.

---

3 Stephen Halliwell, *Between Ecstasy and Truth: Interpretations of Greek Poetics from Homer to Longinus* (Oxford: Oxford University Press, 2011), 88 n. 104, contains useful bibliography on the passage; to which should be added William H. Race, "Phaeacian Therapy in Homer's Odyssey," in *Combat Trauma and the Ancient Greeks*, ed. Peter Meineck and David Konstan (New York: Palgrave Macmillan, 2014), 47–66. Important questions include these: Does the simile point to an irony Odysseus misses, or reflect in some way his own thinking? Does Odysseus anticipate his own emotional reaction? Many textual clues point to a level on which Odysseus, the self-proclaimed master of trickery, is himself orchestrating the whole scene.

4 As numerous studies have shown, Erich Auerbach's thesis in *Mimesis* that the Homeric style does not represent psychological depths misses much that is of value in the poems. See, e.g., Michael Lynn-George, *Epos: Word, Narrative and the "Iliad"* (London: Macmillan, 1988), esp. 1–49.

Like Alcinous, we view the externals of Odysseus' face: cheeks, eyelashes, tears, and eyebrows (8.15, 31). Unlike Alcinous, however, we are guided to consider the reflexive character of his mental experience, emphasized by repeated, juxtaposed uses of the proper name "Odysseus" to denote the Odysseus listening (8.83, 92, 486, 521, 531) and the Odysseus at Troy (8.75,494, 502, 517). The two are of different ages and in different situations, and the one listening has what might be called a higher ontological status than the one Demodocus' song describes. Yet as is the case for a man gazing into a mirror, the two are also one. Odysseus himself suggests this when he says, "I am Odysseus" to the Phaeacians. At this point "Odysseus" is already a referent in their shared communicative framework: thus, more than stating his name, Odysseus is also asserting a relationship between the first-person "I" and the figure about whom they have all just been hearing. His declaration thus includes the idea: "*I* am Odysseus, whose fame you have just heard recounted"; that is, "I and the Odysseus of the songs are the same person."[5]

The question arises: is this scene about self-knowledge, anticipating in a narrative way the mental subject-object reflexivity expressed by the Delphic γνῶθι σαυτόν ("know yourself")? To be sure, the Delphic maxim is generally assumed to postdate Homer, and indeed the reflexive pronoun is never used in Homer to refer to "a psychological aspect of the subject."[6] Nevertheless, this scene might well be seen as exploring the idea of self-knowledge in a sophisticated and psychologically compelling fashion.

Odysseus clearly understands his own experiences as narrative, as his expert narration of his travels in books 9–12 shows; it is

---

5 The alternative, "*I* am Odysseus, *rather than* the Odysseus of the songs," i.e., "*I* am the real Odysseus," has been precluded already by his praise of Demodocus prior to requesting the final song. The praise constitutes an avowal that Demodocus' "Odysseus" is true to his own experience of the recounted (and, for him, recollected) events.

6 Edward Jeremiah, *The Emergence of Reflexivity in Greek Language and Thought: From Homer to Plato and Beyond* (Boston: Brill, 2012) 52, citing earlier work by George Bolling.

therefore possible that Demodocus' narrative prompts within him a change in the story he tells himself about himself. Demodocus' song of the wooden horse emphasizes both the glory of Odysseus and the pathos of the Trojans' fate. Thus, on the one hand, the poet's precis of the song finishes with Ὀδυσσῆα ... αἰνότατον πόλεμον ... τολμήσαντα/νικῆσαι ... διὰ μεγάθυμον Ἀθήνην ("Odysseus braved the fiercest fight and won, with great-hearted Athena," 8.517–20). Yet the song also frames the doom that awaits the Trojans in typically tragic terms, as a failure to make the correct choice against the backdrop of an inescapable destiny (8.511). Odysseus' emotional reaction can thus be understood as originating from a change in the thrust of the narrative by which he mentally contextualizes his own deeds.

Importantly, though, for Odysseus the narrative spun by Demodocus not only lays out his deeds in a particular and possibly novel light; it also confronts him with the one part of him that is, potentially, undying. *Kleos*, after all, for a Homeric hero represents the glory he wins on the battlefield, the sum total of his reputation, and his chief hope for an existence beyond death. As Vernant has put it, "Through the public arena of the exploits in which he was wholly engaged, [the Homeric hero] continues, beyond the reach of death, to be present in the community of the living."[7] Indeed, it is the tactic of the wooden horse as recounted in Demodocus' song that lies behind Odysseus' epic epithet, *ptoliporthos*, "city-sacking."

The scene in consideration thus incorporates a paradox analogous to that found in later philosophical discourse about self-knowledge, namely, the paradox that knowledge of the self entails both recognition of one's (mortal) limitations, and participation in the divine or transcendent. For the Homeric hero, however,

---

7 Jean-Paul Vernant, "A 'Beautiful Death' and the Disfigured Corpse in Homeric Epic" (originally published in 1982 as "La belle mort et le cadavre outragé") in *Oxford Readings in Homer's Iliad*, ed. Douglas Cairns (Oxford: Oxford University Press, 2001) 320.

transcendence is not about the divinity of the soul, but rather consists in the achievement of "undying glory" (*kleos aphthiton*) in epic. Thus, the paradox for Odysseus is this: even as he suffers the pain of disenchantment with his own "story," he participates (as audience) in one of the notionally infinite number of song performances that he believes will collectively preserve and magnify his self forever.

CHAPTER ONE

Self-Knowledge in Plato

Rachana Kamtekar

1.1. INTRODUCTION

Socrates' account of the defining moment of his life, when he learned that Apollo's oracle had declared him the wisest of men (*Apology*),[1] recalls the inscription, "Know yourself," in the temple of Apollo at Delphi:[2]

> Having heard these [words], I wondered, "Whatever does the God mean, and what is he riddling? For I know (*sunoida*) myself to be wise about nothing great or small. What then does he mean by

---

1 Plato, *Apology* 21a. References to Plato's text are to the standard Stephanus pagination followed by both original-language editions and most translations. Translations in this chapter are all my own, using the Oxford Classical Texts of Plato, ed. J. Burnet (vols. 1–4: 1900–1902), but the reader may find it convenient to consult John M. Cooper and D. S. Hutchinson, eds., *The Complete Works of Plato* (Indianapolis: Hackett, 1997).

2 In Plato's *Protagoras* Socrates says the ancient sages inscribed (*grapsantes*) their wise sayings in the temple (343b); while we might be skeptical that the ancient sages did the inscribing, Socrates seems to take for granted the existence of the inscriptions.

saying that I am the wisest? For I don't suppose he lies; it is not permissible for him."[3]

Socrates has (some) self-knowledge, the very thing the inscription enjoins all to acquire (which prior to Socrates' intellectualist take on it might have been understood as "Know your place"), yet the content of this knowledge, that he knows nothing great or small, is now being questioned by the oracle's pronouncement that he is wisest among men. In response to this conflict between what he knows of himself and what the oracle says about him, Socrates tries to refute (*elenchein*) the oracle by examining (*exetazō/exetazesthai*) those with a reputation for knowledge.[4] But he finds that the politicians and poets, who know nothing fine, and the craftsmen, who know only their crafts, take themselves to know about virtue when they do not.[5] On seeing this, he realizes that although he knows nothing fine and good, nothing of human and social virtue,[6] at least he lacks the "most blameworthy"[7] false conceit of knowledge that keeps one from seeking knowledge, and his awareness of his own ignorance in this matter is rare enough, and valuable enough, to earn it the title "human wisdom."[8] This is what the oracle means by saying Socrates is the wisest among men: he is wisest in human wisdom. Socrates reckons that in examining himself and others, he is doing as the god commands him.[9] He considers the unexamined life not worth living for a human being.[10] Does examination itself make a life worth living, or is examination necessary for recognizing one's own ignorance, which is a precondition for seeking the

---

3 *Apology* 21b2–7.
4 *Apology* 21b–c.
5 *Apology* 22a–e.
6 *Apology* 20c.
7 *Apology* 29a–b.
8 *Apology* 20d.
9 *Apology* 30a, e.
10 *Apology* 38a.

("divine") knowledge of what is fine and good?[11] We will return to this question below, in section 1.2.

In contrast with the *Apology*, the *Phaedrus* has Socrates saying that he *lacks* self-knowledge:

I am not able to know myself as per the Delphic inscription . . . whether I turn out to be some beast more complicated and raging than Typhon or a gentler and simpler animal, by nature sharing in a divine and modest lot.[12]

Which is it—does Socrates have or lack self-knowledge?

On the assumption that the self-knowledge Socrates has ought to be different from the self-knowledge he lacks, this chapter explains the differences in content between the two kinds of knowledge, and describes the two kinds of inquiry directed at each kind of self-knowledge. We may distinguish two questions corresponding to two ways of hearing the injunction to know oneself. (1) Concerning one's *state*: is one knowledgeable or ignorant? good or bad? (2) Concerning one's *capacities*: what is one's nature such that one is able to become good or bad, and knowledgeable or ignorant, namely, what are one's capacities to inquire, desire, anger, and so on? Are all of these equally essential to what one is? While an answer to (2) may be implicit in any answer to (1), several ("early") Platonic dialogues pursue only (1), examining various important subjects about which Socrates and his interlocutors may be knowledgeable or ignorant, and other ("middle" and "late") dialogues pursue (2), determining the soul's basic constituents and exploring their behavior in different conditions. Both kinds of inquiry treat the self that is to be known (namely, the state or the set of capacities) as capable of being quite different in reality from the way it appears to itself. The answer to (2) includes the claim that

11 Plato, *Sophist* 230a–c.

12 *Phaedrus* 229e5–30a6.

the best element of the self is its capacity to know, which when it actually knows is in its best condition itself and makes the soul as a whole good, but—unlike later Platonists and many interpreters (see section 1.3)—Plato's answers to (1) and (2) do not reduce the self that is known to the knowing self.

1.2. KNOWLEDGE OF ONE'S STATE

In Plato's *Charmides*, Critias proposes that temperance is to know oneself,[13] and that the person who is temperate has knowledge of what he knows and what he doesn't know.[14] Some commentators complain that this discussion changes the topic from knowledge of the self to knowledge of knowledge.[15] But if Socrates' human wisdom/knowledge of one's own ignorance is the very self-knowledge enjoined by "Know yourself," this is not a change of topic, and in the *Charmides*, Critias and Socrates agree that knowledge of knowledge (and presumably of ignorance) causes its possessor to have self-knowledge.[16] The idea seems to be that self-knowledge, understood as knowledge of one's own knowledge or ignorance, is an application of knowledge of knowledge and ignorance to one's own case.

In the *Charmides*, Socrates argues that knowledge of knowledge and ignorance is not possible, or, if it is possible, is not beneficial—as one would expect of a virtue like temperance. How do these arguments bear on Socrates' knowledge of his own ignorance,[17] and his practice of cross-examining others to test their knowledge or ignorance? In

---

13 *Charmides* 164d.

14 *Charmides* 167a.

15 Julia Annas, "Self-Knowledge in Early Plato," in *Platonic Investigations*, ed. D. J. O'Meara (Washington, DC: Catholic University of America Press, 1985), 134. Cf. M. M. McCabe, "It Goes Deep with Me: Plato's *Charmides* on Knowledge, Self-Knowledge, and Integrity," in *Philosophy, Ethics, and a Common Humanity: Essays in Honour of Raimond Gaita*, ed. Christopher Cordner (New York: Routledge, 2011), 167.

16 *Charmides* 169e.

17 *Apology* 21b.

the relevant passages of the *Charmides*, Critias proposes (and Socrates elaborates):

(1) Self-knowledge is knowledge (*epistēmē*). Although all the other knowledges are about something other than themselves,[18] temperance/self-knowledge is uniquely of itself and all the other knowledges.[19]

The knowledge of knowledge Critias is describing is not a second-order knowledge that a person with first-order knowledge of some particular subject matter, for example, medicine, possesses in virtue of possessing that first-order knowledge. Rather, just like any first-order knowledge, knowledge of knowledge is treated as independent of any other (body of) knowledge, and is what it is in virtue of its subject matter, in this case, knowledge.

(2) A knowledge of itself and all other knowledges would have to be a knowledge of non-knowledge as well (as, e.g., medicine, knowledge of health, is also knowledge of sickness).[20]

(3) Only the possessor of this knowledge of knowledge and of ignorance can know whether he himself or anyone else has knowledge or not.[21]

(Here the words *ti tis oiden kai oietai, eiper oiden, kai ti au oieitai kai men eidenai, oiden d'ou* clearly echo Socrates' account of the way in which he is the wisest).[22]

---

18 *Charmides* 166a.

19 *Charmides* 166e5–6.

20 *Charmides* 166e7–8.

21 *Charmides* 166e–67a.

22 *Apology* 21d.

Socrates counters:

(4) The ability to know knowledge and ignorance is sui generis (*atopon*)[23] among abilities: there is no sight that is of itself and other sights but not of color, similarly for sound, desire, fear, opinion.[24]

(5) Knowledge is knowledge of something because of the sort of power it (viz., the knowledge) has, as a result of which (*hōste*) it is knowledge (viz., grasp) of that thing.[25]

(6) Similarly, the greater is greater than something because of the sort of power it has, as a result of which it is greater than the smaller.[26]

(7) If the greater were greater than itself, it would also be less than itself.

(8) In general, anything that has a power over itself in relation to itself (*pros heauto*) will also have that nature which is had by the object over which it is a power.[27] For example, if sight, the object of which is color, is itself to be seen, sight must be colored.

(9) But how are we to determine whether all powers are over something distinct, or there are some that can be of themselves?[28]

The issue is whether all powers are like relative magnitude (e.g., being greater than), which relate relata of contrary natures (the greater, the smaller) and so preclude the power from being related to itself—for that would require it to have contrary natures.[29] Knowledge would not

---

23 *Charmides* 165c4 and 168a10.

24 *Charmides* 167c–68a.

25 *Charmides* 168b.

26 *Charmides* 168c.

27 *Charmides* 168d1–3.

28 *Charmides* 170a.

29 *Charmides* 168e.

be like this if, for example, the key features of the objects of knowledge that makes them knowable are their immateriality and unchanging-ness, at least if knowledge (or the subject of knowledge qua knower) is essentially immaterial and unchangeable.[30]

A possible lesson of (1) to (9) is that Socrates' knowledge of ignorance should not be thought of as knowledge (*epistēmē*), strictly speaking, for that would have to be of what its object *is* (i.e., the object's nature), and the same knowledge would have to be of both its object and the opposite. Perhaps, instead, it should be thought of as some sort of recognition or awareness, which need not be of opposites;[31] sight, after all, is of color but not of the absence of color. Socrates goes on to argue:

(10) Supposing knowledge of knowledge to be possible, knowledge of knowledge (as distinct from knowledge of some particular subject matter, like medicine or shoemaking) would enable its possessor to know *that* someone is knowledgeable, but not *of what* he is knowledgeable.[32]

How can the knowledge of knowledge enable the knowledge or recog-nition that someone is knowledgeable independently of any knowledge (recognition) of the subject area over which this someone is knowl-edgeable? Perhaps the thought is that the person with knowledge of

---

30 Julia Annas suggests that "knowledge of knowledge peters out because there is no way of interpret-ing it as knowledge of something in the way Socrates requires; and it is clear that the requirement can only be met if knowledge is conceived of as a relation between a subject and a distinct object, existing separately from the knower" (Annas, "Self-Knowledge in Early Plato," 135). By contrast, I suggest that the requirement isn't for subject and object to be distinct, but rather for subject (*qua* having a given power) and object to have natures such that the power is a "fit" for both subject and object.

31 Cf. Hugh Benson, "A Note on Socratic Self-Knowledge in the *Charmides*," *Ancient Philosophy* 23 (2003): 31–47. Benson argues that whereas knowledge must be of opposites, mere awareness need not be. Benson takes the *Charmides* arguments to show that Socrates, since he lacks knowledge, can only recognize ignorance, not knowledge; this corrects Socrates' assumption in the *Apology* that cross-examination enables him, while being ignorant himself, to identify both ignorance and knowledge (Benson, 33 and 40–45).

32 *Charmides* 170a–c.

knowledge knows what knowledge is (or, more in line with the idea that knowledge of knowledge and ignorance is a recognitional ability, knows knowledge to be unerring and of what is).[33] Might this enable him to identify other knowers without knowing their special subject matter? It's hard to see how: would he cross-examine them? About what? Even if they prove irrefutable, this does not establish them as knowledgeable. Without answers to these questions, it is difficult to determine whether the *Charmides* upholds or corrects Socrates' assumption in the *Apology* that despite his ignorance about things great and small, he is able to identify the knowledgeable as well as the ignorant. Further, these considerations also raise the question whether, by cross-examination, Socrates is only able to establish *that* the person refuted is ignorant, not what his ignorance is—contrary to his judgment in the *Apology* that he, the politicians, poets, and craftsmen, are ignorant of human and social virtue.[34]

However, even granting the possibility of knowledge that someone is knowledgeable or ignorant without knowledge of what he is knowledgeable or ignorant about, Socrates argues next:

(11) Knowledge of knowledge, and mere knowledge that
      someone is knowledgeable, would not be beneficial, as befits
      a virtue like temperance, for it is by knowledge-what that
      one identifies an expert in a given area: for example, it is by
      medicine that one knows whether one (oneself or another)
      knows the healthy and the sick, and such knowledge-what is

---

33 *Theaetetus* 152c.

34 Cf. Charles Kahn, "Plato's *Charmides* and the Proleptic Reading of the Dialogues," *Journal of Philosophy* 85 (1988): 541–49. Kahn concludes that these arguments show that one may only have knowledge of knowledge or ignorance, or "second-order" knowledge, in case one has first-order knowledge of the subject matter that defines a branch of knowledge. For, Kahn argues, Socrates' success at identifying his interlocutors' ignorance presupposes his possession of knowledge in the domains on which he examines them—viz., matters of human excellence and good and bad, generally. Cf. Kahn, "Plato's *Charmides*," 546–48.

the thing that would enable us to remove error from our lives by assigning tasks to the relevant experts.[35]

Socrates lacks this beneficial knowledge.[36] The thin knowledge of ignorance and knowledge Socrates is supposed to have in the *Apology*, although rare, necessary for the pursuit of knowledge, and in cases like Socrates' actually motivating the pursuit of knowledge, is no very great thing. Perhaps Plato means to show Socrates refusing Critias' aggrandizing offer to make him a paragon of temperance. Perhaps he means to credit Socrates with modesty—not the virtue proper, but a "human modesty."

It's time to step back and ask: while it makes intuitive sense that knowledge of one's limits—including one's ignorance—should be a part of self-knowledge, why does Socrates focus on knowledge of one's knowledge and ignorance to the exclusion of practically everything else? What about knowing one's likes and dislikes? Values and goals? Why does Socrates not inquire into these in the pursuit of self-knowledge (or to get others to pursue it)?

There are two parts to the answer. First, as Plato tells Socrates' story, Socrates seems initially to have acquired that part of self-knowledge which is knowledge of his knowledge and ignorance as an unintended (albeit natural) consequence of his wide-ranging pursuit of knowledge about the way things are, not because he sought self-knowledge in the first place. In Plato's *Phaedo*, Socrates says that as a young man he was keen on the study of nature, but it led him to unlearn even the ordinary knowledge he previously had, as a result of which he hypothesized Forms and examined their consequences and possible grounds.[37] Plato's

---

35 *Charmides* 169b and 171b–72a.

36 Cf. Richard McKim, "Socratic Self-Knowledge and 'Knowledge of Knowledge,'" in "Plato's *Charmides*," *Transactions of the American Philological Association* (1985): 59–77. McKim adds that this beneficial knowledge cannot be attained by Socrates' methods of cross-examination; I don't think the text speaks to this question.

37 *Phaedo* 96a et sq.

Parmenides shows a young Socrates discovering the many problems with this hypothesis as he is cross-examined by Parmenides. Socrates likely also cross-examined other people even before the oracle (likely in the 430s B.C.E. and before war broke out in 431). Nicias says that it was only as a child (*pais*) that Socrates didn't question you and make you give an account of your whole life;[38] in the 430s Socrates would already have been in his thirties, more than a decade past childhood.[39] A reason for him to cross-examine other people before the oracle is suggested by the *Protagoras* (dramatic date ca. 433 B.C.E.), where Socrates (at least initially) cross-examines Protagoras to determine whether he has the knowledge that would qualify him to teach Hippocrates virtue. This is a sufficient reason to cross-examine someone even without a god-given mission to expose people's ignorance. Finally, the fact that Socrates pursues the question "What does the oracle mean?" by trying to refute (*elenchein*) it with the example of someone wiser than himself[40] suggests that he is familiar with the practice of pointing out contradictions in order to motivate a deeper interpretation.[41] As a consequence of his pursuit of knowledge, Socrates becomes aware of his ignorance, and presumably of the ignorance of some others, but it is the oracle's judgment that makes his purported wisdom and experienced ignorance itself an object of inquiry for him. Nor are Socrates' post-oracle cross-examinations only for the sake of exposing ignorance. Thus in the *Charmides*, Socrates assures Critias that he refutes Critias' statements for the same reason he would refute his own: lest he think he knows something he does not, *and* for the sake of the truth, which is a good common to mankind.[42] And in the *Gorgias*, he tells his Gorgias that he would rather be refuted

---

38 *Laches* 187d–88a.

39 This is why Nicias can't be talking about the beginning of Socrates' "elenctic mission," as claimed by C. D. C. Reeve, *Socrates in the "Apology"* (Indianapolis: Hackett, 1989), 21.

40 *Apology*, 21b.

41 *Protagoras* 339a–48a.

42 *Charmides* 166c–d.

than refute, for being refuted would deliver him of a false belief.[43] So Socrates' focus on knowledge of one's own knowledge and ignorance is a consequence of his pursuit of knowledge in the first place.

Second, Socrates seems to think that the way to knowledge of what we believe or value is to cross-examine ourselves as we would in order to inquire into the truth about things, for we don't (otherwise) know what we believe.[44] For example, in the *Gorgias* Socrates says Polus denies (*ouch hōs ge phēsin*) that doing what one sees fit is having great power, even as Polus says that he affirms it (*phēmi*);[45] Socrates says Polus (and everyone else) believes that doing injustice is worse (for the agent) than suffering it, even as Polus insists that suffering injustice is worse[46] (cf. Diotima telling Socrates that he says love is not a god, contrary to Socrates' plain assertion that love is a god).[47]

Socrates' method of cross-examination explains why one might reasonably conclude that people don't know what they believe. The schema of a Socratic examination is as follows: Socrates asks the interlocutor a question, to which the interlocutor replies with some p (where usually this is because p seems to him to be how things are, although sometimes p is a hypothesis granted for the sake of inquiry). Socrates elicits from the interlocutor further assertions q, r, s, t, and so on, and then shows that these assertions entail not-p. Socrates then asks the examinee which of p or the other assertions he wishes to revise, or tells him

---

43 *Gorgias* 458a.

44 Tad Brennan, "Reading Plato's Mind" in the forthcoming *Keeling Colloquium in Ancient Philosophy*, ed. Fiona Leigh, argues that the "autobiographical" Letter 7 presents Plato as concerned with a thicker kind of self-knowledge (thicker than knowledge of one's own knowledge or ignorance) when he cites his beliefs and values to explain his plans and justify his conduct with respect to both Dionysius, tyrant of Syracuse, and Dion, once their friend and then Dionysius' nemesis. This explanation form—actions in light of values—is similar to that found in the character sketches in *Republic* 8 and 9. I've come to the conclusion that such accounts don't require self-*knowledge*—they are available to the massively self-deceived as well, for all they require is that what seem to one to be one's beliefs and values seem to explain one's actions.

45 *Gorgias* 466e.

46 *Gorgias* 474b.

47 *Symposium* 201e–2d.

that p has been proved false, or that, contrary to his avowal that p, he has been shown not to believe that p. What warrants the last of these claims is that presumably the interlocutor hasn't all along been holding p and not-p firmly in view (interlocutors are routinely surprised or annoyed by Socrates' cross-examination), but has been ignoring q, r, s, t, or what follows from or is presupposed by them or by p, and paying attention only to some of these. In such a situation the interlocutor doesn't know what he believes, not only in the sense of "all the things he believes" but also he doesn't know, about any of the specific beliefs p or q, r, s, t, whether he believes them or not—if believing it involves accepting its entailments, acting on it, and so on. In a sense, what one *does* believe is determined (produced as well as discovered) by finding out what *to* believe through cross-examination.

However, inconsistency detection falls short of identifying which member(s) of the set p, q, r, s, t the interlocutor does and doesn't believe, so how can Socrates know this about his interlocutor, rather than just that somewhere in him lies some ignorance? We might think that Socrates' dialectical skill enables him to identify which beliefs an interlocutor is committed to because they are entailments of things he already believes, but entailments by themselves don't settle which of two conflicting beliefs the interlocutor believes. Does Socrates say what people believe on the basis of his experience examining people and finding no one can hold onto certain beliefs? Or because he believes that the truth lies within each of us and he has some kind of handle on this truth?[48]

---

48 Gregory Vlastos, "The Socratic Elenchus: Method Is All," in *Socratic Studies*, ed. Myles Burnyeat (Cambridge: Cambridge University Press, 1994), 1–37, argues that since inconsistency detection cannot determine what the interlocutor believes, Socrates must be making a "meta-elenctic assumption" based on long experience, viz.: "Whoever has a false moral belief will always have at the same time true beliefs entailing the negation of that false belief" (Vlastos, "Socratic Elenchus," 25). From this assumption Socrates "could infer securely that any set of moral beliefs which was internally consistent would contain exclusively true beliefs" (26). Socrates' own beliefs are internally consistent, so he can attribute them to his interlocutor even contrary to the interlocutor's avowals. In the *Meno*, Plato develops the theory that we already possess all knowledge in some latent form, so that what we call learning is really just recollecting what we already knew (*Meno* 81a–86b), in order to secure Socrates' "epistemologically naïve" assumption (Vlastos, "Socratic Elenchus," 28–29).

Our discussion so far has treated cross-examination of an interlocutor as the same sort of examination one might conduct on oneself, and indeed Socrates says that both can happen in the same conversation. However, Raphael Woolf observes that the dialogues never stage Socrates examining himself—except in the *Hippias Major*, where a "someone" who turns out to be Socrates questions Socrates and critiques his answers.[49] Woolf explains this absence by arguing that cross-examination of beliefs requires distance from the beliefs examined but believing makes such distance impossible. So I cannot both believe that p, and genuinely be open to p's being false, at the same time. (To believe that p, on this view, is to believe that p is true—as opposed to, for instance, to be answerable for p, or to judge p more likely than the alternatives.) But this makes Socratic self-examination impossible. Woolf worries that his argument makes a mystery of how Socrates comes by his knowledge of his own ignorance in the first place,[50] but we need not be mystified. First, Socrates describes thought as a silent discussion that the soul has with itself about the objects under consideration,[51] and having Socrates speak his thoughts out loud to himself would undermine verisimilitude. Second, in his discussions Socrates engages with many cognitive attitudes other than beliefs so committed they can't be examined without losing their status: for example, the hypothesis that virtue is knowledge and its consequences;[52] the appearance, from one perspective, that the good person is the one able to do F and not-F when he wants, even though the contrary appears from another perspective;[53] the impression of temperance that possession of this virtue produces in the mind of the temperate person.[54] So,

---

49 Cf. Raphael Woolf, "Socratic Authority," in *Ancient Philosophy of the Self*, ed. Paulina Remes and Juha Sihvola (Dordrecht: Springer, 2008), 86–92.

50 Woolf, "Socratic Authority" 103–7.

51 *Theaetetus* 189e–90a.

52 *Meno* 87b & sq.

53 *Hippias Minor* 372d–e, 376c.

54 *Charmides* 159a.

third, if Socrates needs to examine a firmly held belief of his own, he should be able to temporarily weaken his commitment to its truth and consider it as a hypothesis or appearance if this is necessary for open-minded cross-examination. But, fourth, it is not even clear that cross-examination requires this, since we may believe quite strongly both p as well as the q, r, s, t that (escaping our notice) entail not-p; once we notice this, however, even if we weren't previously open-minded, our new awareness of our ignorance can open our mind.

1.3. Knowledge of One's Capacities

Following his confession of ignorance of whether he is "more complicated than Typhon" or "simpler . . . [and] sharing in a divine . . . lot,"[55] Socrates argues that all soul is immortal[56] and then gives an account of what the human soul is like in structure, likening it to a winged chariot, drawn by two horses representing the appetites and anger, and driven by a charioteer that representing reason.[57] Later, in the *Phaedrus*, Socrates explains that the soul, as a natural thing, should be studied according to "the method of Hippocrates and the true account": for each thing, determine whether it is simple or complex; if complex, enumerate its simples; for each simple, determine its power to act, and on what, and its power to be affected, and by what.[58] The arguments for the division of the soul in *Republic* 4 and 10 show that a thing may be analyzed into simples by considering cases in which its opposed attitudes or movements require positing distinct subjects to be the bearers of these attitudes or movements;[59] to determine the powers to act and be affected of each simple, it would seem, requires considering

---

55 Plato, *Phaedrus*, 229e–30a.

56 *Phaedrus* 245c–e.

57 *Phaedrus* 246a–56e.

58 *Phaedrus* 270d.

59 *Phaedrus* 436b–41c.

each simple in different circumstances: for example, embodied—in humans, virtuous as well as vicious, in nonhuman animals—and disembodied. *Republic* 4's cases of opposition divide the soul into three: an appetitive, angering, and reasoning part.

These texts may seem to have answered Socrates' question about what he is by nature, yet at the end of the *Republic* Socrates says that for the soul to be known as it is in truth, it should be considered separated from the body (whereas the discussion has so far considered the embodied soul, bringing up cases of psychological conflict and character types from experience), and in its love of wisdom.[60] He privileges one condition and one activity—philosophy—for determining the true nature of the soul and suggests that among the questions that will be answered by studying the soul's philosophy is whether it is simple or multiform.

Myles Burnyeat has proposed that the *Timaeus* and *Phaedrus* explore the two alternatives sketched in this passage of the *Republic*, of an essentially simple, rational soul, and an essentially tripartite one.[61] The *Phaedrus* depicts the human soul as tripartite in both its embodied and disembodied conditions,[62] but in the *Timaeus* the soul is purely rational prior to (its first) embodiment, and it is human embodiment that provides the occasion for tripartition.[63] We can take this suggestion further. Both dialogues are following the *Republic*'s instruction to "look at the soul in its love of wisdom," namely, in its activity of contemplating Forms (*Phaedrus*) or being/becoming rational by understanding the rationality of the cosmos (*Timaeus*). In looking at the soul in its philosophy, the *Timaeus* is looking at how things must be set up—in the world, and locally, in the body—to give an embodied soul the opportunity to do philosophy and thereby return to its

---

60 *Republic* 611e–12a.

61 Cf. Myles Burnyeat, "The Truth of Tripartition," *Proceedings of the Aristotelian Society* 106 (2006): 1–23.

62 *Phaedrus* 246a–56e.

63 *Timaeus* 42a–b, 43a–44b, 69c–72d.

simple condition, whereafter its understanding seems to be just like that of the soul of the world. And the *Phaedrus* is looking at both what a complex soul's motivations must be for philosophy to be possible, and how philosophy affects the various motivations of a complex soul. Plato warns that the *Phaedrus* account is not of what the soul's constitution is, but of what it is like,[64] and that the *Timaeus* account, the subject of which is a likeness of a model and, as such, unstable, is itself also unstable.[65] Neither dialogue decisively answers the question, "Is the soul simple or complex?"; rather, one begins with the assumption that the soul is simple and the other that the soul is complex, and both explore some consequences for the soul's philosophy. What does receive an answer of a sort is the question of what the capacities are of each of the simples (on the different hypotheses) relevant to the soul's philosophy.

The famous image in the *Republic* of the human soul as a composite of a human being, a lion, and a many-headed beast,[66] with the rational part of the soul as the human being within, likewise points in two ways. On the one hand, the rational part is the human being. On the other hand, Socrates remarks that because the human body is a likeness of the human being within, those who see only the outside and not the inside have the (incorrect) appearance (*phainesthai*) of a single human animal (588d10–e1).[67]

I want to suggest, in closing, that *Alcibiades I* also directs us to "look at the soul in its philosophy" in order to know itself, with philosophy described somewhat less commitally than in *Timaeus* and *Phaedrus*, as "looking at all the divine, god and understanding".[68]

---

64 *Phaedrus* 246a.

65 *Phaedrus* 29b–c.

66 *Republic* 588b–e.

67 *Republic* 588d10–e1.

68 *Alcibiades* 133c. While I don't want to stake out a position on the authenticity (or not) of this dialogue, I do want to note that all the elements of its account of self-care and self-knowledge are found in the uncontroversially authentic dialogues *Phaedo, Gorgias, Theaetetus,* and *Republic*. Some will see

In *Alcibiades I*, Socrates supposes that to know how to care for ourselves and make ourselves better, we need to know what we are, as enjoined by the Delphic oracle.[69] He reasons that since the person is not the body, but rather the soul that uses and rules the body,[70] the injunction to know ourselves means that we should know our souls.[71] And the way in which we come to know ourselves is suggested by analogy with how an eye comes to see itself: by looking at the part of itself by which it sees, reflected in the eye of another. Similarly, we come to know ourselves by knowing that part of our soul by which we know, for that is where wisdom, which makes a soul good, comes about.[72]

It may seem that here at least Socrates identifies the true self with the subject that engages in inquiry and achieves knowledge, committing himself on the question so carefully but inconclusively explored in the *Republic, Phaedrus,* and *Timaeus.* Yet Socrates doesn't need to say this to answer his initial question, namely, "How shall we make ourselves better?,"[73] for that is answered by "by attending, caring for, and being guided by the part of the soul in which wisdom, which makes the soul good, comes to be."[74] Nor does he need to say it to answer "What are

---

this as doctrinal convergence favoring authenticity, and others will see it as favoring skepticism on the grounds that these loci are the sources of the pastiche that is *Alcibiades I*:

(1) The care of the soul is connected with the pursuit of wisdom and truth (*Apology* 29d–30b).

(2) Socrates is not his body (*Phaedo* 115c–16a.), and so must be his soul.

(3) The soul is akin to the pure, eternal, and unchanging Forms it knows; this soul is ruler over the body (*Phaedo* 179d–80a).

(4) The soul is the proper subject of perception, using eyes, ears, etc. as its instruments (*Theaetetus* 184c–e.).

(5) Knowledge of the soul's true nature is to be found by looking at the soul in its love of wisdom (*Republic* 611d–e.).

69 *Alcibiades I* 128e–9a.

70 *Alcibiades I* 130c.

71 *Alcibiades I* 131e.

72 *Alcibiades I* 132d–33c and 130d–e.

73 *Alcibiades I* 128e–29a.

74 *Alcibiades I* 133b.

we?" in a way that is relevant to answering that initial question, for if there is some part of us cultivation of which makes us good, it doesn't follow that we are just that part. In fact, thinking that we are only that part could obscure knowledge of our moral and intellectual state, as well as of any internal challenges we might face in becoming good, whereas acknowledging that we are composed of a better and worse part (if we are) would empower our aspiration to be good and enable a more accurate description of our state, good or bad.[75]

And in fact Socrates does not answer the question "What is the self?" by "the subject of knowledge/inquiry" in *Alcibiades I*. Like the *Republic, Phaedrus,* and *Timaeus, Alcibiades I* apologizes for the imprecision of its account of the soul. *Alcibiades I*'s condition for greater precision about the self is knowledge of what "itself" is, not just, as in the present discussion, what each self (*auton hekaston*) is;[76] however, the fact that the soul is more authoritative (*kuriōteron*)[77] than anything else in us suffices to identify the soul with the self, which is user and ruler of the body and its possessions. All this suggests that although further precision about what the self is is possible, it will not be found in this discussion. In this case, we should not expect the eye analogy to precisify what self is any more than "soul."[78] What the eye analogy does instead is to suggest *how* we should pursue the question, "What is soul?": just as an eye sees itself by looking into another eye and in particular at the pupil, the best part of the eye, the part with which it sees, so, too, a soul will know itself by looking at that good-making part of a soul in which wisdom comes to be.[79] Certainly the eye won't see itself at all if it looks at some nonreflective part of the face or eye, and the pupil is the part of the eye responsible for the eye's best (and indeed

---

75 *Republic*, 430e–31a.

76 *Alcibiades I* 130c–d.

77 *Alcibiades I* 130d5.

78 *Alcibiades I* 132b. We've answered that question.

79 *Alcibiades I* 133a–b.

defining) activity, seeing. But it would be a mistake to conclude that the eye *is* the pupil. Similarly, if we don't pay attention to the wisdom-seeking part of our soul, we will miss what our soul—distinctively and importantly—is; we will miss the defining capacity of human beings. But it doesn't follow that other parts or capacities are in any sense not us.[80] As to how we come to know the wisdom-seeking part of the soul, the eye analogy suggests—as we might expect from the *Republic*'s "observe the soul in its philosophy" and the *Phaedrus*' "of each simple, observe what it acts on and is affected by"—*Alcibiades I* directs us to the activity and objects of wisdom.

Many modern readers of the *Alcibiades I* have remarked that it treats self-knowledge as (in Annas' words) "not of the paradigmatically subjective, the embodied individual; [but rather] of the paradigmatically objective, so that the true self turns out to be God, the ultimate reality."[81] But viewing *Alcibiades I*'s self-knowledge in the context of dialogues that pursue self-knowledge in the sense of knowledge of one's soul, which is a set of capacities one has qua human, its objective and universal (rather than subjective and individual) answer comes as no surprise. Individuals differ in their states, not their capacities.

---

80 A recent expression of this (widespread) view is in Pauliina Remes' claim that the proper object of self-knowledge is the subject of thought and reasoning, not the mover of the body (although the boundary between self and world is complicated by the fact that the self's instruments include body, language, and reasons). Pauliina Remes, "Reason to Care: The Object and Structure of Self-Knowledge in the *Alcibiades* 1," *Apeiron* 46 (2013): 285.

81 Annas, "Self-Knowledge in Early Plato," 133.

CHAPTER TWO

Aristotle's Requisite of Self-Knowledge

Christopher Shields

2.1. RYLE'S DILEMMA IN ARISTOTLE'S FRAMEWORK

Long after Aristotle's death, one of his most ardent admirers posed a problem, a dilemma of sorts, about our ability to know ourselves:

> Should I, or should I not, put my knowing self down on my list of the sorts of things that I can have knowledge of? If I say "no," it seems to reduce my knowing self to a theoretically infertile mystery, yet if I say "yes," it seems to reduce the fishing-net to one of the fishes which it itself catches. It seems hazardous either to allow or to deny that the judge can be put into the dock.[1]

---

1 Gilbert Ryle, *The Concept of Mind* (Chicago: University of Chicago Press, 1949), 187.

This was Gilbert Ryle, writing in the mid-twentieth century, recounting a problem which had by then become standard fare. This is perhaps why Ryle did not think it necessary to move beyond metaphor in posing his problem. Unfortunately, colorful and evocative as its metaphors may be, Ryle's dilemma proves no less elusive than the self whose knowledge it specifies as forever beyond our grasp. Why may a judge not be judged, or a net itself not be netted?

Ryle's general worry may none the less be brought into a sharper focus. Shall we say that the knowing self knows itself? If not, then the knowing self itself remains forever unknown; in this case, our theories of the self are doomed to remain forever jejune. Yet if the self may come to know itself, then as we seek self-knowledge, we seem engaged in a markedly misdirected activity, as if we were fisherman setting nets routinely set to catch fishes in a misplaced effort to catch those very nets themselves; and something—Ryle does not say just what—seems oddly amiss in such a procedure. Perhaps his concern is that in asking the knowing self to know itself we are asking a tool to turn its activity upon itself instead of upon its appropriate objects, as if attempting to wield a hammer in an effort to pound not a nail but the hammer itself: each time we lifted the hammer to pound the hammer, it would move aside, out of its own trajectory, rendering it hopelessly impotent when directed upon itself. Taking that together, then, either we cede up front that the knowing self is unknown to itself or we will perforce discover that its own operation precludes its turning its activity upon itself. In either case, the self eludes its own ability to know. If that is so, then, unfortunately, we must despair in the face of the Socratic invocation of the Delphic injunction: "Know yourself." Socrates admonishes (γνῶθι σεαυτόν; v. *Chrm.* 164d; *Prt.* 343b; *Phdr.* 229e; *Phlb.* 48c; *Laws* 2.923a; *I Alc.* 124a, 129a, 132c). Perhaps we would like to follow his admonition: but how?

Ryle did not pose his dilemma with Aristotle expressly in view, but one can appreciate that it finds a natural home within Aristotle's general framework of human thinking—and in two distinct ways, one quite general and the other highly specific and idiosyncratic. This general framework embraces an *act-object conception of thought*, of precisely the sort undergirding and to some extent motivating Ryle's dilemma. On Aristotle's approach, a subject such as Socrates thinks something, for example, *that justice is to be sought*, when and only when Socrates stands in relation to some suitable object of thought. This Aristotle infers on the basis of a parallel he draws between thinking and perceiving. Just as one perceives an object of perception by standing in an appropriate relation to some suitable object of perception, an *aisthēton*, so one thinks when one stands in relation to an object of thought, a *noēton* (*De Anima* 3.4, 429a13–15). Abstracting from the modality of these cases, we see a sameness of structure: thinking (like perceiving), consists in a subject *S*, a thinker (like a perceiver), standing in a relation *R*, thinking (again, like perceiving), to some object of thought (or, of perception). So, in each case: *S* stands in *R* to *o*.

This comparison thus ushers in a worry. One might suppose on its basis that just as our seeing eyes do not manage to see our seeing eyes, except indirectly, say in a mirror, so our thinking selves do not think our thinking selves, at least not in any direct way. We do not think ourselves as we think other objects of thought: we are objects of our own thoughts and perceptions only incidentally, if at all, through the aid of a reflective intermediary. Indeed, here Aristotle's analogy seems to make special difficulties for the knowing self: it, the knowing self, cannot catch itself knowing in the mirror whereas the eyes, at least, can and do catch themselves seeing.

Fairly plainly, the act-object conception of knowing, whatever its merits or demerits, does not *by itself* engender Ryle's problem of self-knowledge. After all, the act-object conception taken by itself is silent on the question of whether thinking may or may not be reflexive; and here any comparison to tools operating on themselves may appear highly inapposite. Hammers cannot hammer themselves, it is true, but that is because hammering is evidently a non- or irreflexive relation. By contrast, there seems to be no general reason to suppose that thinking must be irreflexive; on the contrary, thinking seems ideally suited to be reflexive, since, unlike seeing, it can turn its mental gaze where it will, including—absent some argument to the contrary—upon itself. More to the point, Aristotle several times insists that thinking and perceiving are disanalogous on just this point, since thinking is completely plastic, unrestrained in its objects, whereas perceiving is limited in range and scope (*De Anima* 3.4, 429a29–b9). If thinking can think "all things," as Aristotle says it can (*panta; De Anima* 3.4, 429a18), then presumably it can think itself, and can also think of itself thinking.

This, though, brings us to the second, idiosyncratic point in Aristotle pertinent to Ryle's dilemma. Aristotle maintains, in a challenging passage that has occasioned a number of distinct interpretations, that the reason (or mind, *nous*) is "in actuality none of the things that exist before it thinks" (*De Anima* 3.4, 429a22–24).[2] His reasons for asserting this derive precisely from his contention that the mind (*nous*) is ultimately plastic: he thinks that were it to have a determinate nature of its own, the mind would be precluded from ranging over various objects, because its own nature would occlude or hinder it, in the way that the physical structure of our eyes renders us incapable of seeing colors in the infrared spectrum or the physical structure of our ears renders us temporarily incapable of hearing after we have been subjected to deafeningly loud noises. This commitment in turn induces Aristotle to introduce a worry that begins to sound very much like one tending in the direction of Ryle's: "And there is a further difficulty: is reason (*nous*) itself an object of reason? For either reason will belong to other things, if it is an object of reason itself not in virtue of something else, and the object of reason is one in form, or it will be something mixed with it that makes it an object of reason just as other things are" (*De Anima* 3.4, 429b26–29). This sounds as if Aristotle is posing the following simple problem: how is it that the mind comes to operate

---

2 For an examination of Aristotle's reasoning in this passage, see Christopher Shields, "Intentionality and Isomorphism in Aristotle," *Proceedings of the Boston Area Colloquium in Ancient Philosophy* 11 (1995): 307–30.

on itself? If it is bereft of any positive nature of its own, then how can it know itself? What will there be, so to speak, *there* to be known? As it turns upon itself, it eludes itself, because its own plasticity renders it unsuited to be an object of its own operation.[3]

Taken together, then, Aristotle's general framework, together with his idiosyncratic conception of the ultimate plasticity of mind, leaves him with a Rylean problem: how can the knowing self know itself, if it has no nature to be known and so recedes from view each time it turns its attention upon itself?

Aristotle does not address the Rylean problem head on. That is, although he does reflect on the mind's capacity to have itself as one of its own objects in *De Anima* 3.4, Aristotle nowhere poses and answers an abstract puzzle about the possibility of *self*-knowledge. What he does do, however, turns out to be vastly more interesting: in reflecting on the requisite of self-knowledge for human friendship, Aristotle reflects deeply on the question of what a human being must know about herself—her nature, her character, her virtuous dispositions—in order to enter into stable, long-term loving relationships. This sort of self-knowledge confronts the Socratic injunction in a deep, material manner suited to the exigencies of human social living. It also, then, en passant resolves the Rylean puzzle which seeks to render self-knowledge unattainable.

2.2. INDIRECTION 1: AN UNPROMISING LOOK IN A MIRROR

The seeing eyes do not see themselves directly, but only indirectly in a reflection. They see themselves, and perhaps even see themselves seeing,

---

3 This seems to be the final verdict of S. H. Rosen, "Thought and Touch: A Note on Aristotle's *De Anima*," *Phronesis* 6 (1961): 127–37: "Precisely then if the *psyché* is itself formally indeterminate, it cannot think itself, since to do so would be to determine the indeterminate." He thinks that this in turn has the unhappy consequence that Aristotle's treatment of "the noetic *psyché* leads to the Platonic doctrine of the incapacity of the *psyché* to see itself directly (136)." We shall see some reason to doubt this inference.

when they focus directly on themselves in a mirror. The eyes might equally see themselves reflected elsewhere, when peering, for instance, into the reflecting eyes of a lover. So, we might also see our eyes seeing in the seeing eyes of another. To take Aristotle's own analogy further, then, perhaps the knowing self knows itself only by knowing its own reflection in the knowing activity of another. On this approach, we would attain self-knowledge, but via a reflective rather than reflexive mechanism.

This Aristotle in fact seems to suggest in an intriguing passage of his *Magna Moralia* 2.15,[4] in the context of responding to a worry about friendship. The worry arises in response to a problem about the presumed self-sufficiency of happiness. If we believe that a happy, flourishing life, a *eudaimon* life, is lacking in nothing, then we think that happiness suffices for a good life. Yet even happy people need friends: a life bereft of friends is inferior to a life replete with friends. Indeed, friends seem *required* for happiness in life. So, one might conclude, either, contrary to our account of happiness (eudaimonia), the happy life is not self-sufficient, or contrary to the evident facts, friendship does not make a life better. Aristotle's response:

> But the self-sufficiency about which we are conducting our inquiry is not that of god but of humans, the question being whether the self-sufficient human will require friendship or not. If, then, when one looked upon a friend one could see the nature and attributes of the friend, . . . such as to be a second self, at least if you make a very great friend, as the saying has it, "Here is another Heracles, a dear other I." Since, then, it is both a most difficult thing, as some of the sages have said, to attain knowledge of oneself, but also most pleasant—for to know oneself is pleasant—and, as we are, we are not able to see what we are from ourselves (and that we cannot do so is plain from the way in which we blame others without being aware that we do the same things ourselves) . . .

---

4 Aristotle, *Magna Moralia*, ed. F. Susemihl (Leipzig: Teubner, 1883).

Although the text of this passage is troubled, it none the less contains some rich suggestions about Aristotle's understanding of friendship, happiness, and self-knowledge. Its primary interest in the present context resides in its striking suggestion that a dear friend is a sort of "second self" or "another I" (*heteros einai egō*; ἕτερος εἶναι ἐγώ, 1213a12), whose apprehension provides us a valuable epistemic access to ourselves. The value of knowing another, Aristotle implies, derives from the sad but indisputable fact that we tend to be opaque to ourselves. As evidence, suggests Aristotle, we may witness our tendency to find fault in others for indulging in the very activities we ourselves perform: we are irritable that our neighbor is irritable, and we complain that our spouses complain too much.

Fortunately, we can overcome our tendency to self-opacity by seeing ourselves reflected in our friends:

> As, then, when we wish to see our own face, we do so by looking into a mirror, in the same way, when we wish to know ourselves, we can obtain that knowledge by looking at our friend. For the friend is, as we assert, another I. If, then, it is pleasant to know oneself, and it is not possible to know this without having someone else for a friend, the self-sufficient person will require friendship in order to know himself.

We see ourselves by seeing our friends, because in seeing them we see our second selves. From this angle, we learn that far from precluding its possibility, the self-sufficiency of eudaimonia positively *requires* friendship. To be complete, we must have self-knowledge; and to have self-knowledge, we must have the benefit of our friends, our second selves in whose reflected activities we see ourselves. In seeing ourselves reflected in our friends we thus manage to come to the pleasant self-knowledge that has otherwise been occluded from view.

So far, it must be said, Aristotle's gambit seems unpromising. He may, of course, be right to contend that the self-sufficiency and completeness of eudaimonia presupposes rather than precludes human friendship. What is striking, however, is that in making this case

Aristotle evidently cedes the second horn of Ryle's dilemma: we cannot, he seems to suggest, know ourselves directly or reflexively, and so *must* have friends if we are to attain self-knowledge. It is *only* by knowing ourselves as reflected in our friends that we can know who we are. This is to say, then, that self-knowledge can only be reflective and never reflexive. Yet, so far at least, we have been given no reason for supposing that this is so. To the extent, then, that Aristotle presumes this without argument, his case remains unconvincing: why should we agree that the knowing self knowing itself is like a net netting itself or a hammer hammering itself? When someone rubs her thumb with her forefinger she touches herself. Why must thinking be like seeing and not like touching? What, if anything, requires that it be irreflexive? Indeed, in another context, Aristotle himself is perfectly happy to contend that successful thinking *is* like touching (*Metaph.* 1051b24–25).

What is more, in this passage Aristotle seems to concede that *direct* self-knowledge is impossible—that we cannot know ourselves directly, but rather only indirectly—even while allowing that self-knowledge is pleasant. Such a presumption is at any rate evidently required for his defense of friendship here, which seems simply to be this: (1) eudaimonia requires self-knowledge; (2) self-knowledge is available only by reflection; (3) such reflection is afforded only by friends; hence, (4) friends are required for eudaimonia. If all that is correct, then directed self-knowledge is unattainable. The pleasure attendant on self-knowledge, then, is not derived exclusively from one's self. While this is no form of contradiction, it does introduce a sort of tension into Aristotle's approach. Presumably—although perhaps the matter is underdetermined[5]—the sort of self-knowledge the sages held to be pleasant was not refracted or reflected, but rather direct. This would be, for instance, the sort of knowledge Plato ascribes to the sages

---

5 Probably Aristotle intends to refer to no sage in particular but rather reflects the practice of ennobling an aphorism by offering it a venerable pedigree. See H. Parke and D. E. W. Wormell, *The Delphic Oracle* (Oxford: Blackwell, 1956), 1:389.

when he names them as the sources for the oracle's admonition (*Prt.* 343a–b).[6] The indirect knowledge that Aristotle offers in this passage is rather inferential, or quasi-inferential, as in the so-called *rouge test*, when a primate or a small child comes to realize, often with a startle, that the eyes in the mirror are its own eyes reflected.[7]

There is a more pressing problem in Aristotle's presentation in this passage: he assumes, but does not argue or otherwise establish, that self-knowledge cannot simply be reflexive, that it cannot be immediate, that it cannot be attained noninferentially by an agent's own immediate grasp of her own psychological states and not through the medium of a mirror. For at least some range of states, this seems very odd indeed: one need not rely upon the reactions of one's friends to learn that one is hungry. Doubtless our friends do teach us about ourselves, but it seems a grotesque distortion to insist that our friends are *always* better placed to offer us knowledge of ourselves than we are ourselves, that we *cannot* learn of ourselves from ourselves but *must* rely on glimpses of our attributes as they arise in others.

2.3. Indirection 2: A Second Look in the Mirror

Should we conclude, then, that Aristotle adopts this extreme view, without developed argument, and concedes that direct, unmediated self-knowledge is impossible? In some passages, Aristotle seems to come close to offering just this view, perhaps because he understands his act-object conception of knowledge in a manner prefiguring Ryle. So, for instance, in a suggestive passage of his *Metaphysics* 12.9, Aristotle contends that "it appears that knowledge and perception and belief and understanding have only other things as their objects and are of themselves only as a byproduct" (*Metaph.* 1074b35–36; φαίνεται

---

6 Plato lists seven sages, including both Thales and Solon, as sources (*Prot.* 343a–b).

7 For this test devised to measure self-awareness in small children and some primates see G. G. Gallup, "Chimpanzees: Self-Recognition," *Science* 167 (1970): 86–87; and Jens B. Asendorpf et al.,

δ' ἀεὶ ἄλλου ἡ ἐπιστήμη καὶ ἡ αἴσθησις καὶ ἡ δόξα καὶ ἡ διάνοια, αὐτῆς δ' ἐν παρέργῳ). It is reasonable to understand Aristotle here as very nearly asserting the thesis that all thought, like all perception, is in the first instance directed on some object other than itself, with the result that it thinks of itself only as a byproduct, or perhaps in a secondary or derivative way (*en parergō*; ἐν παρέργῳ). This comes near to stating, then, that thinking can no more be reflexive than visual perception: when thought thinks itself, it does so by grasping itself in something other, in its primary object. This in turn seems to imply that thinking is not and cannot be reflexive: the thinking self, then, will think itself if at all only indirectly, as it is reflected in another, primary object.

This passage occurs, it should be stressed, in a complex characterization of God's self-awareness,[8] but the mental states here recounted are perfectly general and certainly not restricted to those God exhibits. If taken at face value, then it seems to assert—rather than to establish—that thinking is necessarily indirect, because never self-reflexive. So, one may wonder why Aristotle holds to this position, if in fact he does.[9] Nor, even if he does, would this give us a determinate reason for thinking that the thinking self cannot think of itself: the self thinks but is not identical with the process of thinking. The putative non- or irreflexivity of thinking does not preclude its being turned upon the self manifesting it. If one is to complete his argument in the *Magna*

"Self-Awareness and Other-Awareness II: Mirror Self-Recognition, Social Contingency Awareness, and Synchronic Imitation," *Developmental Psychology* 32.2 (1996): 313–21.

8 Sandbach offers a clear overview of the structure of the passage, arguing unsuccessfully, though, for an unnecessary emendation. See F. H. Sandbach, "A Transposition in Aristotle, *Metaphysics* Λ c. 9 1074 b," *Mnemosyne*, 4th ser., 7 (1954): 39–43.

9 This is how Oehler understands the passage. See Klaus Oehler, "Aristotle on Self-Knowledge," *Proceedings of the American Philosophical Society* 118 (1954): 493–506: "Since the real function of thought is understood by Aristotle to be intentional, not reflexive, their self-reference can only be accidental or secondary. . . . It is the sort of self-reference which can come about only through reference to a distinct object" (497). Two questions naturally arise in light of these contentions: (1) why should one support a direct move from "intentional" to "not reflexive" (since nothing about intentionality itself is incompatible with reflexivity)? and (2) supposing that is so, what would self-reference constrained to "come about only through reference to a distinct object" consist in? Are we forever constrained to refer to ourselves by referring to an object we see in some manner of mirror?

Moralia in any sort of convincing way, then, what is needed is either a technical reason for holding that thought can never be reflexive or some other ground for supposing that unmediated *self*-knowledge is impossible. So far, at least, Aristotle has provided neither.

It is, moreover, striking, that Aristotle develops his contention that the happy person requires friends in two further passages, the first of which, in *Nicomachean Ethics* 9.9, eschews the appeal to self-knowledge altogether. In this chapter, we once again find Aristotle debating the question of whether a good person requires friends. Now, however, his solution is comparatively measured and also grounded in a completely different way:

> Surely it is strange, too, to make the blessed man a solitary; for no one would choose to possess all good things on condition of being alone, since man is a political creature and one whose nature is to live with others. Therefore even the happy man lives with others; for he has the things that are by nature good. And plainly it is better to spend his days with friends and good men than with strangers or any chance persons. Therefore, the happy man needs friends.

Aristotle moderates his response of the *Magna Moralia* in two distinct ways.

First, and most crucially for the present context, he now bases his claim regarding the need for friendship not in any putative facts about self-knowledge, but rather in a claim about the political character of human beings. In saying that humans are political animals, Aristotle seeks to locate the need for friendship in facts about human nature. Consequently, the appeal to self-knowledge falls away altogether. Second, Aristotle offers as evidence for the goodness of friendship its *choiceworthiness*: the value of friendship is indicated not because it affords self-knowledge, but rather because it contributes in ascertainable ways to the human good. In a different way, then, these two grounds orient the value of friendship in features given objectively, by nature, and not by any instrumental value friends might have for the attainment of self-knowledge. In *Nicomachean Ethics* 9.9,[10] Aristotle relies not on mirrors, but on natures. He does so, finally, in a way which seems to implicate him in a clear non sequitur. As stated, the argument asserts that friends are external goods and human beings need external goods to be happy, and infers on that basis that friends are required for happiness; but it does not follow from the fact that a human being requires external goods for eudaimonia that the external goods needed will include the good of friendship. Minimally, some further contention is needed to bridge this gap.

The approach to friendship in this chapter, then, may appear to have no relevance to an inquiry into Aristotle's approach to self-knowledge. In fact, though, this appearance proves illusory. Its relevance to questions of self-knowledge emerges in a striking way in a more developed, parallel passage in the *Eudemian Ethics* 7.12.[11] There Aristotle grafts his thoughts about self-knowledge in the *Magna Moralia* onto the objective framework of the *Nicomachean Ethics* in an illuminating way. The *Eudemian Ethics* appeals once again to the reflected self-knowledge afforded by friends, but now from a new angle. It emerges, Aristotle now implies, that the two accounts considered thus far are complementary approaches to the same problem. This sheds new and distinctive light on Aristotle's approach to self-knowledge.

Here the problem about the relation of self-sufficiency to friendship is set once more, but now in a way which seems sensitive to the non sequitur of the *Nicomachean Ethics*:

> We must also consider self-sufficiency and friendship, and the relations they have to one another. For one might doubt whether, if a man be in all respects self-sufficient, he will have a friend, if one seeks a friend on the basis of some need and the good man is perfectly

---

10 Aristotle, *Ethica Nicomachea*, ed. I. Bywater (Oxford: Oxford University Press, 1963).

11 Aristotle, *Ethica Eudemia*, ed. R. Walzer and J. Mingay (Oxford: Oxford University Press, 1991).

self-sufficient. If the possessor of excellence is happy, why should he need a friend? For the self-sufficient man needs people neither because they are useful nor because they cheer him; nor in general does he need society: his own society is enough for him. This is most plain in the case of a god; for it is clear that, needing nothing, a god will not need a friend, nor will a god have a friend, supposing that he does not need one.

The answer provides a fresh twist, one yoking Aristotle's talk of reflected self-knowledge in the *Magna Moralia* to the more objective approach of the *Nicomachean Ethics*:

> It is manifest that living, as an activity and goal, is perception and knowledge; consequently, living together (*to suzēn*; τὸ συζῆν) is common-perception (*to sunaisthanesthai*; τὸ συναισθάνεσθαι) and common-knowledge (*to suggnōrizein*; τὸ συγγνωρίζειν).... And self-perception and self-knowledge are most desirable to everyone, and hence the desire for living is congenital in all; for living must be regarded as a kind of knowledge ... so that to wish to perceive one's self is to wish oneself to be of a certain definite character—since, then, we are not in ourselves possessed of each such character, but only by participation in these qualities in perceiving and knowing— for the perceiver becomes perceived in that way and in that respect in which he first perceives, and according to the way in which he is and the object that he perceives; and the knower becomes known in the same way—therefore it is for this reason that one always desires to live, because one always desires to know; and this is because he himself wishes to be the object known.

In this passage, Aristotle reverses direction altogether. He runs through a series of theses, individually striking and cumulatively unlike either of the passages on the value of friendship quarried thus far. He here contends first that the desire to be known is natural and inborn, because the desire to live in common is natural and necessary for flourishing in actuality. The desire to be known is thus introduced as a teleologically given hypothetical imperative. Such knowledge, however, he further contends, requires knowing in common (*to suggnōrizein*; τὸ συγγνωρίζειν), because living together (*to suzēn*; τὸ συζῆν) requires both knowing in common and perceiving in common (*to suggnōrizein* and *to sunaisthanesthai*; τὸ συγγνωρίζειν and τὸ συναισθάνεσθαι). Call these jointly *common cognition*. That social life requires common cognition seems plausible, not least for the reason that living together demands all manner of cooperative activity, ranging from the utterly pedestrian to the highly nuanced and nimble. If this is correct, then the form of life which is congenital to all humans, according to Aristotle, requires common cognition and mutual knowledge.

Now, then, comes the reversal: common cognition and mutual knowledge require self-knowledge *as a grounding condition*. I know, for example, that you and I are alike in virtue only if I know my own virtue as well as yours; and, more prosaically, you know that I know that we intend to meet after the opera only if you yourself have the requisite self-knowledge of your own intentions. It follows, then, on Aristotle's approach, that self-knowledge is a requisite for human flourishing: far from precluding mutual interdependence, the self-sufficiency of eudaimonia actually requires social living and so also then both common cognition and mutual knowledge. Both of these, however, presuppose perceptual self-awareness and self-knowledge.

This is why Aristotle concludes that knowing oneself is most choiceworthy, and that because of this the desire for living is natural (or congenital) for all (*Eth. Eud.* 1244.25–26). Put concisely, Aristotle's argument is this, coming in three subphases: (1) Human life, regarded as actualized and as an end (*to zēn to kat' energeian kai hōs telos*; τὸ ζῆν τὸ κατ' ἐνέργειαν καὶ ὡς τέλος), *is* knowing and perceiving. Everyone desires life; hence, everyone desires knowing and perceiving. (2) Humans by nature seek to live in common. Living in common is possible only if those living together have mutual perception and mutual knowledge. Hence, everyone finds mutual perception and mutual knowledge most choiceworthy (*hairetōtaton*; αἱρετώτατον). (3) Mutual perception and mutual perception are possible only if those who live in common have self-perception and self-knowledge. Hence, humans by nature find self-perception and self-knowledge choiceworthy and pleasant.

There is much to explore in this argument, but two points of explication must suffice for present. It will sound odd and forced to hear Aristotle contending in the first phase, "It is manifest that living, as an activity and goal, is perception and knowledge; consequently, living together (*to suzēn*) is common-perception (*to suaishthanesthai*) and common-knowledge (*to suggnōrizein*)." Life does not seem to *be* perception and knowledge; rather, living beings seem to perceive and to know. Aristotle means precisely what he says, however. He introduces this contention by claiming that *considered as an activity and a goal, or end (to zēn to kat' energeian kai hōs telos)*, living (*to zēn*) is knowing and perceiving. Here he is drawing on the sort of view articulated most clearly in *De Anima* 2.4, where he maintains that "living *is* being for living things" (415b13), together with his insistence in the same chapter that the soul is not only a formal cause of the body but also its final cause (415b1, b17; *telos*). Together these theses begin to explain Aristotle's striking contention that living, considered as an activity and goal, is knowledge and perception: human beings are essentially knowers and perceivers and what they do they do for the sake of knowing and perceiving. Second, the argument takes the form of a teleological hypothetical syllogism. Put in its most concise form, Aristotle here argues that in order for a human being to attain her best state, for her to flourish—which, of course, she has a natural impetus to do—she must live in common, and so know and cognize in common, and so, therefore, have self-knowledge. His point is, then, finally, not that friends are used as instruments to self-knowledge, but, on the contrary, that self-knowledge is a requisite for friendship, an external good that humans by nature seek.

2.4. CONCLUDING DIRECTIONS

If so much captures Aristotle's most sophisticated view, then his account of friendship highlights in instructive ways both the source and the value of self-knowledge. His contention that self-knowledge is most choiceworthy and pleasant is not the bromide one finds retailed in some later appeals to the injunction of the Delphic oracle. It is rather a highly theoretical contention derived from some substantive and controversial theses about human nature and social living.

His final view is not that to see oneself reflected in another qualifies as a form of self-knowledge, nor even that seeing oneself reflected is a necessary or primary source of self-knowledge. On the contrary: to see one's features, whether attractive or abysmal, exemplified in another, and to see at the same time that the other sees that her features are exemplified in oneself, requires mutual knowledge and mutual perception (*to suggnōrizein* and *to sunaisthanesthai*). The mutual cognition required for human flourishing thus presupposes rather than generates self-knowledge. Aristotle does not, in the end, envisage a subject gazing narcissistically at an object in a mirror and inferring some traits or other back to the subject from the object seen to be gazing at its image. Instead, he envisages subjects knowing themselves, mirroring one another in a shared subjectivity presupposing the kind of self-knowledge reflected in mutual knowledge and perception. So much seems highly apposite. After all, we see ourselves as *ourselves* in a mirror only when we are aware of ourselves as seeing ourselves in a mirror. Otherwise, we are merely seeing another.

To conclude, then, where we began: Ryle's worry is a real worry; but Aristotle's solution is a real solution. When we know ourselves we know as well what we are not: we are not self-netting nets. Nor, more generally, are we tools of any kind only ineffectually turned upon the tools we are. Rather, we are human animals, and so in our very natures social beings, beings whose fullest and finest attributes implicate us in a mutual knowledge and mutual perception born inescapably of self-knowledge and self-perception. It is unsurprising, then, that self-knowledge is most choiceworthy and highly pleasant to each and every one of us. Without it, we could not flourish. Indeed, without self-knowledge we could not be the beings we know ourselves to be.

Acknowledgment

I thank Ursula Renz for her incisive and helpful comments on an earlier draft of this paper, together with the participants in the rich and stimulating conference on the topic of this volume held in Konstanz in July 2014.

CHAPTER THREE

Self-Knowledge in Later Stoicism

Marcel van Ackeren

Zeno, the founder of Stoicism, was attracted to philosophy by reading about Socrates.[1] This influence became so important that the Stoics "are willing also be to be called Socratics."[2] But how did the Stoics conceptualize self-knowledge, which was central to Socrates? They adopted central aspects from Socrates, which is most obvious in the works of Epictetus. They adopted central intellectualistic ethical claims and the general practical ambition of philosophy, including the notion of philosophy as an art of living and also the importance of the cross-examination.[3]

1 Cf. Diogenes Laertius, "Diogenis Laertii Vitae philosophorum," ed. Miroslav Marcovich, in *Bibliotheca scriptorum Graecorum et Romanorum Teubneriana*, vol. 1: *Books I–X*; vol. 2: *Excerpta Byzantina* (Stuttgart: Teubner, 1999–2002), 7.2, 28, and 31–32.

2 Philodemus, "On the Stoics," *Cronache Ercolanese* 12 (1982) *XIII*, 3. Cf. Francesca Allesse, *La Stoa e la tradizione socratica* (Naples: Bibliopolis, 2000). Cf. Rene Brouwer, *The Stoic Sage: The Early Stoics on Wisdom, Sagehood and Socrates* (Cambridge: Cambridge University Press, 2013).

3 Cf. Anthony A. Long, *Epictetus: A Socratic and Stoic Guide to Life* (Cambridge: Cambridge University Press, 2002), ch. 3.1.

The central ethical claim that false or inconsistent beliefs make people unvirtuous and miserable[4] is linked to self-knowledge by an error theory: "Every error involves a mental conflict. . . . every rational soul is naturally averse to conflict; but as long as someone is unaware of being in conflict, there is nothing to prevent him from acting inconsistently. Yet, once he is aware, he is strongly constrained to abandon and shun the conflict."[5]

This error theory also explains certain features of the Stoic methods of self-inquiry. Epictetus, for example, believes that perfectly consistent beliefs are true beliefs and that true beliefs are the negation of refuted beliefs; he claims that cross-examination leads to true beliefs.[6]

Expertise in argumentation and refutation[7] is thus part of the art of living.[8] To Socrates and the Stoics an art is a consistent account (*logos*) of the nature (*physis*) of a subject's (*ergon*) totality, allowing someone to give reasons (*aitiai*) and proceed with precision. Each art also involves knowledge about the norms that are appropriate concerning the *ergon* and what is best for it.[9] Philosophy as an art of living demands self-knowledge, because "each individual's own life is the material of the art of living."[10]

Stoic theories on self-knowledge are thus strongly influenced by the Socratic heritage, but they also gave self-knowledge some distinct characteristics, of which (1) some concern the object of self-knowledge, (2) some its ethical and political consequences, and (3) some its

---

4 Cf. Arrian, *Epictetus Enchiridion*, 5.

5 Arrian, *Epictetus Discourses*, 2.26.1–5.

6 Cf. Long, *Socratic and Stoic Guide*, 83. Cf. Gregory Vlastos, "The Socratic Elenchos," *Oxford Studies in Ancient Philosophy* 1 (1983): 27–58.

7 Cf. Arrian, *Epictetus Discourses*, 2.26.1–4.

8 Cf. Sextus Empiricus, *Against the Ethicists (Adversus Mathematicos XI)*, trans. Richard Bett (Oxford: Clarendon Press, 2000), 170. Cf. Stefan Radt, *Strabons Geographika*, 10 vols. (Göttingen: Vandenhoeck & Ruprecht, 2002–11), 1.1.1. Cf. Diogenes Laertius 7.89 and *Stoicorum Veterum Fragmenta* 3.560.

9 Cf. Plato, *Ion*, 530c–33c and 540b; Plato, *Gorgias*, 463a–64c and 501e–504a.

10 Arrian, *Epictetus Discourses*, 1.15.2.

epistemological analysis. The following will focus on Roman Stoics and especially on Marcus Aurelius, because this allows (4) highlighting the most original feature of late Stoicism: the self-dialogue, which becomes the vehicle for practicing philosophy and gaining self-knowledge. The *Meditations* are unique because they are the first real self-dialogue of an author with himself. To Marcus, acquiring self-knowledge does not require other human beings, such as midwives (Socrates) or friends (Aristotle). This will lead to (5) conclusions concerning the "I," Stoic psychic monism, and the "Self."

3.1. WHAT AM I?

According to Marcus Aurelius, self-knowledge should provide insight into one's own nature, namely the following:

(1) Human beings are completely part of the corporal cosmos.

(2) The most important and leading faculty of the soul (*hegemonikon*) is part of the cosmic reason.

(3) Cosmic reason is shared by all human beings, making the cosmos a community.

(4) Contributing to communities is the supreme action-guiding goal.

Interpreters have debated whether Marcus' anthropological account is Neoplatonic, and therefore dualistic,[11] or orthodox Stoic, that is, sticking to physiopsychic holism. There are two groups of chapters. The first group mentions a tripartition of flesh/body (*sarcs/soma*), soul (*psyche/pneuma*) and reason / leading faculty (*nous/hegemonikon*).[12]

---

11 Cf. Francesca Alesse, "Il tema delle affezioni nell'antropologia di Marco Aurelio," in *Antichi e moderni nella filosofia de età imperiale*, ed. Aldo Branacacci (Naples: Bibliopolis, 2001). Cf. Giovanni Reale, *The Schools of the Imperial Age* (Albany: SUNY Press, 1990), 89–100.

12 Cf., e.g., Marcus Aurelius, *Meditations*, trans. R. Hardie (Ware: Woodsworth, 1997), 12.14, 12.3, 8.56.

The second group mentions an allegedly Platonic dualism between body and soul.[13]

Neither is easy to explain, and especially their relation is problematic. Taken together, Marcus' claims are unprecedented in the history of Stoicism. One might argue that Marcus is not a professional philosopher and that he is not aware that his distinctions are unorthodox. However, Marcus is best interpreted as being an orthodox Stoic. Although he makes the above-mentioned distinction, he keeps assuming that all the above-mentioned—including reason—are corporeal.[14] Thus, his distinctions do not rest on a Platonic metaphysical-ontological dualism. Epictetus,[15] and even more so Marcus, liked to express Stoic views in Platonically colored language. However, this is meant to express that only the leading spirit and virtue matter, and especially that the leading spirit should decide independently.[16]

Self-knowledge is about one's own nature as "a rational and sociable creature."[17] These two characteristics cannot be separated, for the Stoic monistic conception views body, soul, and reason not only as part of the corporeal world, but also holds that there is "only one universal soul"[18] and "one substance and law and one reason common to all intelligent creatures."[19] Reason is something that connects human beings with each other, as it is shared by and common to them. However, a community need not be constituted by the use of reason,

---

13 Cf. ibid., 10.1, 6.32, 3.7, 10.11, 6.17, 10.24, 8.3, 8.60.

14 Cf. ibid., 5.26, 11.20. Cf. Anthony A. Long and David N. Sedley, *The Hellenistic Philosophers*, vol. 1 (Cambridge: Cambridge University Press, 1987), 53 B. Cf. Sextus Empiricus, *Adversus Mathematicos*, 7.2.

15 Cf., e.g., Arrian, *Epictetus Discourses* 1.3.3–6, 1.9.11. Cf. Long, *Socratic and Stoic Guide*, 158.

16 Cf. Marcus Aurelius, *Meditations* 3.16 and 8.3; Christopher Gill, "Marcus Aurelius' Meditations: How Stoic and How Platonic?" in *Platonic Stoicism—Stoic Platonism: The Dialogue between Platonism and Stoicism in Antiquity*, ed. Mauro Bonazzi and Christoph Helmig (Leuven: Peters, 2007); Marcel van Ackeren. *Die Philosophie Marc Aurels*, vol. 1: *Textform—Stillmerkmale—Selbstdialog*; vol. 2: *Themen—Begriffe—Argumente* (Berlin: de Gruyter, 2011), ch. 3.

17 E.g., Marcus, *Meditations*, 5.29.

18 Ibid., 12.30.

19 Ibid., 7.9.

for the reasonable nature of one's soul is something that already "comes from the common polis."[20] The cosmic reason and cosmic community are prior to individual reason and specific communities.

Early Stoics seem to have favored the view that only sages and gods, that is, those with perfect reason and knowledge, are full citizens, which need to be distinguished from other, less reasonable fools who are mere inhabitants of the cosmic polis.[21] Marcus, on the contrary, considers everyone who is at least capable of reason a full citizen. He does not distinguish sages from fools.

The reasonable and sociable nature of human beings also determines the purpose (*ergon*) of human beings: in order to achieve happiness, they need to act in a way that benefits the community. Marcus Aurelius demands "to view things in such a way as to take account at the same time of what use each thing serves in what kind of a universe, and what value it has in relation to the whole, and what value to man as a citizen of the most exalted of cities, of which of all other cities are, as it were, mere households."[22]

Self-knowledge as knowledge of one's own reasonable and political nature therefore entails normative elements. This leads to the theory of goods.

3.2. WHAT IS GOOD FOR ME?

Orthodox Stoic ethics is based on a threefold division of goods or value: good things (*agatha*), bad things (*kaka*), and indifferent things (*adiaphora*). The good is equated with the beneficial and useful, and only virtue is good and therefore both necessary and sufficient for happiness. Likewise, only vice is bad. The group of indifferent things subsumes all things like wealth, beauty, power, health, and pleasure.[23]

---

20 Ibid., 4.4.

21 Cf. Katja M. Vogt, *Law, Reason, and the Cosmic City* (Oxford: Oxford University Press, 2008).

22 Marcus Aurelius, *Meditations*, 3.11.

23 Cf. Diogenes Laertius, "Diogenis Laertii Vitae philosophorum," 7.101–2.

Indifferents are further divided into things that are more in accordance with one's own individual nature and thus preferable, those that are not and therefore are to be avoided, and finally those that are completely indifferent and thus neither to be preferred nor avoided.[24]

However, there is the deviating Stoic position advocated by Aristo of Chios—a pupil of the founder Zeno—who argued that all indifferents should be treated equally, meaning that they should neither be preferred nor avoided.[25] David Sedley has remarked that the history of philosophy, like other historical accounts, is written by its winners,[26] and the winners made Zeno's position the orthodox one and Aristo's position heresy,[27] though his position is not completely unfaithful to the Socratic-Cynic roots of Stoicism.[28]

In late Stoicism there was a renewal of Aristo's position. In the case of Epictetus it is not easy to decide whether he adopted Aristo's position, or whether he is simply not applying the orthodox distinction.[29] Marcus, however, clearly goes back to Aristo. He argues that "justice will not be maintained if we care for indifferent objects,"[30] and speaking of indifferent things, Marcus never mentions that some should preferred.[31] This might have even been the result of a

---

24 Cf. Long and Sedley, *Hellenistic Philosophers*, 58 C–D.

25 Cf. ibid., 58 F–G.

26 Cf. David N. Sedley, "The School, from Zeno to Arius Didymus," in *The Cambridge Companion to the Stoics*, ed. Brad Inwood (Cambridge: Cambridge University Press, 2003), 14.

27 Cf. Diogenes Laertius, "Diogenis Laertii Vitae philosophorum," 7.161. Cf. Sedley, *The School*, 14–15. Cf. Cicero, *De Finibus Bonorum et Malorum*, ed. L. D. Reynolds (Oxford: Oxford University Press, 1998), 3.50.

28 Cf. Plato, *Euthydemus*, 278–81. Contra, cf. Tad Brennan, *The Stoic Life: Emotions, Duties, and Fate* (Oxford: Oxford University Press, 2005), 119.

29 On the one hand, Epictetus never clearly adopts the distinction between preferable indifferents and those to be avoided. On the other hand, however, there is one passage in which he mentions Chrysipps' argument for it and distinguishes different values of indifferents on the basis of whether they are in accordance with nature or go against it. Cf. Arrian, *Epictetus Enchiridion*, 36; Arrian, *Epictetus Discourses*, 1.2.7, 1.2.10; Pierre Hadot, *The Inner Citadel: The Meditations of Marcus Aurelius* (Cambridge, MA: Harvard University Press, 2001) vs. Geert Roskam, *On the Path to Virtue: The Stoic Doctrine of Moral Progress and Its Reception in (Middle-)Platonism* (Leuven: Peters, 2005), 17–133.

30 Marcus Aurelius, *Meditations*, 11.10, 11.24, 2.12, 6.32.

31 Cf. e.g. Ibid., 7.31; 6.41; the only exception is Marcus, *Meditations* 11, 1.

direct influence, for in a famous letter the young Caesar confessed to his teacher Fronto that he read Aristo instead of doing his rhetoric homework.[32]

There are misunderstandings or even prejudices concerning Stoic ethics, namely that their philosophy is devoid of political aspects, or that the polis they refer to is only the abstract conception of the cosmos as a polis mentioned in the previous section, and not to any specific political community with tangible politics. Some commentators even have claimed that the Hellenistic and late ancient philosophers abandoned political aspects in their philosophy, and focused on self-knowledge and a purely individually construed art of living, because the political context became less democratic and more totalitarian.

But self-knowledge and the related care for one's own soul are not meant to exclude political engagement. Marcus, like Seneca,[33] not only distinguishes between the cosmic city and specific political communities,[34] but also makes political usefulness the criterion for what is good: "Now my nature is that of a rational and sociable being: As Antoninus my city and fatherland is Rome, as a human being, it is the universe; so what brings benefits to these is the sole good for me."[35] In turn, Marcus considers cooperation the most important type of action.[36]

This emphasis on political and social aspects is based on a physical theory that takes connectedness and cooperation to be essential.[37] Marcus is very fond of *composita* with the prefix "together" (*syn-*)— there are about 150 occurrences of them in the *Meditations*, and many such words are coined by him.

---

32 Cf. Marcus Cornelius Fronto, *Epistulae*, 1.214.

33 Cf. Seneca, *De Otio*, 4,1.

34 Cf. Marcus Aurelius, *Meditations*, 3.11.

35 Ibid., 6.44.

36 Cf. e.g. ibid., 2.1, 5, 16, 8.59, 9.1.

37 Cf. ibid., 3.11, 3.4, 4.26, 4.4.

The emphasis on connectedness and cooperation seems to be inconsistent with the very often recommended "retreat" (*anachorese*). Marcus knows two forms of retreat, and there is no contradiction because both primarily have epistemological meanings:

a. In accordance with his anthropology, Marcus demands an internal retreat of the leading spirit from the influence of rough movements of the body, so that its judgments are not blurred by impressions that might lead to wrong (value) judgments.[38]

b. Marcus demands a retreat from other persons, for he assumes that other persons are not necessary to be cross-examined and to acquire self-knowledge.

To Marcus, self-knowledge can be acquired through self-dialogue. To Socrates, on the contrary, it was important to keep in mind that one needs the help of another person to acquire self-knowledge.[39] Epictetus' position seems to be intermediate: "Since he [Socrates] couldn't always have someone to test (*elenchein*) his judgments or to be tested by him in turn, he made a habit of testing and examining himself, and was forever trying out the use of some particular preconception."[40]

3.3. ARE MY IMPRESSIONS TRUE?

Self-knowledge is related to epistemology in at least two ways, and both depart from the original Socratic notion of it.

First, self-knowledge can be understood as self-awareness, which is the very foundation of each human being and animal. The Stoics held that all animals were familiar with themselves, their own constitution (*sustasis*), and the function of their parts and organs as soon as they

---

38 Cf. e.g. ibid., 4.3, 8.48.

39 Cf. Plato, *Theaetetus*, 150e.

40 Arrian, *Epictetus Discourses*, 2.1.32–3.

were born.[41] This is the first pillar of the famous theory of "approbation" (*oikeiois*) in Stoicism, the other being self-affection, which follows from those perceptions that are pleasing.[42] Second, self-knowledge amounts to more than knowing one's own rational and social nature, for we do have preconceptions (*hypolepseis*) about the good. But as we are not necessarily aware of our preconceptions, self-knowledge entails gaining this self-awareness of the preconceptions and then developing them.[43]

The Stoics demand awareness and cross-examination of one's own sense perceptions, so that the (value) judgments that result from them are correct. Here, cross-examination becomes an internal task, since its primary objects are one's own impressions (*phantasiai*). Self-knowledge is related to the core of Stoic epistemology, as the cross-examination of impressions is concerned with the criterion for truth.[44] For of "impressions, one kind is cognitive, the other incognitive. The cognitive, which they [the Stoics] say is the criterion of things, is that which arises from what is and is stamped and impressed exactly in accordance with what is."[45] Gaining knowledge requires the cross-examination of one's own impressions and only assenting to those matching the criterion, thereby gaining a state of mind that grasps what is (*katelepsis*).[46]

However, impressions and their cross-examinations are also ethically important, as sense impressions tend to lead to judgments about the goodness or badness of what we experience.[47] Yet value judgments belong to a sphere that is entirely up to us and to the realm of free

---

41 Cf. Hierocles, 1.48–2.3.

42 Cf. Hierocles, 6.40–52; Diogenes Laertius, 7.85; Anthony A. Long, "Hierocles on Oikeiōsis and Self-Perception," in *Stoic Studies* (Cambridge: Cambridge University Press, 1996), 250–63.

43 Cf. Long and Sedley, *The Hellenistic Philosophers*, 30 E; 60 D.

44 Cf. Angelo Giavatto, *Interlocutore di se stesso: La dialettica di Marco Aurelio* (Hildesheim: Olms, 2008), 37.

45 Diogenes Laertius, 7.46.

46 Cf. Cicero, *Academica*, 2.145.

47 Cf. Marcus Aurelius, *Meditations*, trans. R. Hardie (Ware: Wordsworth, 1997), 8, 7.

judgments, whereas sense impressions are involuntary and thus not left to us. "In the same way as we exercise ourselves to deal with sophistical questioning, we should exercise ourselves daily to deal with impressions; for these too put questions to us."[48]

That is why the Stoics argue that the leading faculty of the soul (*hegemonikon*) needs to retreat from relying on the senses and cross-examine impressions. However, this does imply that all sense impressions are wrong or to be ignored. This would involve some form of Platonism. Again, some chapters in the *Meditations* (e.g., 3.16, 9.7) might be seen as pointing in that direction, but Marcus is emphasizing the Stoic theory that sense experience is not necessary and sufficient for appropriate judgments.[49] Therefore, all impressions should be examined, and only the leading faculty is free and supposed to judge. But there is no total rejection of sense experience in Marcus. Impressions that are based on sense data and that are clear and distinct should be tested, but might be given assent to.[50] He even makes use of sense impressions with respect to exercises of imagination; for example, he asks himself to imagine that dear things will perish in order to reduce fear or future grief.[51] Assenting to wrong impressions does not only mean erring in that particular judgment, but also amounts to self-deception, and the most fatal form would be to deny that the leading faculty is free.[52]

Self-knowledge can become more internal and reflexive in the sense of being less dependent on other persons, the interpersonal dialogue, and cross-examination by others, because the Stoics believe that it

> is within yourself that you bear him [God] ... God has not only fashioned you, but has entrusted you to the care of yourself alone....

---

48 Arrian, *Epictetus Discourses*, 3.8.1–4.

49 Cf. Marcus Aurelius, *Meditations*, 3.16.

50 Cf. ibid., 8.49; 8.7.

51 Cf. e.g. ibid., 10.28; 3.1. Cf. Seneca, *Epistulae morales*, trans. R. M Gummere (Cambridge, MA: Harvard University Press, 1917–25), 49.10, 12.8, 61.1, 93.6, 101.10.

52 Cf. Marcus Aurelius, *Meditations*, 4.7;3.9.

If God had committed some orphan to your care, would you so neglect him? He has committed you to yourself and he says: "I had no one more trustworthy than you. Keep this person for me in the way that is his nature: reverent, trustworthy, upright, undismayed, unimpassioned, and undisturbed."[53]

Apart from being a central part of general epistemology, self-knowledge becomes as important as it is because the universal nature (or providence or God) takes care of humans and animals not by directly guiding them, but by entrusting human beings to themselves, so that their soul—their daemon—and knowledge may guide them.[54] The idea that cross-examinations can be carried out by one individual alone leads to the most original development—the self-dialogue.

3.4. What Is the Form of Self-Knowledge?

It is characteristic of Marcus' approach, and constitutive for his views on self-knowledge, that his writings have the form of a self-dialogue and that he discusses the role of self-dialogues. Though the term "self-dialogue" is not quite common English, the verbal communication of a person with herself is best kept distinct from "monologue," which also sounds like ancient Greek, but became a widely used term during the time of the Renaissance as the opposite to "dialogue." Up to Hegel, the term "monologue" referred to the speech of performers alone on stage. There are only few exceptions: "monologue" can be found in a lexicon of obscure Greek words form the fifth century (Hesychius) and in the works of some twelfth-century Byzantine authors who referred to that lexicon (e.g., Zonaras and Pachymeres, Georgios). To Henricus Stephanus, *monologistoi* are persons who spend time alone,

---

53 Arrian, *Epictetus Discourses*, 2.8.11–23.

54 Cf. Seneca, *Epistulae*, 121.18. Cf. Arrian, *Epictetus Discourses*, 1.14.12–14. Cf. Marcus Aurelius, *Meditations*, 3.6; 8.27; 3.5.

praying. Finally, there are two titles: the *Monologion* by Anselm and the *Monologien* by Schleiermacher.

Most of the ancient monologues are not self-dialogues, as they do not have a dialogical structure, nor does the speaker address herself, but other persons who are absent: gods or the dead or the audience. Self-dialogues are as old as Greek literature; they even appear in the *Iliad*, as the heroes are alone due to contingent external factors. In those cases, the self-dialogue is something that more or less happens to them, or becomes necessary because there is no one else to talk to. Self-dialogues in the *Iliad* all feature the same central line, which expresses the surprise of the heroes: "But why does my heart (*thymos*) debate (*dielexato*) this with me?"[55] Though already linked to decision-making, the self-dialogue was then not a consciously used technique of persons to get to know or influence themselves. Since Plato, however, philosophers have recommended the self-dialogue, and there are many reports of philosophers conversing with themselves.[56]

Seneca himself did not write self-dialogues proper, that is, the verbal and written protocol of a self-dialogue of an author,[57] but texts that were meant to address and inform someone else and supposed to be published. But he discusses them: To Seneca self-dialogues imitate or substitute for the interpersonal dialogue or being together with another (*contubernium*).[58] Self-dialogue and interpersonal dialogue can also intermingle—which is what he likes about the textual form of letters[59]—but the interpersonal dialogue remains the foundation.[60] He

---

55 Odysseus (*Il.* 11, 404–410), Menelaus (*Il.* 17, 91–105), Agenor (*Il.* 19, 533–70) and Hector (*Il.* 22, 99–130) have these self-dialogues. Odysseus' (*Od.* 20, 18–21) self-dialogue is different.

56 Cf., e.g., Plato, *Phaedo*, 77e; Pyrrhon (DL 9, 64); Kleanthes (DL 7, 171); Diogenes of Oinoanda (74); Lukrez (III).

57 Not even *On Anger* (3.36) is a self-dialogue in that sense.

58 Cf., e.g., Seneca, *Epistulae*, 6.6, 55.9.

59 Cf. ibid., 38.1, 40.8, 55.9, 71.4.

60 Contra. Cf. Robert J. Newmann, "Cotidie meditare: Theory and Practice of the Meditation in Imperial Stoicism," *Aufstieg und Niedergang der Römischen Welt*, III, 36.3 (1989): 1473–517.

gives examples and admonitions to pursue therapeutic self-dialogues in order to control emotions or to exercise self-observation.[61] Epictetus, like Seneca, did not engage in self-dialogues, but recommends them as a substitute for an interpersonal dialogue.[62] He also grants self-dialogues a more independent and additional worth, as they fully actualize the human potential, by helping man to become like Zeus, who also talks to himself.[63]

The texts of Epictetus and Seneca have a "double focus," for they are addressed to actual persons who are different from the speaker or author, and are meant to be heard or read. Marcus' *Meditations*, on the contrary, was not meant to be published, Marcus is not addressing someone else, and the book does not simply consist of sentences collected by others (*hypomnemata*), as Foucault has suggested.[64] The dialogue of Marcus is free from all interpersonality. In fact, it is the first self-dialogue of an author that has survived. The unique form of the text has puzzled commentators, but it reflects his Stoic philosophy. There are different types of self-dialogues to be found in the *Meditations*:

(1) The words of two interlocutors are given in the text.[65] Either (1a) one interlocutor is asking, the other is answering[66]— though the questions can be admonitions, asking for actions and not answers[67]—or (1b) one interlocutor is recognizable as a teacher and the other as a student.[68] Sometimes (1c) both interlocutors state their opinions.[69]

---

61 Cf., e.g., Seneca, *Epistulae*, 20.4, 26.1–4, 35.4.

62 Cf. Arrian, *Epictetus Discourses*, 2.1.32–33.

63 Cf. ibid., 3.14.2–3, 3.3.6–7, 4.1.131; Arrian, *Epictetus Enchiridion*, 53.

64 Cf. Michel Foucault, "L'écriture de soi," *Corps écrit*, No. 5, L'Autoportrait (1983): 3–23.

65 Cf. Marcus Aurelius, *Meditations*, 2.1; 4.13.

66 Cf. ibid., 8.40.

67 Cf. ibid., 4.13.

68 Cf. ibid., 5.32.

69 Cf. ibid., 8.32.

(2) In the second main group only the speech of one interlocutor
     is given, but two interlocutors are mentioned by name. There
     are two subclasses, chapters (2a) using "you" and "I,"[70] and
     (2b) ascribing the capacity to engage in a dialogue to other
     (internal) entities like the soul,[71] the leading faculty,[72] impres-
     sions,[73] or bodily organs.[74]

(3) The last main group consists of chapters using "we."[75]

The verbalization of the self-dialogue is important, and it is carefully
done, consistently applying different philosophical strategies, of which
two are particularly interesting. Both demonstrate Marcus' skills as an
author and philosopher, and both are couched in the typical Socratic
question-answer scheme.

First, grammar is used for philosophical purposes, as Marcus chooses
different grammatical persons for different aims. The grammatical
"you" is addressed in admonitions.[76] The "you" generally allows the
author to distance himself from a certain way of thinking, feeling, and
acting. Quite often, the "you" is addressed using the imperative form.
The grammatical "I" is used to reinforce a certain way of thinking and
acting. The "I" is used in cases of self-identification and is accompanied by the indicative mood. The first person is also used when Marcus
wants to analyze himself.[77] The "I" is the subject of the "critical analysis of convincing impressions."[78] This is part of a general method that

---

70 Cf. ibid., 4.10, 7.2.

71 Cf. ibid., 11.1, 10.35.

72 Cf. ibid., 9.39, 6.8.

73 Cf. ibid., 7.17, 4.19.

74 Cf. ibid., 10.35.

75 Cf. ibid., 4.4, 5.8.

76 Cf. ibid., 3.4–6, 3.13–15, 4.11. There are only few exceptions where a "you" is addressed in a calm,
nonparanetic way (Marcus Aurelius, *Meditations* 3, 7–8, 9, 26), and only one instance of an "I" being
addressed in a harsh, cynic way (Marcus Aurelius, *Meditations*, 8, 24).

77 Cf. ibid., 5.13, 2.2.

78 Ibid., 8.26.

Marcus recommends for all kinds of purposes and objects; it proceeds diaeretically,[79] distinguishes between material and causal aspects of every process and being,[80] and thereby reaches a view of the world that is in accordance with nature.[81] Therefore, self-analysis in the form of a self-dialogue is the reflexive version of this general analytical method, and self-knowledge is its result.

Second, there are constitutive aspects of the self-dialogue, because Marcus is recommending dialogues between psychic capacities. Self-dialogues are about becoming a certain person with certain beliefs, virtues, and feelings and committing certain actions.[82] Here Marcus uses the two methods again, that is, self-identification and self-distancing. It is noteworthy that there are only a few chapters in which the *hegemonikon* is addressed directly, for it is the very entity that thinks and verbalizes.[83]

But why is all of this necessary? The self-sufficiency of the leading spirit is endangered by the impressions and preconceptions. Every moment of our life they tend to lead us to false value judgements, consequently to wrongdoing, and ultimately to misery. Therefore, the leading faculty needs to control and free itself by controlling these other psychic activities. And this is something that happens in the form of a "self-dialogue." Note, however, that Marcus does not want the reason to encapsulate itself; instead, the *hegemonikon* should stay in contact with the impressions and be open to natural ones.[84] Marcus stresses that this internal self-dialogue is important and a permanent task: living means having impressions, and they may lead to judgments without having validated them.[85] Epictetus has called for an art of controlling impressions.

---

79 Cf. ibid., 2.11.
80 Cf. ibid., 4.21, 7.29.
81 Cf. ibid., 9.38.
82 Cf. ibid., 10.39, 7.29, 12.25.
83 Cf. ibid., 11.1, 2.17, 5.14.
84 Cf. ibid., 5.26.
85 Cf. ibid., 4.3, 7.66, 6.8, 8.13.

Not only does the *Meditations* entail the theory, the reader also gets an insight into how this kind of art may be practiced.

To sum up, there is one form of an internal dialogue that is natural, because psychic capacities communicate without the individual being conscious about it. And there is an artful and deliberate philosophical internal dialogue, which has to be learned and which is about shaping this natural communication and its agents. Self-knowledge as an important aspect and goal of the art living means pursuing this second deliberate internal dialogue. But the first, natural form of self-dialogue is the object of this second form.[86]

3.5. Conclusions: The "I," Psychic Monism, and the "Self"

Some general conclusions may be drawn with regard to the assumptions that underlie the notion of self-knowledge and the self-dialogue. Unlike the monologue, the notion of a self-dialogue requires a seemingly paradoxical situation, for it needs at least two interlocutors, yet one person functions as both of these interlocutors. Older commentators (e.g., Leo) have assumed that one Cartesian "I" is talking to "another I." But maybe there is more to it than grammatical role play or the duplication of a Cartesian, and therefore anachronistic, idea. Marcus does not mention the belief that he consists of one "I" or maybe two or three; instead, he is assuming that there are various aspects or capacities in him, which communicate with each other. However, if the self-dialogue requires two interlocutors, it might be in conflict with Stoic psychic monism, that is, the doctrine that the soul is a unity without a persistent partition. But there is no need to assume that the two interlocutors are separately existing, persistent entities or parts of the soul, and only that assumption would be at odds with psychic monism.

There is a related problem, because Marcus demands that the leading faculty of the soul observes *and* controls itself. However, this is

---

86 Cf. ibid., 2.1.

problematic only from an essentialistic point of view, because that which observes and that which is observed is the same. From an essentialistic perspective, in order to have a dialogue, some kind of division is required. Yet we may also think of the interlocutors as roles or capacities or maybe aspects of the soul that are not persistent. And these capacities can communicate. Once the communication is verbalized, we might be allowed to call the result consciousness.[87]

Similarly, it would be wrong to think that self-knowledge and self-dialogue in this case involve the idea of a *Self*. The self-dialogue does not require this notion; a self-dialogue does not aim at constituting a *Self*, nor is the *Self* the proper object of self-knowledge. There simply is no *Self* in the text, and there might be none in Marcus. He, like all ancient thinkers before him, used the term "self" just as a reflexive pronoun.

Nonetheless it might be profitable to use the self as an anachronism, as Christopher Gill has done. He construes and distinguishes concepts like "objective-participant self" and the "subjective-individualistic self"[88] and applies them to ancient texts. While Foucault[89] stressed the subjective individualistic concept by assuming that the self that we should care about is the sum of all self-references, Gill argued plausibly that Marcus clearly falls within the former category.[90] If later concepts are used in the study of historical texts, one needs to keep in mind that these later concepts are tools and not part of what these tools are applied to—that is simply part of the interpreter's self-knowledge.

---

87 With regard to Homeric self-dialogues, cf. Christopher Gill, *The Self in Dialogue* (Oxford: Oxford University Press, 1998), on the basis of Harry G. Frankfurt, "Freedom of the Will and the Concept of a Person," *Journal of Philosophy* 68 (1971), 4–16, and Daniel Dennett, "Conditions of Personhood," in *The Identity of Persons*, ed. Richard Rorty (Berkeley: University of California Press, 1976), 175–196.

88 Christopher Gill, *The Structured Self in Hellenistic and Roman Thought* (Oxford: Oxford University Press, 2006).

89 Cf. Michel Foucault, *The Hermeneutics of the Subject: Lectures at the Collège de France (1981–1982)*, trans. Graham Burchell (New York: Palgrave Macmillan, 2005).

90 Cf. Christopher Gill, trans., *Marcus Aurelius Meditations*: Books 1–6 (Oxford: Oxford University Press, 2013), xxviii.

CHAPTER FOUR

Self-Knowledge in Plotinus: Becoming Who You Are

Pauliina Remes

Following Socrates, self-knowledge is in two ways important for philosophy. First, it is a prerequisite for other kinds of knowledge. Second, and perhaps even momentous, it is conceived as ethically beneficial. This idea gets its most familiar expression in the Aristotelian essentialist conception according to which identifying the kind of life proper to human beings will be crucial for the ethical quest of living a good and happy life.

Another and no less influential figure central for the history of self-knowledge is the late Platonist Plotinus (207–260). For Plotinus, becoming self-knowledgeable is an integral part both of moral development and of knowledge acquisition. He introduces a notion that has appealed to many contemporary philosophers, namely selfhood understood as forged through *appropriating* certain aspects of our nature. Self-knowledge, for him, is a way of becoming who one really is. But unlike in later theories, in antiquity this development is, and should be, guided by truths about our human nature; it is not as in modernity a matter of developing one's authentic individuality. Even in antiquity, however, self-knowledge is processed by individuals. Coming to know oneself in terms of human nature is thus a form of individual self-realization.

Plotinus' significance for the theme is grounded in the way he distinguishes the notion of self, or "us" (*hēmeis*), from the notion of soul. Given such a distinction, it becomes possible to ask questions about ourselves in a new way. In what follows, I begin with a reconstruction of Plotinus theory of the "we," by which he conceptualizes something distinct from the notion of soul, a self (section 4.1). We shall see that in Plotinus' concept of the self, two assumptions come together. Structurally considered, the self is a point of reference or a target of identification. Second, however, Plotinus also associates the notion of "we" with the notion of the intellect as constituting our truest nature, or self. These assumptions constitute a crucial background for Plotinus' views on self-knowledge discussed in two contexts in the *Enneads*.[1] First, Plotinus examines an epistemological issue, the way in which a thinker's thinking is accompanied with an awareness of itself as the thinker (4.2). Second, the main focus of my discussion will be on a practical, ethically motivated self-knowledge (4.3). Focal are particular kinds of relation to ourselves, a look within, and the ethical call to "sculpt" or transform ourselves. The idea of self-transformation, in turn, depends upon the capacity of self-determination, giving Plotinus' theory a voluntarist twist (4.4).

---

1 The *Enneads* (= *Enn.*) are Plotinus' collected works, edited by his pupil Porphyry into fifty-four treatises organized in six books, or groups of nine (Gr. *ennea*) treatises. The references give first the book or group (from I to VI), then the number of the treatise within that group (1–9), and finally the chapter and line number (e.g., 4.12–15). Passages are quoted, with occasional adjustments by the author of the chapter, from *Plotinus in Seven Volumes*, with an English translation by Arthur H. Armstrong, Loeb Classical Library (Cambridge, MA: Harvard University Press, 1966–88). Hereafter cited as *Enn.* The Greek edition used is Plotini, *Opera*, vols. 1–3, Scriptorum Classicorum Bibliotheca Oxoniensis, ed. Paul Henry and Hans-Rudolph Schwyzer (Oxford: Oxford University Press, 1964–83).

4.1. The *Hēmeis*: Who Are We?

Plotinus philosophy of self is an interpretation of his questioning the
theme of, as he puts it, "Who we are?" Many of Plotinus' passages
seem, at the first glance, to suggest a reply according to which human
beings are rational rather than bodily creatures. The question would,
thereby, be translatable as the classical question about what is the distinctive and essential human nature. But the way in which Plotinus
proceeds makes it clear that the question is richer, and grows into an
inquiry about the feature in virtue of which we are selves. According
to him, human beings are special in their capacity for two different
kinds of life, one according to their nature as the composite, the other
as their higher soul or intellect.[2] This essential duality of our nature
leaves room for normative self-identification: we can choose to identify ourselves either with the composite or with the intellect, and to
live a life according to it. As we shall see, this room, left for voluntary
and normative choices as regards who we want to be or develop into,
creates another sense of "we" or self, as that which chooses: the point
that has the power of self-identification.

On some occasions Plotinus emphasizes our nature simply as higher
souls or intellects:

> But we, who are we (*hēmeis de—tines de hēmeis*)? Are we that which
> draws near and comes to be in time? No, even before this coming to
> be we were there, men who were different, and some of us even gods,
> pure souls and intellect united with the whole of reality; we were
> parts of the intelligible, not marked off or cut off but belonging to
> the whole, and we are not cut off even now.[3]

Working within the Platonic distinction between being and becoming, Plotinus locates human selves in the former. While the bodily part

---

of us is in the realm of becoming, via the intellect a part of human nature is on the level of being. It is this aspect that is the unchanging and eternal core of us.

In a similar tone, Plotinus often emphatically denies that we would be our bodies: The body depends upon us and is attached to us, but " 'We ourselves' refers to the dominant part."[4] The self is not identified with the body, because the body is not an independent being, but something that needs, for its activities and organization, a life- and reason-giving principle. But we cannot merely identify the self as the soul and conclude that Plotinus would think that the soul is our self. "We" most properly applies only to a part of it, the intellect.[5] His insistence on our authentic nature as intellects seems to go, however, against our experience: why are human beings, in fact, embodied, and why do they spend most of their time preoccupied with this aspect of their nature? Plotinus introduces a metaphorical myth to answer the problem: embodied individuality is a result of alienation, the soul's "fall" from the intelligible origin.[6] We have, in a sense, alienated ourselves from our original position within the intellect.

But Plotinus is not merely striving to locate the self ontologically or cosmologically. We come closer to his original approach in passages that describe the human condition not as intellectual, but as that of beings in a middle position:

> We ourselves are not Intellect. We are, then, in accord with it by our rational power which first receives it. . . . it is we ourselves who reason and we ourselves make the acts of intelligence in discursive reasoning. The activities of the Intellect are from above in the same way that those of sense-perception are from below; *we are this, the principal*

---

4 *Enn.* IV.4.18.13–16.

5 Cf., e.g., Richard Sorabji, *Self: Ancient and Modern Insights about Individuality, Life and Death* (Oxford: Oxford University Press, 2006), 34.

6 Cf. *Enn.* IV.8.1.47–50.

part of our soul, in the middle between two powers, a worse and a bet-
ter, the worse that of sense-perception, the better that of Intellect ....
Sense-perception is our messenger, but Intellect is our king.[7]

This passage identifies the "we" as the middle point between perception and intellection. But does this not conflict with the previous passage, since it seems flatly to deny our identity with the intellect? Some
of the tension vanishes once we recognize that in this context Plotinus
does something more than to locate the self within an ontological hierarchy. The aspect of our nature of interest here is the agent or subject
of reasoning and intellection—the way in which we are the origin of
our cognitive functions. The human self is not to be identified with the
power of sense perception, presumably for the Aristotelian reason that
this ability is not distinctive for human beings (even animals perceive),
but neither can it be identified, simply, with intellection since we do
not always use the innate ability of intellection, but have to practice
its actualization.[8] The self is thereby closer to our everyday reasoning
subject that makes use of both perceptual and intellectual abilities.
This capacity is both derived from and empowered by the innate intellect, which already makes it understandable why the intellect can, in a
qualified sense, be said to be our true or original self.

The soul, then, includes many different cognitive capacities, some of
which are more relevant to the question of who we are than others. It is
the recognition of the variety of our abilities, combined with the idea
of us as beings capable of choosing which activities to prioritize and
actualize, that create a distance between who we are, our self, and the
soul. While the latter is something fixed, and can be explicated by giving
a set of powers and qualities, the former is something more dynamic.[9]

---

7 Cf. *Enn.* V.3.3.32–33, 35–40, 45–46.

8 Cf., e.g., *Enn.* I.2.4.25–29.

9 Cf. Raoul Mortley, *Plotinus, Self, and the World* (Cambridge: Cambridge University Press, 2013),
79–93. Contains an interesting discussion on the dynamic verbs, especially that of "having," that structure Plotinus' discussion.

E. R. Dodds called the Plotinian ego "the fluctuating spotlight of consciousness":[10] it can turn its attention either to the higher or to the lower realm. The self is not an entity-like thing, with determinate nature and fixed boundaries, but a focal point that can be placed, more or less voluntarily, in a layer of the soul or in the body. As Gwenaëlle Aubry aptly puts it: "Situated rather than defined, it cannot be substantified."[11] But Dodds' talk about a spotlight of *consciousness* may be anachronistic. While Plotinus is one of the first philosophers to distinguish and use several different words that correspond, or to the very least connect, with phenomena that later came to be called "consciousness" and "self-awareness,"[12] these notions develop gradually in the history of philosophy, and the topic is not nearly as central for him as it is in early modern philosophy. Notably, moreover, none of the above texts actually makes use of the terminology of consciousness. Consciousness is involved more obliquely, as a presupposition. On one occasion Plotinus is explicit that the identification with some activities of the soul rather than others is a matter of perception or awareness (*aisthētikon*);[13] but generally his talk of "we" exhibits certain aspects and activities and omits others. Recently, therefore, the Plotinian self has been called, more befittingly, *the reflexive subject* and described as *that which makes the choice of its identity*.[14] Let us treat these aspects in turn.

---

10 E. R. Dodds, *Les Sources de Plotin* (Geneva: Fondation Hardt, 1960), 6.

11 Gwenaëlle Aubry, "Metaphysics of Soul and Self in Plotinus," in *Handbook of Neoplatonism*, ed. Pauliina Remes and Svetla Slaveva-Griffin (New York: Routledge, 2014), 310.

12 Cf., e.g., Edward Warren, "Consciousness in Plotinus," *Phronesis* 9 (1960): 83–98. For the ways in which Plotinus anticipates but also differs from Descartes, cf. Sara Rappe, "Self-Knowledge and Subjectivity in the *Enneads*," in *The Cambridge Companion to Plotinus*, ed. L. P. Gerson (Cambridge: Cambridge University Press, 1996), 250–74.

13 Cf. *Enn.* V.1.12.5–10.

14 Cf. Aubry, "Soul and Self," 321–2.

4.2. THE THINKER THINKING ITSELF AND ITS
OWN THOUGHTS

The question of whether and how we are conscious of the contents of our own thoughts is discussed in Plotinus within his analyses of the activity of the intellect. It is this discussion, too, that shows Plotinus coming close to a notion of subject, an understanding of self as something more than the collection of our thoughts. His entry point is in the perfect cognition of the intellect, inherent in both the perfect, paradigmatic Intellect, and each individual intellect at the heart of every human soul. The contents of the Intellect are the objects of knowledge, the Platonic Forms, with which the Intellect is also identical. This identity of the knower and the known, or immediacy, is to guarantee infallibility in Plotinus. Ordinary human thinking, in contrast, happens through representations, and representational relationship opens up the possibility of erring.[15] In ordinary human case, knowledge acquisition is an attempt at, first, matching representations with innate paradigms, and, in its second phase, gaining an insight that would not be mediated, either ontologically or epistemologically, by any entity in between the subject and the object of thinking.

In discussing the unmediated relationship of the intellect with its objects, Plotinus takes up two questions relevant for self-knowledge, the intellect's awareness *that it is thinking*, and the intellect's self-awareness of itself *as a thinker*.

The thinker, he claims, has to be one and the same with that which also knows that it thinks:

> Again, the supposition that one intellect thinks and the other thinks that it thinks is certainly not a reason for making several intellects. For even if in these [on our level?] it is one thing for the intellect to

---

15 For this idea and its roots in Plato and Aristotle, cf., e.g., Lloyd P. Gerson, "Neoplatonic Epistemology," in *Handbook of Neoplatonism*, ed. Pauliina Remes et al. (New York: Routledge, 2014), 266–72.

think and another for it to think that it thinks, it is a single application of a mind not unaware of its activities.[16]

While the conceptual differentiation between thinking and thinking that one thinks can and should be made, Plotinus argues for a
one-level and one-activity explanation. In a higher-level solution,
the higher thinking activity itself is in danger of going unnoticed,
unless we postulate a further, even higher activity to make the
lower self-aware, and yet another to explain that one, ad infinitum.
Moreover, it is unclear whether this would count as *self*-awareness,
since the thing that is aware is another than the thing of which it is
aware.[17]

In considering the option that perhaps the intellect only knows,
and neither itself nor any other entity is aware that it thinks, Plotinus
appeals to ordinary human thinking:

> If this happened to ourselves, who always watch over our impulses
> and our thought processes, if we are even moderately serious people,
> we should be blamed for witlessness. But certainly when the true
> Intellect thinks itself in its thoughts and its object of thought is not
> outside but it is itself also its object of thought, it necessarily in its
> thinking possesses itself and sees itself: and when it sees itself it does
> so not as without intelligence but as thinking.[18]

Plotinus argues from the possibility of introspection, of conscious
directing of attention to our own thoughts and motivations, to the
overall structure of mentality/mind involving a self-reflexive aspect.
Since the human mind can self-reflect and become aware of its content, there has to be something that explains this ability. This is why

---

16 *Enn.* II.9.1.33–37.
17 Cf. *Enn.* II.9.1.49–58.
18 *Enn.* II.9.1.43–50.

Plotinus introduces the notion of a paradigmatic mind or intellect that sustains such a feature.

The activities of an infallible thinker are as immediately given to itself as its objects of thinking. It enjoys a privileged access to them, because its own essence, the thinking activity, reveals itself to itself. Ordinary thinkers are not related to all of their own mental states or activities equally infallibly, but can access them with more or less effort, as testified by ordinary life experiences.

We saw already Plotinus' being careful to describe the structure of self-intellection in such a way as not to differentiate the subject of self-thinking from the object of self-thinking, leaving the first unknown. He elaborates on the epistemic problems with such a separation:

> Knowing himself in this way he will think himself as contemplated, not as contemplating, so that he does not know the all or the whole of himself: for what he saw he saw contemplated but not contemplating, and so he will have seen other, but not himself.[19]

To postulate a part of the intellect as that which thinks the other part, and to locate in one the thinker and in the other the object thought creates problems for self-knowledge: there is one part that is not known at all. Worse still, this is the part that we originally wanted to know, namely the thinker as thinking, not merely as being thought of. Her own subjectivity, if we wish to put it in that way, escapes the knower.[20] In this way, the knower's knowledge would be severely delimited, and far from perfect. Plotinus' answer is to claim that in the intellect's thinking activity the thinker, the thinking, and the thought object fall into one. Self-awareness of the knowing "I" is an inseparable part of the thinking activity that coincides with knowledge. Our

19 Cf. *Enn.* V.3.5.13–16.

20 For a fuller discussion, including references to previous scholarship, cf. Pauliina Remes, *Plotinus on Self: The Philosophy of the "We"* (Cambridge: Cambridge University Press, 2007), 156–75.

knowledge of ourselves as thinkers cannot be of the same kind as our knowledge of other, ordinary objects, for if we take our own thinking activity as a thematic or particularized object in a way similar to other objects, it loses the very feature we tried to grasp.

4.3. The Inward Turn and Inner Vision

We now move from self-relations that are given, structural features of the soul's activities to a self-directedness as a particular methodology. Plotinus' treatise *On Beauty* (I.6) holds one of his most memorable exhortations to turn away from the bodily beauties:

> For how shall we find the way? What method (*mēkhanē*) can we devise? . . . Let him who can, follow and come within (*eis to eisō*), and leave outside the sight of the eyes and the bodily splendours that he saw before. . . . We cannot get there on foot; for our feet only carry us everywhere in this world, from one country to another. You must not get ready the carriage, either, or a boat. Let all these things go, and do not look. Shut your eyes, and change to and wake another way of seeing, which everyone has but few use.[21]

The key contrast is between the two kinds of visions, one looking at external bodily objects and one leaving them and concentrating on inner objects. The method devised is further contrasted to traveling: it is not a journey that can be done by physical movement, and the novel things to learn are not reached by change of scenery. Rather, to practice one should close one's eyes and look inward. Finally, we may note two features: first, this capacity of inward-looking vision is a power innate to the soul. Second, actualization of this power is not a given. Quite the contrary, it is an ability that has to be practiced.

---

21 *Enn.* I.6.8.1–2, 4–5, 23–28.

Plotinus raises next the question of what the inner vision of this kind sees.[22] What follows is one of the most famous passages in the *Enneads*. Let us quote it here in full:

> When it [the inner vision] is awakened it is not at all able to look at the brilliance before it. So that *the soul must be trained* [1], first of all to look at beautiful actions, then at beautiful works—not those which the *technai* produce, but the works of the people that are considered good; then to look at the soul of the man who does good action. How then can you see the sort of beauty a good soul has? *Go back to yourself and look* [2]; and if you do not yet see yourself beautiful, then, just as someone making a statue which has to be beautiful cuts away here and polishes there and makes one part smooth and another pure till he has given his statue a beautiful face, so too you should cut away the excess and straighten the crooked and clear the dark and make it bright, and never stop *"working on your statue"* [3] till the divine glory of virtue shines out on you, till you see "self-mastery enthroned upon its holy seat." [4] If you have become this, and see it, and are home with yourself in purity, with nothing hindering you from becoming in this way one, with no inward mixture of anything else, but wholly yourself, nothing but true light, not measured by dimensions, or bounded by shape into littleness, or expanded to size by unboundedness, but everywhere unmeasured, because greater than all measure, and superior to all quantity; when you see that you have become this, then you have become sight. You can trust yourself then: you have already ascended and need no-one to show you: concentrate your gaze and see. This alone is the eye that sees great beauty.[23]

---

22 Cf. *Enn.* I.6.9.1.

23 *Enn.* I.6.9.1–26. With references to Plato's *Phaedrus* 252d7, 254b7, and my structuring numbers.

As regards the method, we can differentiate three phases: The first phase (1) happens before the inward looking. It is the therapeutic practice close to the one described by Diotima in Plato's *Symposium*, one of starting with bodily beauties and advancing to appreciate intelligible beauty. What Plotinus emphasizes are actions. His point seems not so much to be in Plato's shift from particular to universal, as from the goodness of actions to the source of that goodness and virtue, the soul. The first ennobling move is from attaching one's interest in the beauty of actions to the soul of the people doing them.

This third-personal method is followed by a first-person move distinctive of Plotinus' whole outlook.[24] The second phase (2) consists of the already encountered reversion of the direction of vision, from the external to the internal, into oneself and one's own soul. Inquiry of beautiful souls has to target the soul closest to us, our own. Although the passage itself is not explicit about this, we can supply two reasons for the turn: first, given Plotinus' understanding of knowledge as the intellect's nonmediated relationship—or, rather, identity—with its objects of knowledge, combined with the Platonic idea of these being innate to one's reason, we can see why any attempt at truth, knowledge, and intelligible beauty would have to turn, at some point, toward one's own soul. A relationship mediated by representations and language cannot reach the unmediated awareness to be found in inward-directed contemplation. Second, since the self-knowledge described in the passage coincides with self-improvement, with becoming at the same time more aware of one's true nature, and developing to a better, more virtuous person, the method has to include a reflection of the soul one has the strongest moral interests in, that is, one's own soul, not just any soul.

Regrettably not everything that the inner vision sees—presumably our personal thoughts, desires, others mental happenings and character

---

24 Here he may be following late Stoic ideas. Cf., e.g., Marcus Aurelius, *Meditations*, 4.3.

dispositions—is beautiful, and therefore a third step is called for. We see in ourselves vicious intentions, weaknesses, and other kinds of "crookedness," and have to start, as the third phase (3) of the process, purifying these. The terminology used in the context is pregnant with meaning. For example, Plotinus uses the Platonic pair of bright and dark, terms used to refer, respectively, to the intelligible and nonintelligible, to the darkness of nonbeing and to the brilliant light of being to which the philosopher devotes himself, both in epistemic and in moral or political contexts.[25] Both are also optimists about basic human nature: even the crooked soul has some inner tendency for goodness and improvement. Plotinus' distinctive take, however, lies in the methodology proposed: Plato has no developed ideas about introspection— quite the contrary, his few discussions seem to go against the idea that self-knowledge would be acquired by an inward turn or vision.[26]

The passage further recalls, given especially the self-ennobling context, Plotinus' distinctive theory of virtues. After the stage of civic virtues that concern especially action and its moderation, the Plotinian philosopher will continue to a new phase of purificatory virtues (*katharseis*), in which the inner state of the soul is not suffering from any inner discrepancies.[27] In purification, the person sees herself correctly as her soul, and its intelligible part, "cutting away" the body. This cutting away does not mean a radically ascetic approach. Rather, it concerns identification. The body still has desires and needs, but a philosopher will not mistake her selfhood to consist of the body, its inclinations, and through it the demands imposed on us by the external world.[28] Thus the inward turn goes along with a moral change; by

---

25 Cf. *Alcibiades I*, 134d1–e7. Cf. *Sophist*, 254a5–9. The dialogue is sometimes considered spurious. For my interpretation of the dialogue, and references to secondary literature, cf. Pauliina Remes, "Reason to Care: The Object and Structure of Self-Knowledge in the *Alcibiades* I," *Apeiron* 46.3 (2013): 270–301.

26 The initial suggestion in *Charm*. 159–60 is found deeply problematic.

27 Cf. *Enn*. I.2.4–7; esp. 5.28.

28 Cf., e.g., *Enn*. I.2.5.12–15.

becoming who one really is, aware of the intellect within, one gains a stable, higher kind of virtue. The epistemic advancement in self-knowledge is necessary for the advancement of one's virtuousness.

A person who has succeeded in the three-phase method will finally have nothing impending her inner vision, and has reached the *telos* of the many-stage and many-method journey (4). She will see herself as beautiful, pure, and good, and as unified, one. She will understand herself as light or sight rather than a being limited by shape, size, or measure. Only by becoming godlike in this way will the soul see the true object of knowledge, the intelligible Forms, and the Good (One) beyond them in which the intelligible beauty is originated.[29]

The treatise *On Beauty* establishes a method of inward vision at least in partly observational terms. Even though the first three phases must work closely with propositional, discursive reasoning, the wordings Plotinus uses suggest that there is an observational aspect to be combined with rational self-reflection. Looking within is like looking without insofar as it delivers information that reasoning can further make use of: the internal realm of one's mental states and character dispositions. Moreover, both internal and external visions have a voluntary feature: looking is a matter of turning one's attention to whatever one considers as salient. Plotinus insists, further, on the fallibility of this looking. Since this is an ability to be awakened and practiced, its objects are not immediately available to everyone. Normatively, there is a further difficulty in arriving at true knowledge about oneself. Ideally, the inner vision would reveal not only the states of our soul, but the core self, the intellect, and its objects of knowledge, the Forms. To arrive at this vision is not a given, but the endpoint of a long therapeutic journey, accompanied with rational reflection and dialectical philosophizing. The combination of these elements has, further, one aspect very unlike perception: the process of moral development

---

29 Cf. *Enn.* I.6.9.33–44.

transforms the object "looked" at. The object of self-knowledge, unlike ordinary objects of perception, is not independent from our knowledge of it.[30]

Self-knowledge, then, does have a central place in moral and in epistemic development. Coming to a correct self-understanding is the foundation of goodness of character. Without an accompanying moral and therapeutic development, knowledge remains theoretic or secondhand. Infallible knowledge, for a human being, is dependent upon self-realization. But it is important to underline just how the theory proposed differs from a picture more familiar from the early modern period, according to which certain kinds of relationship to some or all of our own mental states would act as a secure fundament for other knowledge claims. First, while self-reflection may temporally precede the acquisition of objective knowledge in Plotinus, self-knowledge does not provide basic beliefs from which one could infer other beliefs, nor is it needed to answer the problem of justification of knowledge claims. Second, in Plotinus, self-knowledge is also dependent on objective knowledge. There is no proper self-knowledge without knowledge of the Forms, without identification with the Forms, the whole of being. A proper advancement of self-knowledge depends upon a gradual growth in one's knowledge in general. Knowledge acquisition changes the self that is the object of inner vision: it makes it not just more knowledgeable, but also more virtuous. The epistemic and moral development must go hand in hand.

4.4. SELF-DETERMINATION

One might argue that this kind of theory defends an inhumane ideal of human telos and externalizes too much of what is human from the true

---

30 In this respect, Plotinus' view is an early predecessor of rationalist or constitutive views on self-knowledge. Cf., e.g., Akeel Bilgrami, *Self-Knowledge and Resentment* (Cambridge, MA: Harvard University Press, 2006), esp. 22–28.

self.[31] One might also raise worries about personal identity: why would a pure intellect that each and every soul has, but that does not seem to contain anything temporal or individual, be *me*?[32] While the method and therapy of the soul must in each case be, both motivationally and structurally, first-personal and individual, Plotinus' theory advances ontological stability, epistemic security, and universality at the expense of individuality. In this, combined with his ideas of intellection as a direct identity relationship of the knower with being, Plotinus is an important link in the development of mystical, apophatic tradition, to be followed by later Neoplatonic interest in the practices of prayer and ritual as a means to the divine. Plotinus develops, however, also another kind of trend within the history of philosophy, one connected to freedom and autonomy. Let us end with some words that qualify Plotinus' view and explicate why attending to our bodily nature is understood as some kind of alienation from our true self. Why exactly is the identification with the highest aspects of our nature seen as a means of overcoming this alienation?

Repeatedly, Plotinus connects the true—and ideal—self with self-determination and mastery over emotions and over destiny. We have already seen him advocate the end of the therapy as a realization of one's unbounded nature, and as that which controls rather than is controlled. "So what is left which is the 'we'? Surely, just that which we really are, we to whom nature gave power to master our passions."[33] The process of self-identification is understood as liberating. As composites, human beings are inside the cosmological, deterministic natural order. But we need not think of ourselves only in such a way, as beings with an externally determined role in the causal framework.

---

31 Cf., e.g., Julia Annas, *Platonic Ethics, Old and New* (Ithaca, NY: Cornell University Press, 1999), 62–70.

32 Cf., e.g., Richard Sorabji, "Is the True Self an Individual in the Platonist Tradition," in *Le commentaire entre tradition et innovation*, ed. M. O. Goulet-Cazé (Paris: Vrin, 2000), 293–300.

33 *Enn.* II.3.9.14–16.

Through identification of oneself as the intellect the human being can, at least in some sense, stay outside the cosmic causal framework, to escape living under destiny.[34] Identification with the body, on the other hand, means that one gives oneself over to external influences.

On one level, the mere identification of a more beneficial regulative ideal has good consequences for the self's choices and life. The possession of knowledge understood as the full set of essences, and probably also a fair number of the principles that govern causal networks, provides rational control: a chance at understanding the cosmos, providing, thus, if not a point of manipulation of that same cosmos (on this there is a scholarly disagreement), at least an insight into its workings and embedded value hierarchies.

On another level, the activity that lies at the end of the process, contemplation or intellection, is a self-determined and self-controlled activity. In intellection, the impulse comes from the intellect itself, not from the world, and the same activity is also directed to itself, to the internal objects of knowledge, rather than to external things outside its control:

> Contemplation alone remains not spell-bound because no-one who is self-directed is subject to spell-binding: for he is one, and the object of his contemplation is himself, and his reason is not misled, but he makes what he ought and his own life and work.[35]

Intellect, then, is that part of us which has ideal autonomy. It is self-sufficient and paradigmatically invulnerable, and a source of human ability for self-determination.

Plotinus seeks the point from which activity, both in action and in cognition, stems, the point of origin that would be under the agent's own control, and secure human autonomy, freedom (*eleutheria*), and

---

34 Cf. *Enn.* II.3.9.21–2, 24–31.

35 *Enn.* IV.4.44.1–4.

self-determination (*autexousion*, using also *eph' hēmin*, "up to us").[36] Through our intellectual abilities we can actualize our potentiality for autonomy. The pursuit of self-knowledge is a process of coming to understand ourselves as this power of choice of what we want to become. While the Aristotelian, essentialist tradition emphasizes realization of one's essence as a key feature of becoming happy, Plotinus picks this notion but gives it a proto-voluntarist reinterpretation. The self is the subject of self-identification, in a sense the whole process of appropriation. In maintaining, however, that only choices for the good can be free, he subscribes to strong teleology as regards possible directions of choice. The normative, and normatively regulative, goal of self-knowledge is to understand one's authentic, essentially good selfhood.

---

36 Central is *Enn.* VI.8. Cf. esp. 1.15–18.

CHAPTER FIVE

Augustine on Self-Knowledge and Human Subjectivity

Johannes Brachtendorf

One of the oldest topics in ancient philosophy is the connection between knowledge of oneself and knowledge of God.[1] It may be found already in prephilosophical wisdom— "Know thyself" was written above the portal of the Apollo temple in Delphi, it is preeminent in Plato's philosophy, and was later fully developed in the later Platonic tradition.[2] Augustine adheres to this tradition. In his early works, he declares knowledge of God and knowledge of the soul to be the foremost concerns of his entire thought,[3] and in his late writings the concept of the human mind as an

---

1 The introduction and sections 5.1–5.3 of this chapter rely largely on a translation and revision of my article "Endlichkeit und Subjektivität: Zur Bedeutung des Subjekts im Denken Augustins," in *Fluchtpunkt Subjekt: Facetten und Chancen des Subjektgedankens,* ed. Gerhard Krieger and Hans-Ludwig Ollig (Paderborn: Schöningh, 2001), 37–53.

2 Cf. Pierre Courcelle, *Connais-toi toi-même: De Socrate à Saint Bernard,* 3 vols. (Paris: Études Augustiniennes, 1974). Cf. Klaus Oehler, *Subjektivität und Selbstbewußtsein in der Antike* (Würzburg: Könighausen & Neumann, 1997).

3 Cf. Augustinus, *Soliloquia,* I.7 and II.1. Cf. Augustinus, *Contra academicos, De beata vita, De ordine, De libero arbitrio,* Corpus Christianorum, Series Latina, 29, ed. William M. Green (Turnhout: Brepols,

image of God plays a dominating role. In his late speculation on the divine Trinity, however, Augustine begins to conceive of this connection in a new way—a way that is accompanied by decisive changes to his notion of the human mind. Subjectivity in the sense of self-knowledge, self-awareness, or self-presence is an important topic in modern philosophy but by no means an invention of modern thinking. Ancient philosophers like Aristotle and above all Plotinus developed subtle and highly elaborate conceptions of this notion. But while the ancient tradition before Augustine understood subjectivity as a feature of the divine, infinite intellect only, Augustine interprets it as an essential property of the human mind. In my opinion, Augustine's most important contribution to the philosophy of mind is his development of a theory of finite subjectivity.

In the following I will expound the connection of self-knowledge and knowledge of God as we find it in Augustine's earlier works up to his *Confessiones*. Here, Augustine's thought is strongly influenced by Plotinus.[4] Then I will turn to the bishop's most complex work, namely *De Trinitate*, to give an account of the arguments that lead him— beyond Plotinus—to his final concept of the human mind.

5.1. SELF-KNOWLEDGE AND SELF-TRANSCENDENCE IN EARLY AUGUSTINE

In Augustine's early writings, self-knowledge primarily means insight into the metaphysical rank of the human mind above the material bodies and below God. As a reflection on the acts of the mind, especially on the conditions of the act of making judgments, self-knowledge leads to knowledge of God.[5] The proof of the existence of God, as developed

1970), II.30, II.44, and II.47. Cf. G. Verbeke, "Connaissance de soi et connaissance de Dieu chez Saint Augustin," *Augustiniana* 4 (1954): 495–515.

4 Cf. also Phillip Cary, *Augustine's Invention of the Inner Self: The Legacy of a Christian Platonist* (Oxford: Oxford University Press, 2000), 31–44.

5 Cf. Augustinus, *De Ordine*, II.30–51. See also Scott Macdonald, "The Divine Nature: Being and Goodness," in *The Cambridge Companion to Augustine*, ed. David Vincent Meconi and Eleonore Stump, 2nd ed. (Cambridge: Cambridge University Press, 2014), 17–36, 34f.

in *De libero arbitrio* II, rests on the idea of a hierarchy of beings.[6] The living, Augustine asserts, is better than the merely existing. Within a living being, the inner sense is superior to the outer senses, because it judges them. On the same ground, reason surpasses the inner sense. Augustine argues further that reason passes all its judgments on perceptual entities, whether theoretical, practical, or aesthetic, by applying immutable and universally valid standards. Since the human mind is a changeable being, it cannot generate these unchangeable standards, but receives them from a higher realm—the realm of immutable truth.[7] According to this argument, self-reflection gives proof of the existence of a divine sphere of principles prior to all judgments of human reason.

The same reasoning can be found in the *Confessiones*, especially in Augustine's report on his confrontation with Plotinus and Porphyry (book 7),[8] and in the so-called vision of Ostia (book 9). However, the mere inference of the existence of a divine sphere is now crowned by a momentary intuition of the divine light. At Ostia, Augustine and his mother Monica encountered the divine for an instant.[9] To achieve this, the noise of the senses had to be left behind, the soul had to fall silent and step beyond its thinking of itself,[10] so that God could be perceived directly and immediately. In the *Confessiones*, self-knowledge culminates in transcending the self toward a direct vision of God, which is attainable only if the soul leaves everything behind, even its thinking of itself.

Modern research on Augustine has shown that his idea of an intellectual ascent to God is Platonic in character and inspired in particular by Plotinus.[11] For Plotinus, the dianoetic part of the soul becomes aware

---

6 Cf. Augustinus, *De libero arbitrio*, II.7–41.

7 Cf. ibid., II.34.

8 Cf. Augustinus, *Confessiones*, VII.11–23.

9 Cf. ibid., IX.23–26.

10 Cf. ibid., IX.25.

11 Cf. Werner Beierwaltes, *Platonismus im Christentum* (Frankfurt am Main: Vittorio Klostermann Verlag, 1998), 180–84.

of its dependence on divine reason (*nous*) through a reflection on its own acts of thinking and judging.[12] Rational insight may be topped off by a momentary intuition of the realm of ideas. Plotinus' highest principle, the first hypostasis, is the pure "one," which is beyond all multiplicity. The second hypostasis is the nous, a unity admitting the slightest possible degree of multiplicity. For Plotinus this means that the nous is perfectly self-related. It is multiple by having knowledge and thus being subject to the distinction between a knowing subject and an object known. The nous is one, however, because it itself is the object of its knowledge.[13] Moreover, knowledge of the nous for Plotinus comprises the whole cosmos of ideas, and in knowing these, it knows itself in a perfect way. Whatever object the nous may think, in thinking its object, it is completely present to itself.[14] Plotinus conceives of the nous as absolute subjectivity. A typical feature of his conception of mental ascent is that in the ecstatic moment of unification with the divine the human intellect becomes part of this absolute subjectivity. While being pulled upward to the intelligible realm, the human soul comes to participate in the unimpaired self-presence of the divine mind. For Plotinus, this means that the soul has to relinquish its humanity, leave behind its finitude, and be transformed into "something other."[15]

Augustine holds that the human mind is capable of self-reflection, in the sense of a consideration of its own abilities, which leads to a mental ascent toward the encounter of the divine. Even the early Augustine, however, did not receive Plotinus' idea of the human mind becoming part of the divine subjectivity at the climax of the ascent. Neither in the reports of his ecstatic experiences in *Confessiones* 7 nor

---

12 Plotinus, *Enneads*, V.3.4.15–23. Hereafter cited as *Enn.*

13 Cf. *Enn*, V.3.5.

14 Cf. *Enn*, V.5.1–2. For an analysis, cf. E. Emilsson, "Plotinus on the Objects of Thought," *Archiv für Geschichte der Philosophie* 77 (1995): 21–41. Cf. I. Chrystal, "Plotinus on the Structure of Self-Intellection," *Phronesis* 43 (1998): 264–86.

15 Cf. *Enn*, V.3.4.10–30.

in the description of his vision of Ostia is the ascent to God linked in any way to the notion of perfect self-presence. Thus, even Augustine's early approach departs from Plotinus in conceiving the human mind as essentially distinct from the divine.

5.2. The Divine Trinity and the Problem of Mental Ascent

The later Augustine was increasingly skeptical about some of Plotinus' ideas. In *De Trinitate*, he shows that the scheme of mental ascent that was so important in his early writings proves to be insufficient as soon as the notion of trinity comes into play. Augustine's concept of the divine Trinity is based on four principles:

1. God is one—*una essentia* or *una substantia*.[16]
2. There are three divine persons. The three persons each bear the character of a substance. This is indicated by sentences like "The Father is God, the Son is God, the Spirit is God," in which each person functions as a subject of so-called *ad se* propositions, that is, essential predications in which the predicate explicates an essential property of the subject. Subjects of *ad se* propositions are ontologically "in themselves" (*in se ipso*), and that means for Augustine that they are substances.[17]
3. The three persons are equal to each other, because their specific *ad se* propositions have the same content: The Father is good, just, and so on, the Son is good, just, and so on, and the Spirit is good, just, and so on, and even simply the same is true of God. According to ordinary logic this would mean that there are three gods, as the propositions "Peter is a man," "Paul is a man," and "John is a man" imply that there are three men. The principle of unity, however, prohibits such a plurality in the

---

16 Augustinus, *De Trinitate*, V.3 and VII.10. Hereafter cited as *Trin.*
17 Cf. *Trin.* VII.2.

divine Trinity. As Augustine says, the equality of the persons is of such power that it becomes a unity.[18] The consequence is that in the divine Trinity each single person represents each other person as well as the totality—that is, God, absolutely. Here two or three, as Augustine puts it, is not more than one.

4. The three persons can be distinguished only through their specific relations to each other, articulated in propositions *ad aliquid relative* (= relational predications). The Father is called Father in relation to the Son, the Son is called Son in relation to the Father, and so forth.[19] Even in the divine Trinity, Augustine asserts, relations presuppose substances to adhere to,[20] but since the trinitarian relations are immutable, Augustine does not consider them accidents.[21]

In book 8 of *De Trinitate* Augustine tries to connect the Plotinian ascent with the concept of the triune God. If God is trinitarian, the soul that moves upward and ecstatically reaches God should see the Trinity. In a fictitious dialogue with the soul, Augustine offers the soul four ways of an ascent to the Trinity; all of them use the Platonic pattern of discursive reasoning and subsequent intuition. The first way is based on the concept of truth.[22] The soul shall understand that "truth" lies at the bottom of all things true and gaze at it. The second way includes an inference from the many good things to the "good itself"; the third shows "justice itself" to be the operative principle in all the just souls,[23] and the fourth rests on "love itself" as the ground prior to all acts of loving.[24] With each of these four ways the ascent fails, not because the

---

18 Cf. *Trin.* V.9.
19 Cf. *Trin.* V.6 and V.12–16.
20 Cf. *Trin.* VII.2.
21 Cf. *Trin.* V.5–6.
22 Cf. *Trin.* VIII.3–4.
23 Cf. *Trin.* VIII.9.
24 Cf. *Trin.* VIII.12–14.

desired view of *veritas, bonum, iustitia*, and *amor* was unsuccessful, for it is indeed attained, but because the divine Trinity did not become visible. The ideas of truth, of the good, of justice and of love are uniform in themselves; they do not reveal anything trinitarian. On the background of Augustine's doctrine of the Trinity, it is easy to see why the mental ascent to the vision of the divine Trinity could not reach its goal. All the four ideas are essential properties of God, that is, predicates that can be said equally of any person as well as of God absolutely. Thus, Augustine explains, they cannot give any indication of a plurality in God. The Plotinian concept of a connection between self-knowledge and knowledge of God such that an inward movement of the mind leads to a vision of God—a concept that the young Augustine appreciated so much—strands at the notion of a triune God.

From book 9 of his *De Trinitate* onward, Augustine develops an alternative strategy that has important consequences for his theory of the human mind. If a direct vision of the divine Trinity is not feasible, indirect access still may be possible, such as a view of God as in a mirror, or in an image. For Augustine, the human mind is the "image of God." For an interpretation of the human mind as *imago Dei*, Augustine could reach back to a tradition that emerged partly from biblical writings (Gen. 1:26: let us make humans in our image and likeness), partly from Platonic sources.[25] Augustine gives this tradition a new meaning by claiming that the human mind is an image of God because it, too, is trinitarian in structure. The triune God is withdrawn from our faculty of intuition, but nothing is closer to the human mind than itself. If the human mind is a trinity, we can perceive in it the triune God as in a mirror or in an image.[26] Augustine makes this the program of the second half of *De Trinitate*. To conduct this project, Augustine has to show that the four principles of trinitarian ontology: unity of substance, threefoldness, radical equality, and relational difference apply

---

25 Cf. Plotinus, *Enn.* V.3.4.21–22.
26 Cf. *Trin.* IX.2 and XV.10.

not only to God, but also to the human mind. This is the meaning of Augustine's theory of the human mind as laid out in books 9–15 of *De Trinitate*. According to Augustine, the key to an understanding of the trinitarian character of the human mind is the notion of its self-relatedness.

Augustine distinguishes three elements in the human mind, namely the mind itself (*mens*), its self-love (*amor sui*), and its self-knowledge (*notitia sui*), and sets out to show that they make up a trinitarian structure. He asserts that these three elements are not related to each other like a whole and its parts or like a substance and its accidents.[27] Evidently, the *mens* is one as God is one: but do *amor* and *notitia* have the status of substances, so that together with the *mens* they form a threefoldness? According to Aristotle's *On Categories*, knowledge (*epistēme*) is a quality of the soul, that is, an accident.[28] As we know from the *Confessiones*, Augustine is well aware of Aristotle's view,[29] but he does not share it. Instead, Augustine advances three arguments to show that *amor* and *notitia* are to be treated like substances. First, unlike accidents they do not simply adhere to a bearer as color and shape adhere to a corporeal being, but through their intentionality they reach beyond the *mens*. Second, love and knowledge can bend backward to the *mens*, turn into self-love and self-knowledge, and thus completely penetrate its bearer, which no accident would be able to do. Third, Augustine claims that *notitia* and *amor* themselves are self-related. For Augustine, knowledge of something always carries along with it knowledge of itself, and love of something necessarily loves itself. Reflexivity indicates a degree of self-sufficiency or being *in se ipso* that no accident can have.[30] Thus, Augustine concludes

---

27 Cf. *Trin.* IX.2–7.
28 Cf. Aristoteles, *The Categories*, trans. H. P. Cooke, Loeb Classical Library No. 325 (Cambridge, MA: Harvard University Press, 1983), 1b, 1–2.
29 Cf. Augustinus, *Confessiones*, IV.28–30.
30 Cf. *Trin.* IX.7–8.

that the mind, its self-love, and self-knowledge are not to be characterized as one substance with two accidental properties, but as a three-in-oneness.

Finally, Augustine maintains the equality and mutual relatedness of *mens, amor sui*, and *notitia sui*. The mind, he claims, loves itself as knowing and knows itself as loving; the mind loves itself completely and knows itself completely—it knows its whole love and loves its whole knowledge. Each of the three elements is in each other, and each pair of elements is included in the third. By this play with the permutations of the three elements, Augustine wants to show that *mens, amor sui*, and *notitia sui* are related to each other in a way that corresponds to the structure of the divine Trinity. If the mind, its self-love, and self-knowledge completely embrace and penetrate each other, then each element represents each other element and the whole, so that two or three are not more than one.[31] At the end of book 9 of *De Trinitate*, Augustine comes to the conclusion that the human mind is a triune being just as God is triune, but for different reasons. With regard to God, metaphysical unity and infinity, combined with the biblical distinction of Father, Son, and Spirit lead to the conception of a trinity. With regard to the human mind, the trinitarian structure is based on its self-relatedness. For Augustine, self-relatedness guarantees the substantiality of *amor* and *notitia*—otherwise there would be no real threefoldness; and it guarantees their perfect mutual penetration—otherwise there would be no unity. Whereas the divine Trinity can be articulated in propositions *ad se* and *ad aliquid relative*, the human mind seems to evade this distinction, because it is essentially in relation to itself (one might say: *ad se ipsam relative*). According to Augustine, self-relation is the way in which an intelligible, but finite being imitates in itself the ontological structure of the trinitarian God. This is the result of book 9 of *De Trinitate*.

---

31 Cf. *Trin*. IX.8.

5.3. The Natural Self-Presence of the Human Mind

For two reasons, Augustine is not satisfied with this result. The first reason is that, according to the argument so far, *mens, amor sui*, and *notitia sui* form a trinity only if the mind is in a state of wisdom, that is, of moral and intellectual perfection. For an equality between *amor sui* and *mens* only occurs if the mind loves itself in the right way, namely more than material goods and less than God. Likewise, *notitia sui* equals the *mens* only if the *mens* interprets itself correctly as an intelligible being ranked between the material bodies and God. In book 10 of *De Trinitate*, Augustine sets out to show that it is not only the wise man's mind that is trinitarian, but the human mind as such. For Augustine, being an image of God is not a privilege of the saint or the philosopher, but an undeletable character of any human being.

The second reason for Augustine's dissatisfaction is that the result of book 9 is open to an objection advanced first by the Hellenistic skeptic Sextus Empiricus.[32] The bishop knows of Sextus' argument probably via Plotinus, who discusses it in order to safeguard the self-relatedness of divine *nous*.[33] In Augustine's assimilation (*De Trinitate* 10), the objection runs as follows. The Delphic injunction "Know thyself" summons us to turn away from the outward world, to seek ourselves, to become aware of what we are, and thereby to develop an adequate self-knowledge. But how can the mind seek itself if it does not already know itself? As Augustine points out, all seeking presupposes a knowledge of what is sought; otherwise the seeker would neither know what he or she is looking for nor realize when the item sought is found. Furthermore, any act of seeking is motivated by love. But, as Augustine asserts, there is no indeterminate love. Love always loves something

---

32 Cf. Sextus Empiricus, *Adversus Mathematicos VII*, trans. R. G. Bury, Loeb Classical Library No. 291 (Cambridge, MA: Harvard University Press, 1983), 284–86, 310–12.

33 *Enn.* V. 3. 1. Cf. Christof Horn, "Selbstbezüglichkeit des Geistes bei Plotin und Augustinus," in J. Brachtendorf, *Gott und sein Bild: Augustins "De Trinitate" im Spiegel gegenwärtiger Forschung* (Paderborn: Schöningh, 2000), 81–103.

and knows what it loves. Thus, the act of striving for self-knowledge, as the Delphic injunction commands, is sparked by a love that must already include the knowledge of that which is sought.[34]

Obviously, the reflecting subject can identify itself only if it knows itself in advance. Otherwise it could not recognize itself amid the many objects it encounters. Higher-order accounts of self-awareness or consciousness are either circular because they presuppose what they purport to explain, or, if the self-knowledge that makes the act of self-reflection possible is in its turn explained as an outcome of another act of reflection, it leads to an infinite regress. Thus, self-knowledge cannot be a result of a separate act of self-reflection.[35]

Is self-knowledge therefore impossible? This is precisely what Sextus Empiricus contends. For him, the claim of self-knowledge is as dubious as any other knowledge claim. Augustine, however, draws another consequence. He admits that not only all striving for self-knowledge but even the understanding of the Delphic injunction presupposes a prior form of self-knowledge; but he asserts that, as a matter of fact, we are able to understand the injunction and to act accordingly. Thus, Augustine concludes, there must be a kind of self-awareness or self-presence that does not come into being through the act of self-reflection, but is prior to it and enables it. This original self-relation, which is the constitutive structure of human subjectivity, manifests itself only secondarily in the mind's ability to turn away from the outward world and to bend back on itself. Primarily it means that the mind always implicitly knows itself and always loves itself. Augustine thus distinguishes two levels of self-relatedness. He calls the basic level of self-presence *se nosse*, which can be understood as intuitive self-awareness,

---

34 Cf. *Trin.* X.4–5 and XIV.13.

35 For a critique of the "reflection model," cf. Dieter Henrich, "Fichtes ursprüngliche Einsicht," in *Subjektivität und Metaphysik*, ed. Dieter Henrich and Hans Wagner (Frankfurt am Main: Vittorio Klostermann, 1966), 192–95. For a discussion of his views in English, cf. Dan Zahavi, "The Heidelberg School and the Limits of Reflection," in *Consciousness: From Perception to Reflection in the History of Philosophy*, ed. S. Heinämaa, Vili Lähteenmaki, and Pauliina Remes (Dortrecht: Springer, 2007), 267–85.

self-acquaintance, or prereflexive self-knowledge; and he calls the secondary level *se cogitare*, which means explicit self-reflection.[36] *Cogitare* is the mode of discursive thinking, in which we think our thoughts successively. Here we can make various things the object of our attention, even ourselves. The Delphic injunction "Know thyself" exhorts us to develop an adequate self-love and self-knowledge on the level of *se cogitare*.[37] The *se nosse*, however, is intuitive, not discursive; here, the self is not one possible content of thinking and willing among others, but the only possible one. As Augustine points out, being present to oneself in a prereflexive, immediate mode is the precondition for understanding the Delphic injunction and for attaining the state of moral and intellectual perfection that is required for an adequate *notitia sui*. To know ourselves in the mode of *se nosse*, however, does not presuppose any learning or education. By its very nature the human mind is always and incessantly acquainted with itself.[38]

Due to its immediacy, the *se nosse* is unquestionable. Obviously we can be mistaken about the nature of the human mind as an intelligible being. In fact, Augustine claims that most people are mistaken, because they get used to material beings and—as a consequence of sin—even expect ultimate happiness from perishable goods, so that in the end they think of themselves as material beings. In Augustine's interpretation, the Delphic injunction has a decidedly ethical meaning. It shall cure us from wrong self-conceptions and make us aware of the intelligible nature of the soul, whose ultimate good only can be another intelligible being, namely God himself. All this, however, is a matter of *se cogitare*.[39] On the level of *se nosse*, there is no error and no deception, because what a human being knows just by being present to itself is not

---

36 Cf. *Trin.* X.7.

37 That it is on the level of discursive thought that our original self-knowledge can be distorted is also emphasized in John M. Rist, *Augustine: Ancient Thought Baptized* (Cambridge: Cambridge University Press 1994), 146f.

38 Cf. *Trin.* XIV.13.

39 Cf. *Trin.* X.11–12.

an abstract notion of the essence of the mind, but simply this: that it is itself. And nobody can be mistaken about her being herself.

5.4. The Unity of Consciousness and the Identity of the Self

From the last books of the *Confessiones* onward, Augustine deals with the astonishing fact that nothing is closer to the human mind than itself, and yet the mind is never completely present to itself. In well-known passages from the *memoria-tractatus* of *Confessions* 10, Augustine points out that we are unable to become fully aware of all the contents of our mind.[40] How is the fragmentary self-presence of the mind compatible with the fact that nothing, not even God, is closer to the mind than itself?[41] In *De Trinitate*, Augustine tackles this question again. He refers to the attempt of reconciling these two observations by declaring the mind divisible; one part of the mind would be present to itself, the other part would not. Augustine considers this attempt preposterous, because divisibility is a character of material beings, not of intelligible ones. "It is absurd to say that the whole of it does not know what it knows: I am not saying 'It knows the whole,' but 'What it knows, the whole of it knows.'"[42] The *mens* does not know everything; it does not even know everything about itself. And yet in knowing what it knows, it always knows as the whole self. What Augustine is after in these reflections is the identity of the knowing self in the flux of its imaginations. To know as the whole self in all the thoughts means to be the identical subject of these thoughts. For Augustine, the identity of the self is grounded in the self-presence of *se nosse*. On the level of *se cogitare*, the mind's self-knowledge remains fragmentary. Its

---

40 Cf. Augustinus, *Confessiones*, X.15.

41 Cf. ibid., X.7.

42 *Trin.* 10.4.6. Cf. Augustinus, *De Genesi ad litteram*, VII.27–28.

inability to understand itself completely is a mark of the finitude of the human self. On the level of *se nosse*, however, the mind's self-presence must be complete; otherwise, the identity of the knowing self would be suspended. The identity constituted by *se nosse* guarantees the unity of consciousness in the sense that all my knowledge, however limited and fragmentary it may be, is *my* knowledge.

Every mental act is accompanied by an awareness of the act. Through this awareness, the self perceives its own reality as the agent of all these acts. Augustine's *se nosse* certainly encompasses the self-perception of the acting mind, but also reaches beyond this. The mind can perceive itself only when mental acts are performed, which is not always the case. Augustine, however, emphasizes that the mind "was seen always to know itself and always to will itself," and that "it must at the same time be seen always to remember itself and always to understand and love itself."[43] According to Augustine, the *se nosse* is continuous. It does not depend on whether *cogitationes* occur or not. By claiming the steadiness of *se nosse*, Augustine wants to account for the continuity of the identical self.

Modern research has rightly pointed out that Augustine received important concepts and arguments from Plotinus.[44] Augustine's claim, for instance, that the mind knows itself as a whole already can be found in Plotinus, but Augustine uses it differently. Plotinus holds that the divine nous thinks the entire cosmos of the Platonic ideas. Referring to Plato's claim that the ideas are themselves living and thinking beings,[45] Plotinus maintains that in thinking the ideas the nous thinks itself as thinking. In thinking any thought, the nous comprises all possible

43 *Trin.* 10.12.19.

44 Cf. Edward Booth, "St. Augustine's "notia sui" Related to Aristotle and the Early Neo-Platonists," *Augustiniana* 27 (1977–79): 27–29; Volker Henning Drecoll, *Die Entstehung der Gnadenlehre Augustins* (Tübingen: Mohr Siebeck, 1999), 288–294; and Frederick E. Van Fleteren, "Augustine's Ascent of the Soul in Book VII of the Confessiones: A Reconsideration," *Augustinian Studies* 5 (1974), 29–72.

45 Cf. Plato, *Sophistes*, 248e.

knowledge; but none of its objects of thought is external to the nous.[46] What it thinks is always itself. For Plotinus, the nous is completely present to itself precisely because its self-knowledge includes the totality of all possible knowledge. Rendered in Augustine's language: What the divine mind knows, the whole of it knows, because it knows the whole. According to Plotinus and the Greek tradition before him, only an infinite mind can be immediately related to itself. Augustine, however, denies this. He claims that even the finite human mind, although it does not know the whole, because its knowledge is limited, is perfectly present to itself in the *se nosse* that constitutes its identity. In contrast with divine self-knowledge, human *se nosse* does not contain any knowledge about the world. This would be a matter of *cogitare*. The mind's self-presence includes nothing more than the perfect and unshakable knowledge that I am myself. Thus, it may not be an exaggeration to say that Augustine's discovery of *se nosse* marks the beginning of philosophical reflection on the finite self. Augustine, so to speak, brought the concept of self-knowledge from heaven down to earth and thereby threw new light on what it means to be a human subject.

5.5. The Self as an Image of God

In *De Trinitate* 10, Augustine further analyzes the *se nosse* and finds three elements in it, which he calls *memoria sui, intellegentia sui*, and *voluntas sui*. These three constitute a trinitarian structure as *mens, amor sui*, and *notitia sui* did in book 9.[47] However, since *se nosse* is prior to *se cogitare*, the trinity of *memoria sui, intellegentia sui*, and *voluntas sui* is the foundational one. Augustine holds that in the natural, everlasting self-presence of *se nosse* we find the clearest likeness of the trinitarian God in the human mind. For Augustine, the mind is an image

---

46 Cf. *Enn.* V.3, 5; V.5, 1–2.
47 Cf. *Trin.* X.14 and X.17.

of the divine Trinity precisely by being a self in the fundamental sense explained above.

Augustine is well aware of the inadequacy of the terms *memoria*, *intellegentia*, and *voluntas*, but sees no better alternative. These terms are inadequate because in their ordinary understanding they denote faculties used by the mind in discursive thinking. To avoid any misunderstanding, Augustine makes a distinction between the "inner" *memoria*, *intellegentia*, and *voluntas* as moments of the *se nosse*, and the "outer," ordinary *memoria*, and so on.[48] In ordinary understanding there is a temporal difference between *intellegentia* and *memoria*. The *intellegentia* grasps a thought, then stores it in the memory, where it can be found and actualized later. In the process of learning, *intellegentia* and *memoria* perform their acts successively. The *se nosse*, however, needs no learning. It is an essential property of the human mind that it is naturally present to itself. For Augustine, this means that the "inner" *memoria sui* and the inner *intellegentia sui* persist simultaneously.[49] The use of the term "memory" indicates the steadiness and permanence in which self-presence resembles any content of the memory; *intellegentia*, however, suggests an actuality, through which self-presence is similar to any actual thought. Augustine even finds a practical dimension in the *se nosse*, namely a perpetual self-affirmation that he calls *voluntas*. As he explains, this will is hard to detect, because it is not manifested in any need. It always has the self that it wants, and like the inner understanding, which is continuously directed at the self, the inner will cannot want (or, which amounts to the same for Augustine, love or affirm) anything else but the self, which it already has.[50] It is important to see that the inner will as a constituent of the

48 Cf. *Trin.* XIV.10.

49 Cf. *Trin.* X.19. For a detailed account of Augustine's conception of memory, cf. Roland Teske, "Augustine's Philosophy of Memory," in *The Cambridge Companion to Augustine*, ed. Eleonore Stump and Norman Kretzmann (Cambridge: Cambridge University Press 2001), 148–58.

50 Cf. *Trin.* X.19.

self is not open to any imperative. For the outer will, which may seek its highest good in different things, it makes perfect sense to demand that it should love God more than anything else, even more than itself. Inner self-love, however, does not compete with the love of God, but makes all loving possible. If, for a moment, the human mind stopped loving itself with the inner will, it would at the same moment cease to exist. According to Augustine, the inner self-affirmation of the human mind is prior to all other acts of will, including religious ones. For only a rational being, that is, a being that has a self, is able to love God. *Memoria sui, intellegentia sui,* and *voluntas sui* constitute the trinitarian structure of the mind's self-presence that must be presupposed in any deliberate self-reflection as demanded by the Delphic injunction, or any deliberate love required by the commandment of the Gospel: Love God above all, and your neighbor like yourself.

Even in *De Trinitate*, Augustine remains faithful to the old idea of a link between self-knowledge and knowledge of God. However, he does not conceive of it in the Plotinian manner any more, as he did up to the *Confessiones*. For the late Augustine, discursive self-reflection with a subsequent transcending of the self is not the way to achieve a vision of the triune God. What is needed to view the divine Trinity as it can be seen during life on earth is not a transcendence but a deeper understanding of the self. Augustine wants us to understand the self by its constitutive immediate and immutable self-presence. In this regard, the mind is like the divine Trinity. If we understand what it ultimately means for a human being to be a self, we see the triune God as in a mirror or in an image.

The *se nosse*, as explained in book 10 of *De Trinitate*, is the most fundamental image of God in the human soul. It is part of human nature. Every human being is immediately aware of itself, since this is what founds a person's identity. This identity is the presupposition for being a moral agent at all. In itself it remains untouched by good or bad decisions and deeds. Thus, on the level of *se nosse*, every human being is and has always been an image of the triune God, sinner and saint alike. Here, humans are essentially similar to God.

But for Augustine, there is also an image of God on the level of *se cogitare*, as explained in book 9 of *De Trinitate*, and this image is restricted to conditions of intellectual and ethical perfection. *Mens, amor sui*, and *notitia sui* form a trinity only if the mind conceives of itself correctly, namely as a rational creature, and if it loves itself correctly, namely less than God and without *superbia*. Only then is there an equality of *amor sui* and *notitia sui* equal to the *mens*, an equality that is one of the four principles of a trinity. The ethical appeal to self-knowledge, moreover, entails degrees of moral perfection. Although the sinner is always aware of himself, he lacks a comprehensive self-knowledge, because he loves himself too much, and therefore is less similar to God. The saint, however, in addition to being acquainted with himself like any rational being, also loves himself in the right way and thus gains an adequate self-conception, which makes him more similar to God. For Augustine, this similarity will be perfect in the afterlife, when the saints see God with uncovered faces.[51] Then the self-knowledge of the human mind will be complete in the full vision of God.

---

51 Cf. *Trin.* XIV.20–24.

CHAPTER SIX

Self-Knowledge in Scholasticism

Dominik Perler

6.1. AN ARISTOTELIAN PUZZLE

All scholastic philosophers agreed that self-knowledge is of crucial importance for human beings, for we could not understand what makes us so special as rational beings if we did not have access to our rational soul and its activities. They also agreed that self-knowledge is indispensable for self-evaluation, for we could not assess ourselves as rational beings with good or bad thoughts, good or bad desires and volitions, if we were utterly ignorant about what we think and desire. But how can we acquire knowledge of our own thoughts and desires? How can we also have knowledge of the soul that produces these activities? How does this knowledge differ from other types of knowledge? And why is it possible at all?

Inspired by Augustine, philosophers in the early and high Middle Ages discussed these questions at great length.[1] With the reception of Aristotle's writings in the thirteenth century, these discussions became part of an all-embracing debate about the possibility and structure of knowledge.[2] In his *De anima*, Aristotle had provided a detailed explanation of how we acquire knowledge, but his explanation seemed to focus on the knowledge of other things. It made clear how we can first have sense perception, then imagination, and finally intellection of material things, namely by assimilating their sensible and intelligible forms. Moreover, it spelled out the cognitive mechanisms that are required for this process of assimilation. But it did not give a detailed account of how and why self-knowledge is possible. In a rather cryptic passage, Aristotle had affirmed that the thinking intellect, the highest part of the soul, "is itself an object of thought, just as its objects are,"[3] but he had not elaborated on this statement. How exactly does the intellect make itself an object of thought? How is it then related to itself? And why does this relation provide self-knowledge?

Given these obvious questions, it is not surprising that medieval Aristotelians attempted to go beyond Aristotle by analyzing the structure of self-knowledge and its relation to other types of knowledge. When dealing with this problem, they focused on three questions. First, they examined the *object* of self-knowledge: is it an act of the intellect, the soul as a whole, or some other object? Their second question concerned the *cognitive process* required for self-knowledge: is this knowledge built upon introspection, upon reflection, or upon some other cognitive activity? Finally, their third question was about the *status* of self-knowledge: is it the most fundamental type of knowledge, or does it depend on the knowledge of other things?

---

1 Cf. Pierre Courcelle, *Connais-toi toi-même: de Socrates à Saint Bernard*, 3 vols. (Paris: Études Augustiniennes, 1974–75).

2 On the new Aristotelian framework, cf. Dominik Perler, ed., *Transformations of the Soul: Aristotelian Psychology 1250–1650, Vivarium*, special issue, 46.3 (2008); Russell L. Friedman and Jean-Michel Counet, eds., *Medieval Perspectives on Aristotle's "De anima"* (Louvain: Peeters, 2007).

3 Aristotle, *De anima* III.4 (430a2–3), trans. D. W. Hamlyn (Oxford: Clarendon Press, 1993).

In the following I will discuss medieval attempts to deal with these questions by focusing on three late thirteenth-century authors: Thomas Aquinas, Matthew of Aquasparta, and Dietrich of Freiberg. They were all inspired by Aristotle's scanty remark about the intellect being "itself an object of thought" but explained self-knowledge in different ways, partly by adding Augustinian elements to the Aristotelian picture. Admittedly, this is only a small part of a long and complex debate, but it will, I hope, show that there was no unified scholastic theory—scholasticism is a large house with many rooms.[4]

6.2. THOMAS AQUINAS: SELF-KNOWLEDGE
AND COGNITIVE ASCENT

Like every Christian author, Thomas Aquinas unhesitatingly affirms that God has full knowledge of himself and that we are made in the image of God.[5] But this thesis does not lead him to the seemingly natural conclusion that we also have full knowledge of ourselves. Why not? He emphasizes that there is a striking difference between the divine and the human intellect.[6] God is a perfect being whose intellect is always fully actualized. That is why he does not need to be actualized by an external thing in order to have knowledge. Everything is all the time fully present to him, including his own intellect with all its acts. He is, as it were, a self-transparent being. Or as Aquinas says: as a fully actualized being God knows himself by his mere essence—nothing else

---

4 For other authors, cf. François-Xavier Putallaz, *La connaissance de soi au XIIIᵉ siècle* (Paris: Vrin, 1991); Dominik Perler and Sonja Schierbaum, eds., *Selbstbezug und Selbstwissen* (Frankfurt am Main: Klostermann, 2014). My discussion will be limited to intellectual self-knowledge, leaving aside forms of sensory self-consciousness and self-awareness. On these forms, cf. François-Xavier Putallaz, *Le sens de la réflexion* (Paris: Vrin, 1991), 39–69; Susan Brower-Toland, "Medieval Approaches to Consciousness: Ockham and Chatton," *Philosophers' Imprint* 12.17 (2012): 1–29.

5 On the image relation cf. Thomas Aquinas, *Quaestiones disputatae de veritate*, q. 10, art. 1, Editio Leonina XXII (Rome: Commissio Leonina; Paris: Cerf, 1970–75). Hereafter cited as *QDV*.

6 Cf. Thomas Aquinas, *Summa theologiae* (hereafter cited as *STh*), ed. Peter Caramello (Rome: Marietti, 1952), I, q. 87, art. 1; *QDV*, q. 10, art. 8; English translation in *The Treatise on Human Nature: Summa Theologiae Ia 75–89*, ed. and trans. Robert Pasnau (Indianapolis: Hackett, 2002).

is required.[7] By contrast, human beings are not fully actualized beings. Their intellect is in a potential state and needs to be actualized by external things. Only when being actualized will it know these things and eventually also itself. That is why human beings do not know themselves by their essence alone.

Two points are noteworthy about this line of argument. First, Aquinas gives a rather restricted account of the fact that human beings are made in the image of God. This only means that they are structurally similar to God insofar as they also have an intellect as a cognitive capacity. But having the same type of capacity still leaves room for different degrees of actualization—having an intellect is one thing, making full use of it is quite another. The second point to be noted is that Aquinas explains the actualization of the human intellect by referring to external things. We cannot know ourselves simply by looking inside because our intellect cannot actualize itself. We rather need to be affected by things that first produce perceptions, then imaginations, and finally intellectual acts. Consequently, our first acts of thinking are not directed at ourselves, but at external things.

How then can we arrive at acts of thinking that are directed at ourselves? And what exactly is their object? These questions can most easily be answered by means of an example that Aquinas himself adduces. Suppose that a stone is lying in front of you. It produces a perception of something gray and round, and this perception gives rise to a first act of thinking:

(1) This stone is gray and round.

It is precisely this act that sets, as it were, your intellect in motion. As soon as your intellect is in this actual state, you can produce another act of thinking, directed at the first one:

(2) I think that this stone is gray and round.

---

7 Cf. *STh* I, q. 14, art. 2; *QDV*, q. 2, art. 2.

Clearly, this act gives you some information about yourself, namely that you are having or performing an act of thinking with a specific content. It is distinct from the first one, as Aquinas unmistakably holds: "So there is one act by which the intellect understands a stone, and another act by which it understands that it understands the stone, and so on from there."[8] The last clause gives rise to the suspicion that there will be an infinite regress. Will there be the further act

(3) I think that I think that this stone is gray and round

and many more acts? And will that lead to a proliferation of acts of thinking? In fact, there can be a series of acts. Some people may go up to a third level of acts, others to a fourth, still others even to a fifth. But this does not amount to a dangerous regress, since not every act of thinking needs to be accompanied by a higher one. Aquinas does not make the strong (and rather implausible) claim that higher-order acts are necessary for each and every act. They are *contingent* acts that are produced at will, and their production can always be stopped.

The fact that Aquinas appeals to a series of distinct acts shows that he subscribes to what is nowadays called a "higher-order theory."[9] We come to know our own acts of thinking not through some kind of inner feeling or sensing, but through higher-order acts that are as intentional as first-order acts. But why is our intellect able to produce higher-order acts? Why can it start a "cognitive ascent" when it moves from the first to the second or to even more levels of acts?[10] Aquinas does not give a detailed answer, but we can see the sketch of an answer when we look at the way he explains cognitive processes in general.

---

8 *STh* I, q. 87, art. 3, ad 2, trans. Pasnau, 193.

9 For an extensive analysis cf. Peter Carruthers, *Consciousness: Essays from a Higher-Order Perspective* (Oxford: Oxford University Press, 2005).

10 I borrow the expression "cognitive ascent" from Robert Pasnau, *Thomas Aquinas on Human Nature: A Philosophical Study of Summa theologiae Ia 75–89* (Cambridge: Cambridge University Press, 2002), 336–47.

The human intellect, he claims in accordance with Aristotle, is a cognitive capacity that can, in principle, think about everything. However, it cannot actually think about a thing unless it receives its form, for it is precisely the presence of a form in the intellect that makes an act of thinking possible.[11] Now suppose that an act of thinking is produced. This act will have its own form. Admittedly, it will only have an accidental form (an act is, technically speaking, an accident that inheres in the intellect), but it will nevertheless have a real form. Since this form will also be in the intellect, a second act of thinking will be possible, namely one that has the first act as its object. And the second act will in turn have its own form, which will also be in the intellect, so that a third act will be possible, and so on. Or for short: for each form present in the intellect there can be an act of thinking. That is why the intellect can start a "cognitive ascent" and produce a series of higher-order acts.

This explanatory strategy enables Aquinas to give a short and elegant answer to the three questions I raised at the beginning of this chapter. The first *object* of self-knowledge is a particular act of thinking or a series of such acts. The *cognitive process* is the cognitive ascent initiated by the intellect once it is in an actual state. And the *status* of self-knowledge is fairly limited. Since it presupposes acts directed at external things, it is not the most basic epistemic phenomenon. Quite the opposite, self-knowledge is founded upon knowledge of external things. Aquinas is very clear about this point: "So our mind cannot understand itself in such a way that it apprehends itself immediately. It is rather by apprehending other things that it arrives at knowledge of itself."[12]

---

11 Aquinas even claims that the external thing is then *in* the intellect—not in a material way, but with "intentional" or "spiritual" existence. For an analysis cf. Myles Burnyeat, "Aquinas on 'Spiritual Change' in Perception," in *Ancient and Medieval Theories of Intentionality*, ed. Dominik Perler (Leiden: Brill, 2001), 129–153; Dominik Perler, *Theorien der Intentionalität im Mittelalter* (Frankfurt am Main: Klostermann, 2002), 42–60.

12 *QDV*, q. 10, art. 8, corp.

Clear and concise as this statement may be, it gives rise to a serious objection. Is the kind of self-knowledge Aquinas describes not very restricted and therefore hardly informative? If acts directed at other things are the only items we can know, we seem to be utterly unable to acquire knowledge of our dispositions and character traits. Thus, I seem to be unable to know that I am an anxious or a brave person, someone with or without talent for learning languages.

Aquinas is aware of this problem and tries to resolve it by pointing out that there is an intimate connection between acts and dispositions. For once we realize that acts of a certain type occur regularly, we can know that we have a stable disposition (*habitus*) to produce them. Aquinas illustrates this point with the example of faith.[13] How can a believer know for sure that he has faith? He can observe his external acts, say his praying, just as other people who pay attention to him can. Moreover, he can immediately think about his internal acts of affirming his faith, something other people cannot do because they only have immediate access to his external behavior. In realizing that acts affirming faith occur again and again, he comes to know that he is in fact a faithful person. Generally speaking, knowledge of regularly occurring acts leads to knowledge of a disposition. The same is true for character traits such as being anxious or brave. Since they are dispositions, they can very well be detected as soon as the relevant acts are detected—nothing beyond the observation of acts, which are manifestations of a character trait, is required.

But how can we know the soul that produces all the acts and character traits? It seems as if we could never have access to it, for there is no such thing as the "naked soul" that we could grasp. Aquinas agrees that the soul is not a special thing that we can immediately apprehend or even look at. But he rejects the idea that we have no access to it. For whenever we grasp an act, we also grasp the soul that is having or performing this

---

13 *STh* I, q. 87, art. 2, ad 1; similarly *QDV*, q. 10, art. 9, ad 8.

act. Take again the religious believer as an example. What does he grasp when he realizes that he affirms his faith? He does not simply grasp an intellectual act of affirmation; he rather grasps that *he* is having an act of affirmation. Technically speaking, he does not grasp an isolated accident, but an accident insofar as it is present in a substance. It would therefore be inappropriate to claim that the object of self-knowledge is nothing but an act. It is an "embedded act," that is, an act that is inseparably connected with the soul and apprehended as being in it. That is why Aquinas does not hesitate to affirm that every person can immediately grasp the existence of his or her soul by apprehending a single act.[14]

However, this cognitive activity does not seem to be very informative. What exactly does the believer grasp when he realizes that he has a soul: a corporeal or an incorporeal entity, a mortal or an immortal one? It seems to be impossible to answer this question. Nothing about the nature of the soul in general or one's own soul in particular seems to become evident through the mere apprehension of its existence. Aquinas fully agrees with this conclusion and emphasizes that knowledge of the *existence* of one's own soul should carefully be distinguished from knowledge of its *nature*.[15] The first type of knowledge comes, as it were, for free whenever an act is apprehended. Easy and natural as it is, it does not provide information about the essential properties of the soul. Consequently, it does not enable us to classify our soul as a special entity. To do that we need the second type of knowledge, which does not come naturally. It requires detailed analysis and a comparison of our soul with other types of entities. This kind of knowledge is quite difficult to obtain and can perhaps never be fully reached. Aquinas dryly remarks that "many are unaware of the soul's nature, and many have even erred regarding the soul's nature."[16]

---

14 *STh* I, q. 76, art. 1; *QDV*, q. 10, art. 9. For an analysis cf. Therese Scarpelli Cory, *Aquinas on Human Self-Knowledge* (Cambridge: Cambridge University Press, 2014), 69–91.

15 *STh* I, q. 87, art. 1; *QDV*, q. 10, art. 8.

16 *STh* I, 87, art. 1, trans. Pasnau, 189.

6.3. Matthew of Aquasparta: Self-Knowledge and Introspection

Matthew of Aquasparta, a Franciscan who studied in Paris around 1270, was fully aware of Aquinas' focus on self-knowledge as natural knowledge of the existence of one's own soul and its acts.[17] But he was dissatisfied with this restricted knowledge. On his view, we should first distinguish various types of self-knowledge and then evaluate which one is available to us. Three types in particular should be taken into account.[18]

First of all, there is knowledge "through argument or reasoning" that we gain when we observe an effect and make the inference that there must be a cause for it. As we can infer that there is fire when we see smoke, we can also infer that there is a soul when we detect an act of thinking. Matthew concedes that we often make this inference, but he does not consider it to be very illuminating since it provides the same information about every soul. Whether I start with my own act or with that of my neighbor, I will merely infer that there is some cause for it—nothing more will be known. Given this limitation, Matthew suggests that we need another type of knowledge, which he calls knowledge "through simple contemplation of the essence." This knowledge, which amounts to Aquinas' second type of knowledge, tells us something about the nature or essence of the soul that produces an act, for instance that it is a substance and that it is incorporeal. Clearly, this type of knowledge is more informative than the first one and enables us to distinguish the human soul from other types of souls. But here, again, we do not learn anything specific about our own soul. We simply come to know what a human soul in general is, be it my own or that of my neighbor, but we ignore the special nature of our own soul. This is the main reason why Matthew thinks that we need still another

---

17 On his relation to Aquinas and other predecessors cf. Putallaz, *La connaissance de soi*, 13–18.

18 Cf. Matthew of Aquasparta, *Quaestiones de fide et cognitione*, q. 5, 300, ed. PP. Collegii S. Bonaventurae (Quaracchi: Collegium S. Bonaventurae, 1957). Hereafter cited as *QC*.

type of knowledge, which he describes as knowledge "through attentive looking."[19] It is a form of introspection that reveals the nature of our individual soul.

It is precisely the possibility of this third type of knowledge that Matthew wants to defend against Aquinas, who denied that the nature of our soul will ever be revealed in this life. But how is introspection possible? Matthew answers this question by spelling out the conditions that need to be fulfilled for successful seeing, be it internal or external.[20] In every case of seeing, he claims, there is (1) a visible object that is present, (2) a power or capacity that is directed at the object, (3) an immediate relation between object and power, and (4) a light that illuminates the object. This can be illustrated for the case of external seeing. Why can you see the stone in front of you? You can do so because there is, first of all, a visible object that is not far away but immediately present to you. Second, you have eyes that are actually directed at the visible properties (color, size, etc.) of that object. Third, there is no obstacle between your eyes and these properties. And fourth, the stone is present to you in clear daylight. Given the fulfillment of all four conditions, you do actually see the stone. According to Matthew, something similar can be said about the case of internal seeing. First of all, there is the soul as a visible object that is immediately present to you. Of course, it does not have properties like color and size, but it has acts of thinking that are immediately present and ready to be grasped. Second, there is an appropriate power or capacity for grasping the acts. This is nothing but the intellect, a power of the soul. It is directed at everything that is actually present to it, including the soul itself. Third, there is no obstacle that prevents the intellect from grasping what is present to it. In particular, there is no material obstacle since the soul is fully immaterial and cannot be covered by anything material. Fourth and finally, there is some kind of inner light that illuminates the soul.

---

19 *QC*, q. 5, 300.
20 *QC*, q. 5, 304–5.

For whenever it is present, it is fully transparent in its activity. That is why it can be fully grasped.

This reference to some form of internal seeing shows that Matthew has a perceptual model in mind when he talks about the third and most informative type of self-knowledge. On his view, we can literally see our own soul and thereby detect what it is—we can see its special nature, just as we can see the special nature of the stone when we look at it. It is therefore not surprising that Matthew uses Augustinian terminology, saying that we can have self-knowledge through a "spiritual conversion": we turn to our soul by using the intellect, one of its powers, and see it as an immediately present thing.[21]

However, Matthew's description of the internal seeing gives rise to the suspicion that it is, after all, not the soul that is seen but some act of the soul. Suppose that you are right now thinking about your next holiday and that you are turning to yourself through a "spiritual conversion." What do you see? It seems as if you were seeing nothing but your act of thinking with its special content. For instance, you realize that you are thinking about a nice day on the beach, in company with good friends. The better you focus on yourself, the better you will be able to spell out the content of your act. But you will hardly be able to have a glimpse at the soul, which is nothing but the hidden cause of the act.

Matthew would disagree with this account of the internal seeing. He would point out—just like Aquinas—that we never grasp an isolated act. We always grasp or even see an act insofar as it is present in the soul. Rather than being a hidden cause, the soul is a *manifest* cause that becomes visible through the act it produces. Using Matthew's metaphorical language, we could say that it is not just the act that is illuminated by the inner light, but the soul as well—both shine up. Thus, when you are focusing on yourself, you do not just see the thought about a beautiful day on the beach. You rather see *your soul* as thinking about a beautiful day on the beach.

---

21 *QC*, q. 5, 304.

But Matthew would go one step further. Unlike Aquinas, he would stress that you do not simply grasp the existence of your soul. Since the soul is illuminated as being in action, you see it with some of its distinctive properties. For instance, you see that it is a causal principle and that it is constantly active since it constantly produces thoughts. You also see that it produces thoughts in a special order. Thus, you may see that the thought about your next holiday is followed by the thought about your dearest friends, which in turn is followed by feelings of affection for your friends. You thereby become aware of the special way your soul produces thoughts and feelings. The important point is that you do not simply see the nature of a human soul in general. You rather see the nature of *your* soul as being in action. That is why introspective knowledge crucially differs from the second type of knowledge, which Matthew introduced as "simple contemplation of the essence." Contemplation abstracts from your own soul and aims at indicating the general features of the soul. By contrast, introspection gives you knowledge of your soul that has its own history and that produces acts in its own way.

It is now clear how Matthew deals with the three main problems of self-knowledge. Its *object* is not just an act of the soul or the soul as an unspecified thing, but the special nature of one's own soul. The *cognitive process* is an internal seeing that reveals this nature. Its *status* cannot be that of foundational knowledge since it is built upon knowledge of external things. If we were never in touch with the material world, our soul could never become active and its nature could never be seen or grasped.

6.4. Dietrich of Freiberg: Self-Knowledge and the Self-Sufficient Intellect

Like Thomas Aquinas and Matthew of Aquasparta, Dietrich of Freiberg studied and taught at the University of Paris and was familiar with the theories of his predecessors.[22] But he openly criticized them, claiming that the intellect as the highest part of the soul "always actually understands" and that "through this understanding it understands itself by its essence."[23] This is quite a radical statement. Dietrich rejects the seemingly uncontroversial thesis that the human intellect cannot always think and understand because it is a mere capacity that needs to be actualized. What are his reasons for this rejection?

His main reason stems from his interpretation of the traditional doctrine that human beings are made in the image of God. This image relation, he affirms, is not simply a similarity relation but a relation of "expression."[24] This means that human beings are expressed by God in such a way that they immediately flow out from him and share with him the same nature. Of course, they are distinct from him, but as far as their intellect is concerned they are not utterly different: they have the same type of intellect and can make the same use of it. Clearly, God's intellect is always fully actualized. Therefore, the human intellect expressing it must be equally actualized. What distinguishes the human from the divine intellect is simply the fact that it is created and therefore not an independent thing. But this does not amount to a limitation of its activity. Like the divine intellect, it is in an actual state all the time.

No doubt, this is a strong thesis that departs from the standard Aristotelian theory, defended by Aquinas and others, according to which the human intellect does not think unless it is triggered by a sensory input. To be sure, Dietrich does not deny that the intellect often uses sensory information when it produces acts of thinking. But his main point is that it does not need this information to become

22 On his intellectual biography cf. Kurt Flasch, *Dietrich von Freiberg: Philosophie, Theologie, Naturforschung um 1300* (Frankfurt am Main: Frankfurt, 2007), 19–59.

23 Dietrich von Freiberg, *De visione beatifica* (hereafter cited as *VB*), in *Opera omnia* 1:22 (theses 1 and 2), ed. Kurt Flasch et al. (Hamburg: Meiner, 1977–85).

24 *VB*, 1:41.

active—it is active by itself. In fact, he clearly distinguishes "rational cognition" based on sensory information from "intellectual cognition" that occurs without there being any sensory basis.[25] When the intellect produces this second type of cognition, it thinks about things in their essential structure, and it is able to do that because it is as active and productive as the divine intellect. It "constitutes" them in their essential structure, as Dietrich claims.[26]

This thesis shows that it would be inadequate to speak about Aristotelianism as the common ground for all medieval authors. Dietrich uses Aristotle as his starting point and repeatedly refers to his theory of the intellect, but he integrates it into a Platonic-Augustinian framework that emphasizes the divine-like status of the human intellect. This status does not only enable it to know the essential structure of all things, it even enables it to know itself. In fact, Dietrich establishes an immediate link between these two kinds of knowledge, asserting that "when it understands itself, [the intellect] also understands all other things by its essence, and it does that in the same way in which it understands itself."[27] It is remarkable that Dietrich does not hold that the intellect first understands all things and then, by some process of introspection or reflection, also itself. Self-understanding and self-knowledge do not follow knowledge of other things. On the contrary, self-knowledge is the starting point from which everything else follows: in knowing itself the intellect also knows other things. How should that be possible?

Dietrich spells out this process with metaphorical language, saying that the intellect is "always fixed on itself" and that this activity enables it to know the essential structure of all things.[28] Unfortunately, this does not make clear how it is fixed on itself and why this turn inward

---

25 Cf. *Quaestio utrum in Deo sit aliqua vis cognitiva inferior intellectu, Opera,* 3:294.

26 Cf. *De origine rerum praedicamentalium* 1.20 and 5.33, *Opera* 3:143 and 190. On this thesis cf. Dominik Perler, *Theorien der Intentionalität,* 155–65, and Flasch, *Dietrich von Freiberg,* 109–65.

27 *VB,* 1:22 (thesis 4).

28 Cf. *VB,* 1:22 and 27.

should provide knowledge of other things. But we can try to make sense of his claim by telling a little science fiction story. Suppose that, some day in the far future, neuroscience will develop a brain-imaging technique that will make every single brain state visible. And suppose that this technique will not only visualize the brain states as such, but also their content. When applying this technique to yourself, you will then see every thought you happen to have. Thus, you will see that you are thinking about your next holidays, about your travel companions, about a nice beach, and so on. In this situation you will clearly know yourself as a thinking thing, but you will also know the things present to you in your thinking. The important point is that you do not first see these things and then your own acts by some kind of reflection. It is rather the other way around: in seeing your brain states you see things present to you. Now let us return to the permanently active intellect. Not only does it always think, it also grasps all of its acts of thinking. All of them are somehow visualized by a wonderful intellect-imaging technique and therefore fully present. And in grasping its acts the intellect also grasps their content, namely the essential structure of all things. It is therefore in knowing its own acts that the intellect knows other things.

I hope this comparison makes clear that the turn inward is the most important step. If we had no access to our own acts, we would be utterly ignorant about the essential structure of things in the world, because this structure is precisely what is revealed as the content of our acts. Obviously, Dietrich's main intention is not to explain how people can have pure self-knowledge, but to make intelligible how they get to know other things by knowing themselves. He therefore gives a new answer to the three basic questions concerning self-knowledge. Its *object* is not only a series of intellectual acts, but also their content and thereby the essential structure of all things. The *cognitive process* is nothing but the grasping of the acts that are fully present in the permanently active intellect. And its *status* is absolutely fundamental; it lays the ground for our knowledge of external things since their essential structure would not become accessible to us if we did not pay attention to what is revealed by our own acts.

6.5. CONCLUSION

I hope this short presentation of three medieval thinkers makes clear that there was a lively debate about the structure and status of self-knowledge and that Aristotle's famous remark about the intellect being its own object did not provide the basis for a unified Aristotelian doctrine. On the contrary, it served as some kind of springboard for developing various theories that were also shaped by the Platonic-Augustinian tradition. But how are these theories related to the Socratic question about self-knowledge? They seem to have little to do with the practical concern that was at the core of the Socratic tradition, for they do not address the problems of how we can know what kind of persons we are, what kind of character we have, and how we can improve it. Scholastic theories rather seem to focus on metaphysical and epistemological problems concerning the object and structure of self-knowledge—problems without any practical relevance.

It would be tempting to see a gap between practical and theoretical problems. But I think that we should resist this temptation. When scholastic authors discussed metaphysical and epistemological problems, they did not want to ignore or dismiss practical problems. Their aim rather was to provide a solid foundation for reflections upon practical issues. This is most evident in Aquinas, who attempted to explain what is required for knowing one's own character. Since the character is a set of stable dispositions, knowing it amounts to knowing the dispositions that become manifest in regularly occurring acts. Hence the grasping of our own acts is the first and most fundamental thing that needs to be explained. It is therefore hardly surprising that Aquinas focused on this epistemological problem. A similar strategy was chosen by Matthew of Aquasparta and Dietrich of Freiberg. According to Matthew, it is vain to admonish people that they should strive to know their own character (or even improve it) as long as it remains unclear how they can have access to the special nature of their soul. And according to Dietrich, it is pointless to claim that knowing oneself is more important than knowing external things as long as the relationship between these two types of knowledge remains obscure. It is only a detailed analysis of theoretical issues that shows how Socratic self-knowledge is possible.

CHAPTER SEVEN

Self-Knowledge, Abnegation, and Fulfillment in Medieval Mysticism

Christina Van Dyke

Self-knowledge is a persistent—and paradoxical—theme in medieval mysticism, which portrays our ultimate goal as union with the divine. Union with God is often taken to involve a cognitive and/or volitional merging that requires the loss of a sense of self as distinct from the divine. At the same time, self-knowledge is portrayed both as a necessary precondition and sometimes as a lasting result of this union; for Christian contemplatives in the Latin West (particularly in the thirteenth to fifteenth centuries), the famous injunction of the oracle at Delphi to "know thyself" thus captures the importance of introspection prior to mystic union and, since such union is fleeting in this life, the need for continued self-scrutiny afterward as well.[1]

---

1 In this chapter, I will focus exclusively on Christian mystics in the Latin West between the late 1100s and the late 1400s. Cf. Aaron Hughes, *The Texture of the Divine: Imagination in Medieval Islamic and Jewish Thought* (Bloomington: Indiana University Press, 2004) and *Mystical Union in*

Mysticism within the Christian Latin West was not a homogenous movement, however, and apophatic and affective mysticism take different attitudes toward the ultimate goal of self-knowledge. Although both traditions portray introspection as important preparation for union with God, the apophatic tradition stresses the need to move past self-knowledge to the *loss of self* (self-abnegation), while the affective tradition portrays union with the divine as involving radical (and even physical) *self-fulfillment*.

Today, mysticism tends to be associated with transcending all attachment to the embodied self, a frequent emphasis in the apophatic tradition. Yet affective mysticism—which emphasizes the passion of the incarnate Christ and portrays physical and emotional mystic experiences as inherently valuable—was in fact the dominant tradition in the later Middle Ages. An examination of both traditions demonstrates that, in addition to constituting a necessary stage on the path toward union with the divine, self-knowledge in medieval mysticism was seen not just as something to be transcended, but (particularly in the works of female mystics) as a means of overcoming alienation from embodied existence.

7.1. SELF-KNOWLEDGE IN THE PURSUIT OF MYSTIC UNION

Before discussing medieval mystics' attitudes toward self-knowledge in any detail, it is important to note three features that make any such discussion problematic. First, there has been significant debate in the last century about what mysticism is.[2] Second, the expression of mysticism varies across geographic regions and changes over time (especially, as we'll see, between the twelfth and the fourteenth centuries).[3] Third,

---

Judaism, Christianity, and Islam: An Ecumenical Dialogue, ed. Moshe Idel and Bernard McGinn (New York: Continuum, 1999) for an overview of medieval Islamic and Jewish mysticism.

2 For a discussion of the complex politics involved in the struggle to define mysticism in the twentieth century, cf. Sarah Beckwith, *Christ's Body: Identity, Culture, and Society in Late Medieval Writings* (London: Routledge, 1993), ch. 1.

3 In particular, the later centuries see a marked increase in the importance of personal piety and feminization of religious imagery. Cf., e.g., Herbert Grundmann, "Die Frauen und die Literatur

the majority of extant mystical literature from this period comes not
from universities, but from monasteries and nunneries (and, in the
later Middle Ages, from the "third order" of beguines and tertiaries,
who served as lay members of religious orders); the texts we possess
today are often secondhand reports of the visions of nonliterate mystics who spoke not in Latin but in the vernacular of their region.[4] Thus,
although self-knowledge is a common theme in medieval mysticism,
it should not be understood as a topic that is addressed in a program-
matic or cohesive way.

One belief that is common to the vast majority of medieval mystics,
however, is that a connection with God that goes beyond the realm
of normal earthly experience is possible (however fleetingly) in this
life, and that this connection is the final goal of human existence. This
belief, together with the characterization of mysticism as inherently
phenomenological ("concerning individual felt experience in addition
to systems of knowledge or belief")[5] and *transcendent* ("involving an
encounter—whether direct or mediated, transformatively powerful
or paradoxically everyday—with God"), provides a framework that
encompasses an appropriately wide range of experiences while still cap-
turing what seems distinctive of medieval mystic thought.

There was, for instance, widespread consensus among the medieval
mystics that contemplative and mystic union requires careful preparation, and that this preparation must involve introspective knowledge of
the self—understood both in general terms as knowledge of the structure of the human self and in personal terms as awareness of individual

---

im Mittelalter: Ein Beitrag zur Frage nach der Entstehung des Schrifttums in der Volkssprache,"
Archiv für Kulturgeschichte 26 (1936): 129–61; and Caroline Walker Bynum, *Fragmentation and
Redemption: Essays on Gender and the Human Body in Medieval Religion* (New York: Zone Books,
1992), 151–80.

4 For some of the issues this raises, as well as the effects it had on how mysticism has been treated
as a subject of history, cf. Amy Hollywood, *Sensible Ecstasy: Mysticism, Sexual Difference, and the
Demands of History* (Chicago: University of Chicago Press, 2002).

5 Nicholas Watson, introduction to *The Cambridge Companion to Medieval English Mysticism*, ed.
Samuel Fanous and Vincent Gillespie (Cambridge: Cambridge University Press, 2011), 1.

desires, behaviors, and vulnerabilities. This emphasis on upward progression via a series of stages originally stems from the Neoplatonic
leanings of the early medieval mystics, but the idea that union with
God requires careful preparation (and self-knowledge) remains constant even as mysticism increases among uneducated laypeople in the
fourteenth century and the will (rather than the intellect) assumes the
central role in guiding us along the path.

Self-knowledge is, in fact, often portrayed as the first step in mystical progress. In the early thirteenth century, for instance, the Flemish
beguine Hadewijch's first vision involves being shown the tree of "the
knowledge of ourselves" as the beginning of her mystical initiation.[6] As
she writes in a letter advising a fellow beguine: "If you wish to experience this perfection, you must first of all learn to know yourselves: in
all your conduct, in your attraction or aversion, in your behavior, in
love, in hate, in fidelity, in mistrust, and in all things that befall you"
(Letter 14).[7]

Self-knowledge is seen as the product of rigorous self-examination,
and a precondition for further growth and development. The late
thirteenth-century Dominican Meister Eckhart claims that in order
to progress spiritually, we need to identify and root out negative self-
orientation. "Examine yourself," he writes, "and whenever you find
yourself, take leave of yourself."[8] The eventual goal of this self-scrutiny
is to transcend attachment to the self altogether (as will be discussed
in section 7.2), but "at the beginning there must be attentiveness and

---

6 "And I understood, just as [the angel] revealed it to me, that the tree was the knowledge of our-
selves. The rotten root was our brittle nature; the solid trunk, the eternal soul; and the beautiful
flower, the beautiful human shape, which becomes corrupt so quickly, in an instant" (*Garden of
Perfect Virtues*). Translated text from *Hadewijch: The Complete Works*, ed. and trans. Columba Hart
(Mahwah, NJ: Paulist Press, 1980), 263. Original text, *Hadewijch: Visioenen*, 2 vols., ed. Jozef Van
Mierlo (Louvain: Vlaamsch Boekenhalle, 1924–25).

7 Hadewijch, *The Complete Works*, 77. Original text, *Hadewijch: Brieven*, ed. Jozef Van Mierlo, 2 vols.
(Louvain: Vlaamsch Boekenhalle, 1924–25).

8 Edmund Colledge and Bernard McGinn, eds. and trans., *Meister Eckhart: The Essential Sermons,
Commentaries, Treatises, and Defense* (Mahwah, NJ: Paulist Press, 1981), 250.

a careful formulation within the self, like a schoolboy setting himself to learn."[9]

One of the central functions of this self-examination is to facilitate humility, which medieval mystics portray as essential for opening oneself up to union with God. As the anonymous fourteenth-century English *Book of Privy Counselling* explains, we are not able to rise immediately to experience of the being of God because of the "rudeness" of our spiritual feelings. "To let thee climb thereto by degree," it continues, "I bid thee first gnaw on the naked blind feeling of thine own being."[10] The first stage in the gradual progression toward union with the divine is coming to terms with the reality of one's own existence.

Mystics diverge somewhat as to the exact results of this self-examination, however. For some, such as Bernard of Clairvaux, this process engenders humility primarily by yielding an understanding of the self as a flawed version of the *imago Dei*. For others (such as Hildegard von Bingen, Hadewijch, and Julian of Norwich), self-scrutiny leads to humility by casting our finitude in sharp relief against the infinite divine. Hildegard (a twelfth-century Benedictine abbess) and Julian (a late fourteenth-century English anchoress) even heighten this gap by emphasizing their gender as well as their frailty, comparing their status as a "poor little female figure"[11] and "a woman, lewd, feeble, and frail"[12] with God's unimaginable greatness. Introspection into our limitations is meant to open us to a deeper awareness of God's unlimited attributes. In general, the idea is that the more conscious we are of our own failings and imperfections, the more we will notice God's ultimate perfection and appreciate God's unfailing love for us. As Hadewijch writes to a fellow beguine: "May God grant you to know

9 Ibid., 254.

10 Barry Windeatt, ed., *English Mystics of the Middle Ages* (Cambridge: Cambridge University Press, 1994), 94. Original manuscript British Library Harley 674 (H), fols. 92r–110v.

11 *Epistola* 2, in *Analecta Sanctae Hildegardis*, ed. J. B. Pitra (Monte Cassino, 1882), 332.

12 Julian of Norwich, "Revelations of Love," in *English Mystics of the Middle Ages*, ed. Barry Windeatt (Cambridge: Cambridge University Press, 1994), 189.

yourself in all things what you are in want of, and may you thus attain to a knowledge of the sublime Love that he himself, our great God, is" (Letter 27).[13]

The idea that introspection is the beginning of spiritual development and that the resulting humility is vital for progress toward union with the divine remains constant throughout the Middle Ages. There are two important shifts in attitudes toward self-knowledge from the twelfth to the fourteenth century, however. First, identifying the self with God becomes increasingly common.[14] This is portrayed not as incompatible with humility, however, but as the culmination of the process of humbling oneself. One can be filled with God—one can *be* God—only when one has realized one's infinitesimality next to God's magnitude. When the female mystic who is the subject of the anonymous tract called the *Sister Catherine Treatise* comes out of her trance and says to her confessor, "Sir, rejoice with me, I am become God!"[15] she is not expressing self-exaltation but rather the replacement of her self with God. As Bernard McGinn notes, this remark (and similar formulations) demonstrates "a widespread yearning to give expression to a new view of how God becomes one with the human person."[16] This understanding takes our status as "images of God" rather literally: we are not just meant to be conforming ourselves increasingly to the (ultimately unattainable) image of God that exists in rude form within us; we can, literally, image God.

---

13 Hadewijch, *The Complete Works*, 107. Cf. *The Complete Works*, 49: "Even if you do the best you can in all things, your human nature must often fall short; so entrust yourself to God's goodness, for his goodness is greater than your failures. And always practice . . . doing your utmost to examine your thoughts strictly, in order to know yourself in all things" (Letter 2).

14 For a book-length treatment of this topic (that focuses particularly on Meister Eckhart), cf. Ben Morgan, *On Becoming God: Late Medieval Mysticism and the Modern Western Self* (New York: Fordham University Press, 2013).

15 Elvira Borgstädt, trans., "The 'Sister Catherine' Treatise," in *Meister Eckhart: Teacher and Preacher*, ed. Bernard McGinn (New York: Paulist Press, 1986), 358.

16 Bernard McGinn, "The Harvest of Mysticism in Medieval Germany (1300–1500)," in vol. 4 of *The Presence of God: A History of Western Christian Mysticism* (New York: Herder and Herder, 2005), 87.

Second, and perhaps noncoincidentally, there is a shift in emphasis over the twelfth to the fourteenth centuries from self-scrutiny's requiring the proper use of reason and resulting in knowledge of one's thoughts to introspection's requiring the will and resulting in proper affections. We can see both of these elements in play in Jan van Ruusbroec's *Mirror of Eternal Blessedness*, where the early fourteenth-century Flemish mystic contrasts the joy of loving God with the humility of the intellect/mind:

> Your heart will open wide to receive new gifts from God with deep desire for newness of life, and your desires will mount up to God like a fiery flame of devotion in thanksgiving and praise. Your mind will meanwhile descend in a sense of unworthiness and of humble self-disdain, and your reason will reveal to you your sins, your shortcomings, and your many failings. . . . For this reason, if you have self-knowledge you should always descend in a sense of unworthiness and self-disdain and then rise again with great veneration and reverence toward God.[17]

In general, although mystics continue to describe union with God as the end goal of a multistage process, there is a gradual shift away from the idea that this process requires intellectual training. What is necessary is careful introspection (of the sort any reflective person is capable of) and well-ordered desire, or love. In the words of the anonymous *Cloud of Unknowing*, "Love, but not knowing, may reach to God in this life." That is, "God may well be loved but not thought" (ch. 8).[18]

---

17 John Ruusbroec, "Spiritual Abandonment and Consolation," in *The Spiritual Espousals and Other Works*, ed. and trans. J. A. Wiseman (Mahwah, NJ: Paulist Press, 1985), 196. Original text, cf. *Werken*, ed. by the Ruusbroecgenootschap, 2nd ed., 4 vols. (Tielt: Uitgeverij Lannoo, 1944–48).

18 The idea that union with God doesn't require being learned (or even formally literate) parallels the well-documented shift from the early twelfth century to the late fourteenth century in general attitudes toward the relation of knowledge and piety. Cf., e.g., Bernard McGinn, *The Flowering of Mysticism* and Bynum, *Fragmentation and Redemption*, particularly "The Female Body and Religious Practice."

7.2. Self-Abnegation and Apophaticism

As mentioned above, virtually all medieval mystics saw the kind of self-knowledge resulting from introspective self-scrutiny as the first stage toward union with the divine. They disagree substantially, however, about the role self-knowledge should play later in the process. In particular, apophatic mystics tended to portray awareness of embodied individuality as a feature of humanity that needs to be transcended in order to join with the God beyond thought. Affective mystics, on the other hand (see section 7.3), viewed their physical and emotional experiences as intrinsically valuable unitive states.

Although today mention of medieval mysticism brings figures such as Meister Eckhart to mind, and it forms part of a continuous tradition that begins at least with Plotinus, in its own day apophatic mysticism was the exception rather than the rule. Centering on the conviction that language and thought obscure rather than reveal the unspeakable truth of the divine, apophatic mysticism characterizes true union with the divine as fundamentally *anti*experiential.[19] Mystics could expect transcendent phenomenal experiences as part of the contemplative life, but they were warned not to be distracted by such experiences or to view them as valuable in their own right.

Meister Eckhart, for instance, enjoined his followers to detach themselves from such experiences, "tartly condemning those who want to see God with the same eyes with which they behold a cow."[20] In his late fourteenth-century *The Scale of Perfection*, Walter Hilton also warns against accepting altered physical sensations as signs of true mystic union, whether "in sounding of the ear, or savoring in the mouth, or smelling at the nose, or else [the sensation of] any perceptible heat as if it were fire, glowing and warming the breast" (1.10).[21] The *Cloud*

---

19 For a detailed treatment of this topic, cf. Denys Turner, *The Darkness of God: Negativity in Christian Mysticism* (Cambridge: Cambridge University Press, 1995).

20 Meister Eckhart, *Essential Sermons*, 61. The sermon referenced is Sermon 16b in Meister Eckhart, *Die deutschen Werke und lateinischen*, vol. 1 (Stuttgart: W. Kohlhammer, 1936), 272.

21 Walter Hilton, "The Scale of Perfection" (Manuscript: Cambridge University Library MS Add. 6686), 284.

of Unknowing goes even further in its admonition against identifying any physical sensation (especially heat) as the true "fire of love" that results from union with God: "For I tell thee truly that the devil has his contemplatives, as God has his" (ch. 45).[22] Although such experiences might occur regularly on the path to true union, they were not to be confused with that union.

Because God transcends all thought, emotion, and sensation, any sort of union with that God also requires moving beyond such things. Eckhart, for instance, consistently stresses the need for human beings to detach from all earthly things—including knowledge: "I say that a man should be set as free from his own knowing as he was when he was not [that is, before that person existed]" (Sermon 52).[23] As he goes on to explain, "The authorities say that God is a being, and a rational one, and that he knows all things. I say that God is neither being nor rational, and that he does not know this or that. Therefore God is free of all things, and therefore he is all things." Knowledge of the self is needed for identifying and rooting out sinful self-orientation; it is necessary for developing the humility that allows us to lose ourselves completely in the hidden darkness of God. Self-knowledge is, however, one of the things that we must ultimately set ourselves free from (with God's help).

An emphasis on self-loss and self-annihilation runs throughout this tradition, portrayed as a necessary part of detaching from the transient things of this world. Indeed, because our attachment to self is so fundamental, these mystics see the loss of self as one of the final stages in this process. In his *Counsels*, Eckhart captures a sentiment common to many apophatics when he says, "You should know that there was never any man in this life who forsook himself so much that he could not still find more in himself to forsake. . . . But as much as you go out in forsaking all things, by so much, neither less nor more, does God go in" (Counsel 4).[24] Emptying oneself is the final step in fully receiving (or becoming)

---

22 Ibid.

23 Cf. Meister Eckhart *Die deutschen und lateinischen Werke*, 201.

24 Meister Eckhart, *Essential Sermons* 250.

God: "[After detachment] there is still one work that remains proper and his own, and that is annihilation of self" (Counsel 23);[25] "Perfect humility proceeds from annihilation of self" ("On Detachment").[26]

Apophatic mysticism has deep Neoplatonic roots, emerging in the Middle Ages via figures such as pseudo-Dionysius and John Scottus Eriugena. Accordingly, it is the intellect that is originally identified as the central aspect of the self—that by which we transcend, and the last of what needs to be transcended. Hadewijch, for instance, praises reason as one of God's greatest gifts to humanity: "It is truly fitting that everyone contemplate God's grace and goodness with wisdom and prudence: for God has given us our beautiful faculty of reason, which instructs us in all our ways and enlightens us in all works. If man would follow reason, he would never be deceived" (Letter 14).[27]

As mentioned above, however, over the course of the fourteenth and fifteenth centuries, the will gains importance. Following on the antinomianist and "Free Spirit" movements, both self-knowledge and self-annihilation are increasingly understood in volitional rather than intellectual terms.[28] Although denounced as a heretic and burned at the stake in 1310, Marguerite Porete is not alone in her belief in that our final goal is the annihilation of the conscious self via the absolute surrender of our will to God's. The result of this surrender is radical self-loss: "The whole is one to her without an explanation (*propter quid*), and she is nothing in such a one. Then nothing more remains for her to do concerning God than remains for God to do concerning her. Why? Because he is and she is not" (*The Mirror of Simple Souls*, ch. 135).[29]

---

25 Ibid., 280.

26 Ibid., 286.

27 Hadewijch, *The Complete Works*, 77.

28 For a history of this controversial movement, cf. Robert Lerner, *The Heresy of the Free Spirit in the Later Middle Ages* (Berkeley: University of California Press, 1972).

29 Marguerite Porete, *Le mirouer des simple ames*, ed. Romana Guarnieri (Turnhout: Brepols, 1986). For a recent English translation, cf. Marguerite Porete, *The Mirror of Simple Souls*, trans. E. Colledge et al. (Notre Dame, IN: University of Notre Dame Press, 1999).

This emphasis on the will's central role in self-abnegation is also echoed in fourteenth-century English works, such as the anonymous *Cloud of Unknowing*. Formal education is not required to surrender the self to God in love. In fact, to the extent that the intellect continues to search for knowledge, it gets in the way of perfect submission and loss of self. Not surprisingly, given their understanding of our final end, apophatic mystics tend to associate the body with weakness and limitation. On the path to union with a God who transcends the senses, emotions, and even thought itself, any lingering attachment to the body and its individuality signals a reluctance to detach. The body is not inherently bad, nor are sensations and emotions inherently negative. Nevertheless, they represent a vital part of the individuality we need to move beyond. Self-knowledge is needed for us to reach our final goal, but it is transcended in our attainment of that goal.

7.3. Fulfillment of the Embodied Self and Affective Mysticism

Affective mysticism, in contrast, developed in large part as a reaction to the persistent gnostic heresy (manifesting in the twelfth century as Cathar or Albigensian dualism) that physicality is inherently negative and that our goal as human beings is to liberate the spirit from the material realm. Although negative attitudes toward matter and the body do appear in affective mysticism (as they do in virtually all religious traditions), this tradition emphasizes Christ's Incarnation and Passion as demonstrating that the human body and the material creation are to be celebrated, not overcome. In particular, strong identification with Christ and his experiences on earth—especially the Passion—allows these mystics with a valid means of both positively conceptualizing and experiencing the embodied self.[30] Sense perception, physical states

---

30 Karma Lochrie, for instance, characterizes affective spirituality precisely in terms of "its corporeality and the imitation of Christ's suffering humanity" Karma Lochrie, *Margery Kempe and Translations of the Flesh* (Philadelphia: University of Pennsylvania Press, 1991), 14.

(such bleeding, weeping, and "closure"), and emotions are understood not as distracting from true mystic union but as a valid way of experiencing it. To this end, self-knowledge is viewed not just as the first step toward union with God, but as one of the most important results of such union.

Although virtually unknown today, in its own day (particularly the thirteenth through fifteenth centuries), affective mysticism was the rule, not the exception. It viewed the relationship between human beings and God in a "newly bodily and emotionally laden way," and "took such experience with special seriousness, making it increasingly central to religious life as the period wore on, devoting considerable literary, visual, and human resources to it, reposing extraordinary trust in its validity, and in the process permanently shaping the sensibilities, and (to a considerable extent) even the content, of western Christianity."[31] As amply demonstrated by the lives of the mystics of this time, true union with God (especially the second person of the Trinity, Christ) was seen to be found not in transcending physical reality but rather in recognizing and glorifying the mundane—including illness and suffering.

Thus, we find not only stories of mystics washing the feet of beggars and invalids, but also records of much more extreme practices, such as Ida of Louvain's refusing to eat anything but moldy bread and Catherine of Sienna eating the scabs and drinking the pus from the sores of lepers. What to the modern reader looks like self-mortification is rarely (if ever) described as such by the figures in question. Instead, their emphasis is on identifying with the suffering of Christ and experiencing union with God in this way.[32] Even the most intense physical

---

31 Watson, introduction to *Cambridge Companion to Medieval English Mysticism*, 2.

32 Caroline Walker Bynum discusses the extreme practices of affective mystics in detail in several of her works, but the essays in *Fragmentation and Redemption* are particularly worth attention, as is her treatment of the importance of food—and especially the Eucharist—in the lives of thirteenth- to fifteenth-century mystics. Cf. Bynum, *Fragmentation and Redemption* and *Holy Feast and Holy Fast: The Religious Significance of Food to Medieval Women* (Berkeley: University of California Press, 1987).

suffering was received with joy by those who viewed it as experiencing God in the flesh.

What's more, these states were not viewed as impeding further intellectual or volitional union. Richard of Saint-Victor, for instance, explained that physical mystic experiences such as visions were useful for an understanding of the divine that would fulfill rather than empty the intellect.[33] Formal education is not seen as necessary for affective union, but intellectual and volitional development were often advanced as ways of drawing even closer to God. Thus, a wide variety of sensory, physical, and emotional states—hearing music and seeing visions, for instance, as well as physical closure (that is, not ingesting or excreting for long periods of time) and feeling ecstatic joy or sorrow—are all seen as an important part of mystic union in this tradition.

One of the primary functions of these experiences in the affective tradition was countering the self-alienation common to fallen humanity. Introspection makes us aware of our fallen nature and our need for connection with God. Humility is a result of this self-knowledge, but so is the recognition that God became human, and thus that our experiences are in a way also God's experiences. Knowing ourselves as bodily subjects is a way of knowing the Incarnated Christ. We become distanced from ourselves when we deny our true nature; conceiving of oneself in purely spiritual or mental terms is deeply alienating to creatures whose primary interaction with reality—created and divine—is physical.

It is not surprising in this context that the Eucharist assumes central importance in the mystic experiences of many figures within this tradition. Christina Mirabilis of Saint-Trond and Ida of Louvain are only two of the mystics who experienced intense cravings for the

---

33 Cf. Richard de St. Victor, *De Trinitate*, in *The Twelve Patriarchs*, trans. G. Zinn (Mahwah, NJ: Paulist Press, 1979).

sacrament. In fact, it became almost common for mystics—especially female mystics—to see flesh or taste honey in the Eucharistic wafer, or fall into ecstatic trances in sight of the elements.[34] According to Caroline Walker Bynum, "Paramystical phenomena were common in female (and increasingly in male) piety in the fourteenth century exactly because the fundamental religious goal was seen to be union with the physical body Christ took on in the Incarnation and daily in the mass."[35] The belief that human beings are most closely joined with Christ's divinity through his corporeity makes the ritual of partaking in that body especially ripe for mystical union—and a union that is simultaneously a fulfillment of the self's humanity.

Affective mysticism took on extreme forms at time, and the vision of the self that it aligned itself with is earthy in a way that modern sensibilities have moved past. Yet in stressing union with God in terms of "God-with-us" just as much as "us-with-God," it offers a hope for a holistic connection to the divine. Mystic union with the transcendent God results in a deeper appreciation for the human nature that Christ took on, and that we share. This acceptance rather than abnegation of the embodied self is perhaps best characterized by a vision of Marguerite of Oingt, in which after intense prayer she received a vision in which she was a tree that, watered by Christ, flowered. And on her newly leafed branches she saw written the names of the five senses. This is a far cry from Marguerite Porete's vision of complete self-abnegation: a state in which she is "nothing."

7.4. Conclusion

Self-knowledge in medieval mysticism is a highly complex topic. There was general agreement in the Christian Latin West that introspection constitutes a vital first step toward the ultimate goal of union

---

34 Cf. Bynum, *Fragmentation and Redemption* and *Holy Feast.*

35 Bynum, *Fragmentation and Redemption*, 66.

with the divine, and also that self-scrutiny was necessary for developing the humility that allows us to open ourselves to God. Yet, as discussed above, we can distinguish between the attitudes toward self-knowledge in the apophatic mystics, who stressed self-abnegation, and the affective mystics, who saw their experiences as self-affirming. The distinction between affective and apophatic mysticism was not recognized at the time; much medieval mystical literature combines apophatic and affective elements. The distinction does prove useful, though, for correcting the modern impression that mysticism involves transcending attachment to the self and all of its attendant phenomenology.[36] Rather than merely constituting a stage on the path toward self-less union, mystic experiences can also be seen as a fulfillment of the embodied self in communion with God.

Acknowledgment

I owe many people thanks for comments and questions on this project, especially participants at the University of Konstanz "Self-Knowledge" workshop (July 2014), L'Abri Fellowship International, the University of Leeds Center for Philosophy of Religion seminar, the workshop "Analytical Existentialism" at the University of Ghent (October 2014), and the University of Notre Dame Center for Philosophy of Religion reading group. This publication was made possible in part through the support of a grant from the John Templeton Foundation. The opinions expressed in this publication are those of the author and do not necessarily reflect the views of the John Templeton Foundation.

---

36 Evelyn Underhill, together with William James one of the most influential authors on mysticism in the modern age, is relentless in her criticism of affective mysticism, attributing episodes of ecstatic union and physical sensations to "the infantile craving for a sheltering and protecting love" that is "frequently pathological, and . . . often found along with other abnormal conditions in emotional visionaries whose revelations have no ultimate characteristics" (*The Essentials of Mysticism and Other Essays* [Oxford: Oneworld, 1995], 20 and 23).

CHAPTER EIGHT

Socratic Self-Knowledge in Early Modern Philosophy

Ursula Renz

In the second half of the seventeenth century, reference to Socratic self-knowledge became a frequent move in philosophical texts. The Delphic injunction "Gnothi sauton" or "Know thyself!" is, for instance, explicitly appealed to in Hobbes' *Leviathan*, in Guelincx's *Ethics*, and in Shaftesbury's *Soliloquy*, but it is present also in Spinoza's *Ethics* and in the writings of many French philosophers.[1]

Behind this seemingly rhetorical gesture is, I think, a real concern. As Aaron Garrett has recently argued, we may get a better understanding of seventeenth-century ethics if we think of it in terms of the ambition to provide metaphysically or epistemologically grounded self-help.[2]

---

[1] See Aaron Garrett, "Self-Knowledge and Self-Deception in Modern Moral Philosophy," in this volume.

[2] Aaron Garrett, "Seventeenth-Century Moral Philosophy: Self-Help, Self-Knowledge, and the Devil's Mountain," in *Oxford Handbook of the History of Ethics*, ed. Roger Crisp (Oxford: Oxford University Press, 2012), 230.

Given this suggestion, we should not only hesitate to apply the division between theoretical and practical philosophy to seventeenth-century philosophy, but should also abstain from comparing the texts of this period with later eighteenth-century treatises on the nature and origin of moral norms. Instead, we had better read those texts as kinds of self-help manuals aiming at providing the reader with a new view of both the world and herself. By accepting this view, the reader not only gets into a better position to deliberate on the goals and means of her actions, but also gains a firm grasp of the very ends of a good life.

I am quite sympathetic with this interpretation, and only want to refine it a little bit. While Garrett's focus was on the moral lessons of early modern philosophy's concern with self-help, more can be said about its epistemological presuppositions. My point is this: if seventeenth-century philosophical texts truly aimed at providing a conceptual framework for self-help, rather than at developing a philosophical theory, they may be expected to contain some epistemological considerations indicating *how* they were meant to provide readers with some resource for self-help. They must, as it were, communicate their didactic principles.

It is against this background that I approach the issue of Socratic self-knowledge in early modern philosophy. Assuming that many texts aimed at an enhancement of their readers' self-knowledge, I discuss three types of questions. (1) How is *improvement of self-knowledge* meant to be supported by one's reading of a certain text? To what extent does the intended improvement of self-knowledge rely on anthropological knowledge, or on a posteriori considerations concerning the limitations of man's power? And what relation is assumed between first-personal and third-personal perspectives? (2) What kinds of facts about herself must the ideal reader of a text acknowledge in order to improve her self-knowledge? (3) How is improvement in the reader's self-knowledge expected to contribute to her happiness?

To set the stage, I will draw attention to two seemingly incidental remarks of Descartes' *Discourse on the Method* and *Meditations*, and take a closer look at Hobbes' lesson in self-knowledge underlying the first part of *Leviathan*, before I shall reconstruct Spinoza's *Ethics* and Shaftesbury's *Characteristics* under this perspective.

8.1. Acceptance of One's Exposure to Epistemic Failure in Descartes

In the first sentence of his *Meditations*, Descartes says: "Some years ago I was struck by the large number of falsehoods that I had accepted as true in my childhood."[3] Likewise, he writes in the *Discourse on the Method*:

> I know how much we are liable to err in matters that concern us, and also how much the judgments of our friends should be distrusted when they are in our favour. I shall be glad, nevertheless, to reveal in this discourse what paths I have followed, and to represent my life in it as if in a picture, so that everyone may judge it for himself.[4]

These seemingly trivial passages by which Descartes tries to persuade the reader to join him in his effort to examine the legitimacy and reach of his a priori knowledge suggest that Descartes' views on self-knowledge are richer than is often assumed. Three points have to be emphasized. (1) There is a lesson to be learned, *before* the epistemological contemplation starts, which Descartes primarily envisages in these writings. To get into the position from which we may reflect upon the necessary truths available through introspection, we have to admit that much of what we initially believe is the result of our credulity rather than of our epistemic power. In other words: we have

---

3 René Descartes, *Oeuvres de Descartes*, ed. Charles Adam and Paul Tannery (Paris: Vrin, 1983–91), 7:17. English: René Descartes, *Philosophical Writings of Descartes*, vol. 2, ed. and trans. John Cottingham, Robert Stoothoff, and Dugald Murdoch (vols. 1–2) and Anthony Kenny (vol. 3) (Cambridge: Cambridge University Press, 1984–91), 2:17.

4 Descartes, *Oeuvres*, 7:3–4; Descartes, *Philosophical Writings*, 2:112.

to acknowledge our exposure to epistemic failure. (2) The quoted passages indicate that this acceptance entails an a posteriori insight. I think Descartes is right in this point. Certainly, knowledge of one's epistemic fallibility is not empirical in the sense that it depends on scientific findings. But it is hardly conceivable how the boundaries of our epistemic powers can be discovered without referring to previous experiences of failure. Nobody is born, as it were, knowing himself to be ignorant, not to mention knowing that one is subject to principal epistemic limitations. It seems impossible, for a color-blind person, to notice her color-blindness without reflecting on the discrepancy between her own experiences and the ones reported by others. (3) In presenting his epistemic path and life "as if in a picture, so that everyone may judge it for himself",5 Descartes describes his case as exemplary. Behind this seemingly merely didactical move is an important epistemological insight: although comprehension of the limitation of one's powers requires reference to some previous experiences of failure, these need not be one's own mistakes. We may as well reflect on the failures of others. That is how narratives work. There are thus certain aspects of self-knowledge that we may get by contemplating the lives of others.

To conclude, even though Descartes' main focus is on that self-knowledge of our mental states which is immediately accessible in introspection, he is also relying on insights usually connected with Socrates, such as acceptance of one's own ignorance, and he also seems to be aware that acquisition of this knowledge presupposes previous experiences of failure. Yet, as the theoretical parts of his writings pay no further attention to these points, it is no coincidence that, unlike Socrates', Descartes' name is mostly associated with the concept of introspective self-knowledge.6

---

5 Descartes, *Philosophical Writings*, 2:112.
6 See also Brie Gertler, *Self-Knowledge* (London: Routledge, 2011), 29–31, for an exemplary reading of Descartes along these lines.

8.2. Knowledge of the Human Condition as Self-Knowledge in Hobbes

Descartes wasn't the only seventeenth-century philosopher who sought to guide the reader's reflection by presenting himself as a model. A similar teaching method is applied in the first part of *Leviathan*, which exposes the anthropological framework of Hobbes' political views. To be sure, this text is not an exercise in first-personal meditation on our ideas. But *Leviathan* too aims at involving the reader in a process of guided self-reflection.[7] Or this is the view I would like to defend in what follows.[8]

To begin with, I suggest taking a closer look at the goal of part 1 of *Leviathan*, which is to consider man insofar as he is "the *Matter* . . . and the *Artificer*" of the state.[9] Following this program, the anthropology of part 1 must provide a double perspective on the human condition. To see how man is the matter of the state, we have to learn more about the psychological properties determining human social life, whereas to understand how man can be the artificer of the state requires that we consider the state as a product of man's deliberate actions. Thus, to think of mankind as the matter and the artificer of the state implies that we think of him as both driven by certain psychological dispositions and guided by his intentions. Looking at the mechanistic framework of Hobbes' approach, these are just two sides of one coin. They cannot be separated without

---

7 In Hobbes scholarship, the role of rhetoric for *Leviathan* has often been examined. See, for example, David Johnston, *The Rhetoric of the Leviathan: Thomas Hobbes and the Politics of Cultural Transformation* (Princeton, NJ: Princeton University Press 1986); Jeffrey Barnouw, "Persuasion in Hobbes' Leviathan," *Hobbes Studies* 1 (1988): 3–25; and Quentin Skinner, *Reason and Rhetoric in the Philosophy of Hobbes* (Cambridge: Cambridge University Press, 1996). In pointing out the didactical goals, I follow the approach of Johnston, who is primarily focusing on the usage of rhetorical means. This is not to preclude, however, that Hobbes did not also consider rhetoric in a much better light, as Skinner has argued.

8 I have argued for this at some length recently, in Ursula Renz, "Self-Knowledge and Knowledge of Mankind in Hobbes' Leviathan," *European Journal of Philosophy*, forthcoming.

9 Cf. Thomas Hobbes, *Leviathan*, ed. Richard Tuck (Cambridge: Cambridge University Press, 1991).

undermining his naturalism with regard to the human condition. Hobbes' ambition is thus to bring the reader of *Leviathan* into a position from which she may grasp her condition from a third-personal point of view while keeping in touch with her first-personal mode of experience.

To the reader, this poses a double challenge. To adopt such a twofold attitude toward herself requires that she contemplate her desires and intentions in light of the mechanist principles she is about to learn when reading *Leviathan*. On the other hand, it implies that she will have to identify the third-personal descriptions of human behavior contained in *Leviathan* with her own first-personal experience. Hence, it is not sufficient that she be convinced of the truth of Hobbes' views on mankind; she must accept them as descriptions of her own condition. The ideal reader must, in other words, proceed from general statements of the form "All men are F" to the corresponding I-thought "I am F," and consider whether she is willing to approve it.

This sheds some new light on the epistemological considerations formulated in the second half of the introduction, where Hobbes defends his anthropological approach by appealing to the Delphic injunction "Nosce teipsum." This imperative, which he translates with "Read thy self" and not, as one might expect, with "Know thyself," teaches us

> that for the similitude of the thoughts, and Passions of one man, to the thoughts, and Passions of all other men, whosoever looketh into himself and considereth what he doth, when he does think, opine, reason, hope, feare, &c. and upon what grounds; he shall thereby read and know, what are the thoughts, and Passions of all other men, upon the like occasions.[10]

---

10 Ibid., 10.

This passage exhibits that Hobbes thinks of self-knowledge in terms of people's learning about the human condition, rather than about their personal mental life. As expressed in the phrase "for the similitude of men," we first and foremost have to acknowledge that we are of the same kind as all other men; that is why we can "read" the passions of other men in ourselves. But this implies that we understand our mental life in light of the knowledge of mankind we may get when reconstructing human psychology from a mechanist perspective. There are two kinds of epistemic processes intertwined here: a process of *identifying oneself as belonging to mankind* and a process of *understanding oneself by means of the causal knowledge of the human condition* that we acquire by reading *Leviathan*. Hobbes apparently thinks that the self-knowledge required by the Delphic injunction is a matter neither of introspection nor of any other kind of immediate knowing of one's mental states, but of identifying general features of mankind in one's own thoughts and passions.

Another epistemic peculiarity is contained in Hobbes' usage of the metaphor of reading. It is constitutive for any process of reading that the signs to be looked at are ontologically distinct from the contents read. In exploiting this metaphor, Hobbes analogously distinguishes between the *activity* of looking into ourselves and the *action* of knowing or reading mankind. Hobbes' translation of the Latin *Nosce teipsum* by "Read thy self" seems to result from a deliberate consideration: his use of the metaphor of reading depicts the structural complexity of the kind of self-investigation Hobbes has in mind—and which he also takes to be requested by the Delphic injunction.

Thus, more explicitly than any other seventeenth-century text, *Leviathan* takes up the original ambition of the Delphic injunction, which was to admonish the visitor of the temple in Delphi to think of herself as subject to the human condition.[11] Unfortunately,

---

11 On this point, see Walter Burkert, *Griechische Religion der archaischen und klassischen Epoche* (Stuttgart: Kohlhammer, 2011), 30.

though, Hobbes' anthropology does not have the theoretical resources for explaining how this process works. So his approach lacks any conception of the epistemic privilege of the first person presupposed in the process of identifying oneself as subject to the human condition, and in his *Objections* to Descartes' *Meditations*, Hobbes even denies that there is such a thing as an epistemic privilege of the first person.[12] Still, when introducing his definitions of the passions, he implicitly relies on the reader's conscious emotional experience. When glory, for instance, is defined as the "joy, arising from imagination of a mans own power and ability,"[13] he is not referring to the human disposition of glory-seeking, but alludes to the energizing feeling we have when we think of our own strength from a first-personal perspective. Here, Hobbes obviously attaches some importance to the notion that the reader relates the psychological descriptions presented in the definition to his own feelings. Taking this at face value, we can ascribe to Hobbes the view that first-personal access to one's own experience is prerequisite for self-knowledge. This does not preclude that his main ambition was to teach the reader to conceive of herself, in a third-personal way, along the lines of his mechanist anthropology.

At the bottom of the didactic pull of *Leviathan* is thus a view on self-knowledge according to which it is the aim of philosophical self-reflection to go beyond one's a priori self-awareness and to consider oneself as subject to the human condition. This, however, is not conceived in terms of one's exposure to epistemic failure, but as a matter of man's irreducible dependency, or vulnerability. Clearly, whatever other reasons Hobbes had to appeal to the Delphic injunction,

---

12 There Hobbes says: "It is quite certain that the knowledge of the proposition 'I exist' depends on the proposition 'I am thinking' as the author himself has explained to us. But how do we know the proposition 'I am thinking'? It can only be from our inability to conceive of an act without its subject. We cannot conceive of jumping without a jumper, of knowing without a knower, or of thinking without a thinker" (Descartes, *Writings*, 2:122).

13 Hobbes, *Leviathan*, 42.

understanding of these properties as descriptions of one's own condition provides a strong motivation for every reader to enter into the covenant.

8.3. SPINOZA'S *ETHICS* AS A GUIDE TO REFORMING ONE'S SELF-UNDERSTANDING

Spinoza's *Ethica Ordine Geometrico demonstrata* is certainly one of the best examples of early modern self-help literature. There, departing from the assumption that the main obstacle to happiness is our tendency to think of ourselves in mistaken metaphysical terms, a series of metaphysical and epistemological considerations aiming at an improvement of our self-knowledge is defended. Among Spinoza's most crucial metaphysical lessons is the insight that human beings are not substances, but either modes or constituted by modes. So he claims in proposition 10 of part 2: "The being of substance does not pertain to the essence of man, or substance does not constitute the form of man."[14] To embrace the categorical difference between substance and modes and to affirm that man belongs "only" to the latter is a prerequisite for many of the metaphysical tenets put forward in Spinoza's explanation for the fragilities and contingences of human life. It has to be mentioned, though, that whereas this conceptual decision obviously echoes the Delphic injunction, which was to remind us of human finitude and mortality,[15] Spinoza's interest is in the irreducibility of dependency, rather than on the issue of death.

Even more important for our concern are the epistemological aspects of Spinoza's approach. Let us begin with a closer look at

---

14 Spinoza's *Ethics*, proposition 10, part 2, henceforth: E2p10. Further abbreviations I use are: "a" for axiom; "app" for appendix, "c" for corollary. Passage from the *Ethics* are quoted from *The Collected Works of Spinoza*, ed. and trans. Edwin Curley (Princeton: Princeton University Press, 1985).

15 Cf. F.-P. Hager, "Selbsterkenntnis," in *Historisches Wörterbuch der Philosophie*, vol. 9, ed. Joachim Ritter and Karlfried Gründer (Basel: Schwabe, 1995), 407.

Spinoza's diagnosis of the reasons for man's tendency to think of himself in mistaken terms. Spinoza discusses this problem in the appendix to part 1 of the *Ethics*, where he describes this tendency as a natural effect of the peculiar epistemic condition of human subjects. While, he says, "all men are born ignorant of the causes of things," they are also "conscious of their volitions and their appetite," expressing their disposition to seek their own advantage (E1app). Following Spinoza, this is why man looks for explanations everywhere and, thus, tends to consider nature and natural things as acting according to some end. But this is also why we consider ourselves as free agents rather than as determined by efficient causes. That people so often fail at drawing the categorical distinction between God and man is due to this epistemic condition: they think of themselves in terms of self-sufficiency, or substance, and in turn ascribe human motivations to God.

Now, while these errors result from man's natural epistemic condition, Spinoza nevertheless contends that they can be overcome. Our epistemic condition can be improved if we understand what's driving us in making these mistakes and if we learn to think of ourselves within a metaphysical framework that prevents us from making the same mistakes again and again. Underlying the *Ethics* is thus a whole program for a reform of our self-understanding.

The question arises on what epistemological presumptions this reform operates. It is in this context that I suggest interpreting Spinoza's views on self-knowledge. Generally, the statements made on this issue in the *Ethics* point into two directions. On the one hand, man is denied full knowledge of several aspects of himself. He can know neither his own body, nor his mind, nor the fact of his own bodily or mental existence, except via the ideas he has of the affections of his body.[16] On the other hand, there are ideas of the essences of every single being and its properties in God. This ensures that it is principally possible

---

16 See also E2p19 and E2p23.

that man have adequate knowledge of himself and his mental or bodily constitution.[17] There is a seeming contradiction between these claims, but this impression vanishes if one looks at the specific concerns behind these claims. The first group of statements addresses the question of our cognitive access to ourselves. To answer this question, Spinoza points to the epistemological implications of his conception of the imagination, which alleges that psychologically speaking all our ideas derive from some idea of an affection of our body. It is only in virtue of these ideas that any human cognition, whether of our mind, our body, or the external world, is possible. Our imagination is thus the very source of all consciousness and knowledge, including, of course, our first-personal view on ourselves.

The second group of statements, in contrast, claims that complete self-knowledge is, in principle, available to us. This is not to say that it comes for free. On the contrary, to have a fully adequate self-conception is a perfection the reaching of which is both difficult and exceptional, as the very last paragraph of the *Ethics* states. But Spinoza thinks that it is nonetheless reasonable to strive for more self-knowledge. It is an achievable goal for the human mind. Moreover, if adequacy comes in degrees, as Spinoza assumes, improvement is possible even in the absence of perfection.

But *how* is improvement of self-knowledge possible according to Spinoza? At this point, I would like to recall Spinoza's doctrine of the three kinds of knowledge. It is well known that he distinguishes between three kinds of knowledge: (1) imaginative knowledge, or knowledge deriving from sense experience and signs, (2) rational knowledge, or knowledge consisting in the common notions of the properties shared by several things, and (3) intuitive knowledge, or complete knowledge of the formal essences of things. So far, we have

---

17 See E2p9c, E2p21, E5p4, E5p4c, and E5p30.

only dealt with imaginative and intuitive self-knowledge. The question arises: is there a role to play for rational knowledge in self-knowledge? It is important to see that the three kinds of knowledge are not just meant to denote three different classes of cognitions, but also address different epistemological problems.[18] Behind the conception of the common notions, or the second kind of knowledge, is the contention that it must be possible to form general concepts that, unlike the universals deriving from imagination, provide us with an adequate grasp of the features of reality, or else we are precluded forever from having adequate knowledge. That it is possible for us to develop such a type of concepts depends, in turn, on two facts: first, that the common notions are not about things, but about the fundamental properties all things have simply in virtue of being real or natural; and second, that the human mind is so complex that it has the capacity to discern those properties. Now, given that the common notions are about properties that we share with all other things, any rational knowledge is, simply in virtue of consisting in common notions, knowledge of ourselves. One might of course question whether this is really self-knowledge, for it is not about our individual selves, but about properties of us insofar as we are real or natural things; nor does it involve a first-personal perspective. Still, to know ourselves in these terms contributes to the improvement of our self-understanding, for in contrast to our imaginative first-personal knowledge, rational self-knowledge is always adequate.

Thus, like Hobbes, Spinoza contends that in order to know ourselves better we need to adopt some kind of external perspective on ourselves. But, unlike Hobbes, he is not satisfied by this option. While he thinks that rational self-knowledge is both useful in social interaction and essential to prudent self-guidance, it is only adequate knowledge of our individual self that eventually

---

18 See also Ursula Renz, "Spinoza's Epistemology," in *Cambridge Companion to Spinoza*, ed. Don Garrett (New York: Cambridge University Press, forthcoming).

constitutes our happiness. That is why, I think, he introduces the idea of a third type of knowledge, which is about the essence of individual entities.

The question remains how intuitive self-knowledge, or adequate knowledge of our individual essence, can be acquired according to Spinoza. As I read the *Ethics*, we acquire this knowledge in no other way than through the second kind of knowledge. If we learn about the properties we share with other things, this always adds something to our understanding of our individual essence. To be sure, we only have the third kind of self-knowledge once we have got *complete* understanding of *all* features determining us. Intuitive knowledge marks the point where we can say, "Now, I see why this thing is the very thing it is. Given its features, which I know in virtue of common notions, it could not have been different in any respect." Likewise, intuitive self-knowledge consists in the perfection of self-knowledge acquired by the completion of our knowledge of all properties determining ourselves.[19]

Spinoza's answer to the question of how improvement of self-knowledge is possible thus relies on the assumption that there is no categorical, but only a gradual, difference between our knowledge of the ontological, physical, and psychological properties of the human condition and the complete understanding of our individual essence or self. While this view is obviously inspired by Hobbes' mechanist anthropology, it departs from the latter in a crucial aspect: for Spinoza, it is complete understanding of our individual essence or of our individual person that constitutes the ultimate goal of our quest for self-knowledge. The *Ethics* thus marks a decisive step toward a more modern, individualized understanding of Socratic self-knowledge.

---

19 For a detailed reconstruction of Spinoza's concept of intuitive knowledge, see also Ursula Renz, *Die Erklärbarkeit von Erfahrung: Realismus und Subjektivität in Spinozas Theorie des menschlichen Geistes* (Frankfurt am Main: Klostermann, 2010), 291–92, as well as the final section of Renz, "Spinoza's Epistemology."

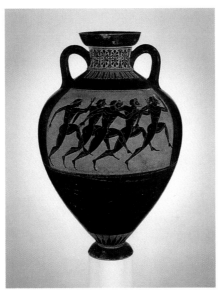

FIGURE 1 Attributed to the Euphiletos painter. Terra cotta Panathenaic prize amphora, ca. 530 B.C. Rogers Fund, 1914. Image acquired from the Metropolitan Museum of Art, The Collection Online.

FIGURE 2 Romare Bearden, *The Sirens' Song*, 1977. Collage of various papers with paint and graphite on fiberboard. 32 × 44 inches. Collection of Dr. Alan and Pat Davidson, New York City. On display in the traveling Art © Romare Bearden Foundation / Licensed by VAGA, New York, NY.

FIGURE 3 Rembrandt van Rijn, *"Self Portrait"*, 1630. 51 × 44 mm. Rijksmuseum, Amsterdam.

8.4. SHAFTESBURY'S INVENTION OF SECOND-PERSONAL SELF-KNOWLEDGE

The philosophers discussed so far all assume that improvement of self-knowledge is a matter of rational reflection about oneself; accordingly, they consider it as a task of philosophy to provide methodological guidance for this reflection. Shaftesbury's writings contained in the *Characteristics* follow this scheme in many respects. The third text, *Soliloquy, or Advice to an Author*, for instance, which is presented as a manual for authors providing moral advice, depicts philosophy as a kind of therapeutic self-reflection following the model of Marcus Aurelius' *Meditations*.[20] Yet, there are also important differences, as we shall see shortly.

Let me begin by pointing out some presuppositions of Shaftesbury's concern with moralist writing. Like Hobbes' usage of the metaphor of *reading*, Shaftesbury's focus' on the activity of moralist *writing* implies a statement on the process by which we acquire self-knowledge. He writes:

> One would think there was nothing easier for us than to know our own minds and understand what our main scope was, what we plainly drove at and what we proposed to ourselves, as our end, in every occurrence of our lives. But our thoughts have generally such an obscure implicit language that it is the hardest thing in the world to make them speak out distinctly. For this reason, the right method is to give them voice and accent.[21]

This passage exhibits more than any other how much Shaftesbury is indebted to the Cartesian legacy. At first, though, it may seem as if he

---

20 See Garrett, "Moral Philosophy," 268, for a discussion of this genre.

21 Anthony Ashley Cooper, Third Earl of Shaftesbury, *Characteristics of Men, Manners, Opinions, Times*, ed. Lawrence E. Klein (Cambridge: Cambridge University Press, 1999), 77–78.

denies that the contents of our minds are immediately known, since he rejects the view that they are plainly given to us. Yet, he does not consider our mental states as something hidden to which we have only indirect access. If it is difficult to know our thoughts, this is because they are presented in an "obscure implicit language." To comprehend them, therefore, we need neither more evidence, nor additional explanations, but a method "to give them voice and accent," to make them explicit, as it were.

Thus, to improve our self-knowledge, we do not have to engage in the labor of scientific investigation. What is required instead, according to Shaftesbury, is that we enter into the somewhat troublesome process of realizing our real commitments. Why is this troublesome? Certainly not because of any *epistemic* difficulty, but rather for the moral conflicts and remorse that often arise when we honestly and conscientiously acknowledge our wishes and desires. Although Shaftesbury discards the notion that we have immediate introspective self-knowledge of our mental states, he is not departing very far from the approach of Descartes' *Meditations*. Both consider philosophy as a matter of guided reflection, and both expect that guided reflection may support the reader in identifying the contents of his mind. Still, there are important differences in their views with respect to the way this goal is reached. For Shaftesbury, to discern one's mental states, introspection is not sufficient; one has to voice them. This is why the acquisition of self-knowledge is a challenge, a moral challenge more precisely, for he who really wants to know his own mind must dare to "tell himself his wishes" and "endure to carry on his thought."[22]

The question remains of what epistemological presumptions Shaftesbury's method relies on. How is philosophical writing expected to provide us with self-knowledge?

---

22 Ibid., 78.

To address this question we have to consider the metaphor of "surgery," which Shaftesbury uses to describe the process of moralist writing. It is important to note here that while his primary focus is on the practice of self-reflection, it is a consequence of this that also the self-relation underlying this practice is described in terms of the relationship between doctor and patient. This, in turn, suggests that the subject be divided into the agent and the patient.

The question arises why we should embrace this assumption. Why is self-division needed for self-knowledge? One way to answer would be that the idea of self-division is appealed to in order to solve a structural problem connected with the usage of the metaphor of surgery. It seems very odd that the very same person is the surgeon and the patient; exempt from extraordinary cases, the process of surgery involves inter-, not intrapersonal relationships. Thus, if self-reflection is like surgery, then a similar division between persons is simply necessary.[23] But this is not Shaftesbury's main reason, I think, as his interpretation of the Delphic injunction shows:

> This was among the ancients, that celebrated Delphic inscription, "Recognize yourself!" which was as much as to say, " 'Divide yourself!' or "Be two!" For if the division were rightly made, all within would, of course, they thought, be rightly understood and prudently managed. Such confidence they had in this home-dialect of soliloquy! For it was accounted the peculiarity of philosophers and wise men to be able to hold themselves in talk. And it was their boast on this account that "they were never less alone than when by themselves." A knave, they thought, could never be by himself.[24]

---

23 See Christopher Shields' discussion "Aristotle's Requisite of Self-Knowledge" in this volume, with regard to the question of why, according to Aristotle, one needs friends to know oneself.

24 Shaftesbury, *Characteristics*, 77.

Shaftesbury argues here that behind the Delphic imperative was the insight that self-knowledge yields wisdom by the increase it effects in our capacity for self-control. This is plausible: the better we know our minds, the more we are indeed in the position to understand and prudently manage our mental lives.

But there is more to be said about this passage, which becomes visible if we compare it with a famous tenet of the *Ethics*. Spinoza, too, contended that the improvement of self-knowledge goes along with an increase in one's power, but his reasons differed essentially from Shaftesbury's. According to Spinoza, this increase of power is first and foremost due to the fact that *any* adequate cognition changes the ratio of one's activity to one's passivity. It is a mere function of the improved epistemic balance to which better self-knowledge amounts. Shaftesbury, in contrast, accounts for the increase in self-control by the psychological assumption that the improvement of self-knowledge changes the mental constitution of the subject. The self of the successful self-knower is not just characterized by a higher degree of self-control, but exhibits a kind of self-agreement, intimacy, or unity that the self-ignorant person lacks; the virtuous self is, he says, "of a piece within."[25] Thus the higher degree of self-control, which the improvement of self-knowledge yields, is due to the higher level of integrity we end up with; it is not simply a matter of our having more power within us.

This constitution, he further assumes, is not reached by the adoption of a more coherent set of doxastic or moral attitudes alone; what is crucial is the experience of self-intimacy. This is also the deeper reason why the notion of self-division is so important to Shaftesbury. Intimacy describes the relation between two persons; whence the idea that self-reflection may come close to an interpersonal relation. The call for self-division is meant to express the need for a self-relation that is, like the

---

25 Ibid.

relation between friends, a second-personal affair. This is certainly an unusual idea, but one that makes sense, I think. Self-knowledge can be conceived as a matter of being more or less intimately acquainted with oneself, and this is why the process of knowing oneself better can be appropriately described as a kind of self-dialogue. Hence self-knowledge is for Shaftesbury neither merely first-personal nor third-personal knowledge, but consists in a sense or feeling we may get of ourselves when we enter into a dialogue with ourselves and consider our mental life from a second-personal standpoint.

8.5. Epilogue

With Shaftesbury, the early modern concern with Socratic self-knowledge has reached new ground. Due to his writings, self-knowledge has become more and more an issue of moral psychology, and no longer of epistemology or anthropology. In the vein of the reception of his approach by Hutcheson and Hume, moreover, the concern with Socratic self-knowledge has increasingly been replaced by the question of what constitutes morality. While this has proved important for the rise of modern moral theory as well as of moral psychology, it has relegated the most crucial insight of Shaftesbury to the fringe: that part of the ennobling effect attributed so often to self-knowledge is due to the intimate relationship we entertain to ourselves when we inquire into our emotions or desires from a second-personal point of view.

CHAPTER NINE

Self-Knowledge and Self-Deception in Modern Moral Philosophy

Aaron Garrett

Pierre Nicole[1] opened his essay "Of Self-Knowledge" by observing that "the most common Precept of *Pagan* and *Christian* Philosophy is this, which orders us to know our selves; and there is nothing in which men agree more than in the Precept of this Duty."[2] Nicole invoked a long-standing philosophical tradition with this assertion that rested on three premises. First, self-knowledge via introspection, reflection, and other sorts of natural reasoning is attainable by human beings through the exercise of their natural reason, and thus natural to us. It is natural in that it arises from our nature and does not depend in a core way on the supernatural. Second, self-knowledge is the proper domain of philosophy, both insofar as it is the special provenance of philosophy to think

---

1 I am indebted throughout my discussion of Pierre Nicole to Beatrice Guion, *Pierre Nicole moraliste* (Paris: Honoré Champion, 2002).

2 Pierre Nicole, *Essais de Morale*, 3 vols. (Paris: Guillaume Desprez, 1701), vol. 1, sec. 1.

about self-knowledge and insofar as philosophy has a special role in acquisition of self-knowledge. Finally, the acquisition of self-knowledge is important, desired, and desirable. It is important that we achieve it, for example, in explaining and facilitating how we fit into the cosmos or world and as a necessary or supporting condition of other important knowledge. It is desirable in itself and also insofar as it is connected with or gives rise to desirable goods of body and mind such as beatitude, felicity, happiness, carelessness, and the like. And human beings do desire to know themselves, at least those who are capable of natural reason.

These commitments, or commitments roughly like them, have been shared by many philosophers and philosophical schools. I will refer to the attainability through natural reason via philosophy of desirable and important self-knowledge as the "self-knowledge tradition." The self-knowledge tradition includes knowledge of our moral virtues and vices, of the motivations for, and outcomes of, our actions that might accrue to us morally (as well as of our virtues more broadly), and of duties connected to our natural and social moral personae. The Stoic, Ciceronian, and neo-Stoic virtues of *constantia*, magnanimity, and strength of mind, Descartes' generosity, Spinoza's *fortitudo*, and so on, drew on a picture like the self-knowledge tradition insofar as they either were coextensive with, or assumed, the desirability, the desire for, and the importance of true knowledge of one's power and virtues through natural reason via philosophy. Consequently one way to understand the connection between the different premises of the self-knowledge tradition was through the acquisition of desirable virtues via philosophy that give rise to happiness and to other desirable and important goods of body and mind. Justus Lipsius' *De constantia*, for example, is a sustained argument that self-knowledge gives rise to the virtue of *constantia* that helps one to be happy throughout this life and makes one likely to merit happiness in the next.[3]

---

3 See Jerome Schneewind, *The Invention of Autonomy* (Cambridge: Cambridge University Press, 1998), 170; and Jill Kraye, "Moral Philosophy," in *The Cambridge History of Renaissance Philosophy*, ed. Charles Schmitt and Quentin Skinner (Cambridge: Cambridge University Press, 1984), 370.

But from the Protestant Reformation to the mid-eighteenth century there was a challenge within theology and moral philosophy that drew extensively on Augustine to question this picture.[4] The challenge was not that self-knowledge was unattainable, but rather that what we naturally take to be *moral* self-knowledge misses the mark due to the fact that we who think we have achieved it have corrupted faculties. The focus was on moral self-knowledge insofar as it was both most important and closest to home, a shared premise of many modern philosophers of many stripes.

Furthermore, it is self-undermining: the more we think we have naturally achieved it and profess it philosophically, the more vicious we become. As Rochefoucauld acidly noted: "The philosophers—and Seneca above all—did not eradicate crime by the advice they gave; they only used it to build up their own pride."[5] The French Moralists[6] argued that self-deceit aided by self-love keeps us from recognizing that self-knowledge is corrupted by self-love. It is unnatural to attain self-knowledge, but it is natural for us to be motivated by self-love and to take self-deceit to be self-knowledge. They thus challenged the self-knowledge tradition by undermining the first premise and to a lesser extent the second: self-knowledge was neither natural nor the special provenance of philosophy (the quote from Nicole is agnostic about the latter). They allowed a modification of the third, that it was important to seek self-knowledge, not as the natural acquisition of virtue but instead as a consequence of recognizing our humility before the supernatural. Any happiness that followed was a grant of grace, not a dessert for virtue. From François de La Rochefoucauld

---

4 I will not discuss Augustine on self-knowledge, but see chapter 5 in this volume. Protestant Augustinianism is of course not identical with Augustine.

5 François de la Rochefoucauld, *Collected Maxims and Other Reflections*, trans. E. H. Blackmore, A. M. Blackmore, and Francine Giguère (Oxford: Oxford University Press, 2007), 1:105.

6 "French Moralists" is a term of art. I just mean by it the French thinkers who were committed to something like the challenge I am describing: (1) primarily Rochefoucauld, Nicole, and Esprit; (2) to a lesser extent Pascal and La Bruyère.

and Nicole to Bernard Mandeville and Joseph Butler to David Hume
and Jean-Jacques Rousseau, many philosophers rejected or modified
the commitments of the self-knowledge tradition and the assumed
connections between our natural self-knowledge, philosophy, and
virtue and happiness.

The French Moralists claimed that our flawed self-evaluations may
appear to us to be accurate judgments, but *that* they appear so might
instead be the consequence of our natural self-interest, limited scope,
laziness, and credulity.[7] As Nicole put it with his characteristic force,
"The World is almost composed of nothing but willful blind People,
who hate and fly the Light, and who labour nothing more than to
deceive themselves."[8] And furthermore, any attempt to gain natural
self-knowledge as the basis for merited virtue was actively morally
pernicious, as it fed and reinforced vice under the guise of virtue. As
Augustine had argued against the Roman philosophers such as Seneca
and Cicero, to try to eradicate self-deceit through natural reason gave
rise to greater and greater self-deceit, hubris, vanity, and hypocrisy—
not to virtue. The legacy of this challenge can be seen in the writings
of many philosophers of the seventeenth and eighteenth centuries,
but in a particularly trenchant form in Hume's suggestion in the conclusion to book 1 of *A Treatise of Human Nature* that the inability
to maintain skepticism itself is due to the inability to maintain an
imposture of mind—that is, to hold onto beliefs and arguments that
go against natural psychology—even if skepticism warranted these
beliefs.[9]

---

7 Jacques L'Esprit, *La fausseté des vertus humaines* (Paris: Guillaume Desprez, 1678), v–vi;
Rochefoucauld, *Maxims*, vol. 1 and *passim*.

8 Pierre Nicole, *Moral Essays, Contain'd in Several Treatises on Many Important Duties*, 4 vols.
(London: Printed for Samuel Manship, 1696), vol. 3, sec. 22.

9 David Hume, *A Treatise of Human Nature*, ed. L. A. Selby-Bigge and revised by P. H. Nidditch, 2nd
ed. (Oxford: Clarendon Press, 1978).

9.1. Calvin, Jansenius, and Hobbes

The extension of the term "philosophy" in the early modern period[10] was, unsurprisingly, quite different from its extension in present-day academic philosophy. As a consequence, authors whom today we do not consider to be philosophers influenced and wrote important works on topics we today consider to be philosophical, and conversely many writings by those we consider important philosophers do not fit easily into what we now consider to be philosophy. In addition, philosophy involved many forms of writing—the dialogue, the reflective personal essay, the maxim, the sermon, the soliloquy, the lengthy commentary—no longer favored in academic philosophical contexts. Due to changes in the extension and the form of philosophy, as well as changes in taste and ideology, some of the thinkers who were most influential have ceased to be viewed as philosophical or at least are not considered central to ongoing debates.

Skepticism about self-knowledge was advanced both by deeply confessionally committed thinkers—theologians and philosophers of an Augustinian bent—and some skeptical philosophers of less overt commitments.[11] As mentioned above, the inability of philosophy, insofar as it was a product of corrupted natural reason, to explain or to achieve grace was a long-standing Augustinian theme and present in Augustine's discussions of the inadequacies of pagan philosophers in the *City of God* and elsewhere. Calvin[12] drew on this Augustinian theme when he stated the central problem of self-knowledge in the opening of the *Institutes*:

---

10 By which I mean England and Continental Europe from the Reformation to the French Revolution.

11 For example, Montaigne and de Gornay. I will concentrate on the neo-Augustinians due to space limitations, but Montaigne and de Gornay are obviously very important as well.

12 Which is not to suggest that all philosophers who focused on self-deceit were Calvinists; cf. the Anglicans Thomas Hobbes and Bishop Joseph Butler.

It is certain that man never comes to clear knowledge of himself, unless he has first contemplated the face of God, and after having considering him, descends to look at himself. . . . Because there is nothing in us that is not greatly contaminated, therefore that which in us is a bit less filthy is taken by us as very pure, so long as we keep our mind within the bounds of a humankind that is wholly polluted, like the eye that is used to seeing nothing but black and judges that which is whitish or even nearly gray to be the whitest thing in the world.[13]

According to Calvin we ought to know God and ourselves. The question is, which first? If we try to know ourselves through natural reason and God afterward, since our faculties are corrupted by Adam's sin, our faculties are undermined by this corruption. But knowing ourselves is of pressing importance even if we wrongly judge something gray to be the whitest thing in the world; in fact, the *Institutes* began with self-knowledge.[14] Since we are thoroughly corrupt, the only way to know ourselves to be corrupt is to recognize something infinitely greater and supernaturally better than us that is only accessible through grace and not via natural reason—the face of God—and to then descend to looking at ourselves having taken in this true standard.

Unlike Descartes' famous argument in the *Meditations* that natural causal reasoning demonstrates that an infinite God exists external to my mind, for Calvin one cannot achieve this self-recognition through natural reason alone. Our natural faculties are corrupt, and the source of this corruption is a choice or volition, Adam's and our sin, which is not rational. As a consequence and wholly unlike Descartes, reason does not weather this corruption but rather is itself a potential source of corrupt evaluation. This gave rise to a skepticism parallel to Descartes' but with an opposing solution. I need to know myself, to

---

13 Jean Calvin, *Institution de la religion chrétienne* (Geneva: Philbert Hamelin, 1554), 3.
14 Thanks to Christian Maurer for pointing this out to me.

know what I am. But I have no natural access to standards on the basis of which I might know what I am. Consequently I misrepresent white as gray. Only once I recognize my incapacity to know myself naturally can I really know myself for what I am, but this involves giving up on the attempt to know myself entirely through natural reason. And once I give this up, I realize that what I really am is, unfortunately, the opposite of what I deceived myself into believing I was when relying solely on natural reason. This skepticism about natural self-knowledge does not lie in denying that there is a fact of the matter about what I am or that there is a prelapsarian state. And since I am both knower and known, I will know myself corruptly and consequently incorrectly access the fact of the matter about myself while thinking I had accessed it correctly; and this is viciously self-justifying.

One of the most influential variants on this argument was found in Jansenius, whose *Augustinus* (1640) argued for an Augustinian revival within the Roman Catholic Church and with it a highly controversial and intricately argued theology of grace through Jesus Christ that brought Calvinist influences into the Catholic sphere. He was of course pivotal for Jansenist philosophers—including Arnauld, Nicole, and Pascal—who sought to combine Augustinian theological influences with philosophical arguments.[15] *Augustinus* included arguments for the limits of human reason and criticisms of pagan philosophy for its hubris and a delicate balancing act on the will.[16] By focusing on the centrality of the will for grace, and more generally by offering a strongly voluntarist theology, Jansenius placed a focus on the passions and volitions as well as questioned their transparency by denying that the passions were rational.

---

15 Although Arnauld stressed that it was primarily a Christian and then an Augustinian movement, not a cult of Jansen. See Brian E. Strayer, *Suffering Saints: Jansenists and Convulsionnaires in France, 1640–1799* (Eastborne: Sussex Academic Press, 2008), 50.

16 Anthony Levi, *French Moralists: The Theory of the Passions, 1585 to 1649* (Oxford: Clarendon Press, 1964), 202–13; Michael Moriarty, *Disguised Vices: Theories of Virtue in Early Modern French Thought* (Oxford: Oxford University Press, 2011), ch. 8.

Hobbes was neither a Calvinist nor a Jansenist; indeed, he was an advocate of the subordination of religion to politics, but he was an important influence on the middle to late seventeenth-century French Moralists and the British philosophers who drew on them. He gave voice to Augustinian, voluntarist, and classical skeptical themes in a moral context while also providing a means of skeptical response to the challenge to self-knowledge. Hobbes was a large influence, often in an alloyed form, in Protestant (and particularly Calvinist and Lutheran) republics and principalities: Pufendorf, Velthuysen, Bayle, and Spinoza are examples. But like Calvin and Jansen, Hobbes held an Augustinian commitment to man as a fundamentally passionate being and *naturally* prone by the passions to act in ways that undermined rationality.

In the introduction to *Leviathan* Hobbes translates the Latinized Delphic command *nosce te ipsum* as "Read thy self" and argued that although the passions are similar in all men, the objects of the passions vary so drastically due to constitution and education that "the characters of mans heart, blotted and confounded as they are, with dissembling, lying, counterfeiting, and erroneous doctrines, are legible onely to him that searcheth hearts."[17] Vainglory, or pride "grounded on the flattery of others; or onely supposed by himself, for the delight in the consequence of it,"[18] was a particularly disruptive and pervasive passion that led one to misjudge one's own capacities and future chances. Insofar as vainglory was the central passion that disrupted life and did so through false judgments of one's self, the problem of self-knowledge was the heart of the Hobbesian problem. This was recognized in particular by Nicole,[19] who saw in Hobbes a philosophical fellow traveler.[20]

---

17 Thomas Hobbes, *Leviathan*, ed. Noel Malcolm, 3 vols. (Oxford: Clarendon Press, 2012), vol. 2, "Introduction," 18.

18 Ibid., ch. 6, 88.

19 See particularly Nicole, *Essais*, "Foiblesse de L'Homme," vol. 1.

20 Indeed one can argue that the places where he dissented from Hobbes—on what appeared to be Hobbes' denial of an uncorrupted state of man prior to the fall (E. D. James, *Pierre Nicole, Jansenist and Humanist: A Study of His Thought* [The Hague: Martinus Nijhoff, 1972], 155–56—are due to a desire to disassociate himself from Hobbes' perceived impiety more than a fundamental disagreement.

For Hobbes, the skeptical solution to the lack of transparency of self was to read oneself through what one had in common with others, which then allowed one to know oneself via what one has in common with others. The best means for doing this was a mechanistic and comparative science of the passions that provided an external test as to the veridicality of judgments of self and others. As mentioned above, the need to understand the particular passions came to the fore when it was no longer assumed that they were all rational or confused rational desires. The science of the passions was the means (along with rhetoric) to convince not entirely rational and passionate agents as to what was in their interest through those of their passions most amenable to reason. And it was a means to provide self-knowledge through reading oneself in a way that equalized one with others and defeated vainglory, that is, that showed that one's basic passions and drives were the same as everyone else's.

9.2. THE FRENCH MORALISTS AND MANDEVILLE

A sequence of Rochefoucauld's maxims reads,

> Self-love is cleverer than the cleverest man.
> We have no more control over the duration of our passions than over the duration of our lives.
> Passions are the only orators who always succeed in persuading. They are so to speak a natural art, with infallible rules.[21]

As mentioned above, self-love was a problem for knowledge in general, but above all for knowledge of self and in particular knowledge of one's

---

Still, as will be argued, there was a fundamental difference in their attitudes toward the role of a science of the passions in self-knowledge insofar as Nicole was also an essayist in the Montaignean mold.

21 Rochefoucauld, *Maxims*, 5:4 –5, 8.

moral self insofar as the ways in which we evaluate ourselves are also how we value ourselves. On Rochefoucauld's account, self-love and the passions associated with it are naturally more motivating than our desire for virtue, our reason, and our long-term interest. Indeed they are *naturally* persuasive; that is, we are psychologically so constituted as to be convinced by them, and they have their own natural rules and force that we cannot control and that justify them whether we are aware of it, whether we are clever or not. This makes self-knowledge not only difficult to maintain but in some sense unnatural to us. And insofar as morality is something we value centrally, the problem of self-deception has its home in morality and in our appraisals and valuations of what matters most to us—us.

Rochefoucauld's forms—the maxim, reflection, and brief essay—were perfectly suited to counteract the difficulty of what Hume referred to as "impostures of mind" in self-knowledge. Since we are only able to sustain self-knowledge very briefly in cases where self-knowledge goes against our natural propensity for self-love, maxims provide a quick shock that forces readers briefly to examine themselves and to recognize their real motivations, but not long enough that one would begin to rationalize the shock away. Rochefoucauld seemed particularly interested in showing that what are held to be virtues are indeed often vices. For example: "It may seem that self-love is deceived by kindness, and that it forgets its own interests when we are working for the sake of people. Yet this is the surest way for it to reach its goals: it is lending at interest, under the pretext of giving; in fact it is a subtle, refined method of winning over everyone else."[22] When we hold that the virtues that we possess, such as kindness, are in opposition to self-love, this is actually a consequence of deep and deceptive self-love and pride.

Rochefoucauld represented the most subversive and extreme pole of this challenge insofar as he highlighted the ubiquity of self-love but

22 Ibid., 5:236.

suggested no wholesale means to combat self-deception. Any recognition was fleeting. Similarly, from the fact that we might recognize that we share passions with others and that those might inform us of our real motivations, it does not follow that we actually will read ourselves and apply what we learn to our own conduct: "The thick darkness that hides it [i.e., self-love from itself] does not prevent it from seeing clearly what is outside itself. In that respect it is like our eyes, which discover everything and are blind only to themselves."[23]

Rochefoucauld's friend and collaborator Jacques Esprit offered a parallel sustained attack on the pagan moral theorists who were the originators of the self-knowledge tradition. In a passage that very well may have influenced a far more famous passage in Hume,[24] Esprit argued that "this Opinion of Philosophers, that *Moral Good* was the principle of whatsoever they did that was virtuous and praiseworthy, proceeded from their Ignorance of the true State of the Heart of Man. For they did not know how its Springs are dispos'd, and never suspected that strange Alteration in him, which hath made reason a slave to the Passions."[25] Pagan philosophers posited an inadequate natural good that was a reflection of their preferences and desires. As a consequence, they represented the moral good in ways that drew on and flattered themselves as possessing the virtues that they promoted due to self-love. In parallel with Rochefoucauld's claim about Seneca, Esprit argued that Cato, the Stoic exemplar, was driven to his supposedly glorious acts by pride and self-love and that those who extolled his virtues were similarly driven by self-love.[26] In other words philosophy tended not to counteract self-deception but to reinforce it.

In his attack on the pagan virtue of magnanimity, Esprit attempted to upend the idea that those who possessed the greatest virtues also

---

23 Ibid., 5:1.

24 Hume, *Treatise*, 2.3.3.4.

25 Jacques L'Esprit, *Discourses on the Deceitfulness of Humane Virtues*, trans. William Beauvoir (London: Andrew Bell, 1706), 9.

26 Ibid., II, ch. 13.

de facto possessed the greatest self-knowledge: "The greatest Humane Virtues are the most Deceitful, and . . . Men's Opinions are very Unjust and Erroneous."[27] "A man who is Magnanimous upon the Principles of Natural Reason, knows that he is so full of Self-love, that he always minds his own Interest in all his Good Actions, and therefore that he hath no real Virtue."[28] In contrast, a magnanimous Christian "acknowledges that his understanding is so full of Errours, and his Will so corrupted and deprav'd, that all his Thoughts and Inclinations are Repugnant to Virtue."[29]

Nicole held similarly that our self-knowledge was severely restricted due to "the general propensity of our corrupt nature,"[30] occluded by our passions and our self-love or *amour propre*. As Nicole, Rochefoucauld, and Hobbes all suggested, what we think of as self-knowledge is often colored to a great extent by others who flatter us and do not point out our flaws, and this allows us to avoid reaching true but unpleasant conclusions about ourselves. In the aforementioned essay "Of Self-Knowledge" and the essay "Of Charity and Self-Love" that follows it, Nicole argued, like Rochefoucauld, that although everyone agrees with the truth of the precept to know oneself, "they are still far from practicing it."[31] Our psychology is poorly suited to making good on this precept. The command to know thyself is offset by an even more proximate desire not to know oneself. In one of his most startling analogies Nicole compares our constant exercise of self-interest in our avoidance of self-knowledge to birds who need to be continually in motion in order not to drop to the earth.[32]

For Nicole, like Calvin and Jansen, self-knowledge is fundamental but painful, and self-love leads us to obscure from ourselves that

---

27 Ibid., 328.
28 Ibid., 337.
29 Ibid., 339.
30 Nicole, *Essais*, vol. 3, sec. 5.
31 Ibid., sec. 2.
32 Ibid., vol. 1, sec. 60.

"Madness (*rage*) and Hell are the center of corrupted nature."[33] Self-knowledge is the knowledge of our corruption that we acquire via first by recognizing the greatness of God and then seeing that we are nothing positive in and of ourselves—indeed we were made of nothing.[34] Our pride may suggest otherwise, but we are the worst judges of ourselves, poor judges of others, and progressively worse as we value ourselves. Nicole, like Montaigne, suggested intellectual and spiritual humility as a response to the labyrinths of self-deception.

The combined effect of this challenge was to attack the first premise of the self-knowledge tradition: that self-knowledge was natural and the product of natural reasoning. Rather, self-deception and the passions are natural—as Esprit put it, "The Heart commonly clubs with the Mind."[35] Second, in Calvin, Jansen, Nicole, Rochefoucauld, and in particular Esprit, the second premise, that philosophy was the special province of self-knowledge, was argued to be destructively mistaken. Philosophy in the absence of supernatural checks tended to exacerbate self-deceit. Self-knowledge *is* important in itself and as a supporting condition for other important kinds of knowledge. But how it is important was modified by the attacks the French Moralists delivered and diverged greatly from the self-knowledge tradition—either toward essayistic humility or toward a science of the passions. And in Esprit and Rochefoucauld, we see a profound challenge to the assumed connection between natural self-knowledge, virtue, and happiness. The morally justified goods that are supposed to be warranted by natural self-knowledge arising from natural reason are rather evils arising from self-deceit.

It was Mandeville though who provided the most thoroughgoing attack on these connections and particularly on the belief that moral

---

33 Ibid., sec. 61.

34 James, *Pierre Nicole*, 117.

35 Esprit, *Fausseté*, 342.

and other goods follow from self-knowledge. He synthesized themes in the French Moralists with Hobbes' science of the passions to effectively amplify the arguments of both. Mandeville opened the *Fable of the Bees* with a characterization of the anatomical attitude toward unmasking self-love:

> As those that study the Anatomy of Dead Carcasses may see, that the chief Organs and nicest Springs more immediately required to continue the Motion of our Machine, are not hard Bones, strong Muscles and Nerves, nor the smooth white Skin that so beautifully covers them, but small trifling Films and little Pipes that are either over-look'd, or else seem inconsiderable to Vulgar Eyes; so they that examine into the Nature of Man, abstract from Art and Education, may observe, that what renders him a Sociable Animal, consists not in his desire of Company, Good-nature, Pity, Affability, and other Graces of a fair Outside; but that his vilest and most hateful Qualities are the most necessary Accomplishments to fit him for the largest, and, according to the World, the happiest and most flourishing Societies.[36]

This suggested an external and experiential evaluation of the passions independent of introspection—à la Hobbes. In the "Search into the Nature of Society," which was appended to the 1723 edition of the *Fable* along with the "Essay on Charity Schools," Mandeville attacked Shaftesbury's attempt in the *Characteristicks* to provide a modern revival of the self-knowledge tradition via an argument for the unity of self-interest and virtue as resulting from self-knowledge—that virtue educes to interest and vice versa in rational and reflective agents. Following the French Moralists, Mandeville lanced moral exemplars

---

36 Bernard Mandeville, *The Fable of the Bees*, ed. F. B. Kaye (Oxford: Clarendon Press, 1924), 1:39–40.

like Cicero and Cato and argued that they acted out of vice and self-deception, not out of virtue and self-knowledge.

But perhaps even more destructively than his predecessors, he argued that self-deception is often for the best and gives rise to happiness. This again had its antecedents in a Calvinist tradition, where God works through our sins to give rise to the best, and in Nicole and particularly Rochefoucauld. And as with them, the best in no way redounded to us morally as individuals. But unlike all except Rochefoucauld, the future reckoning of sins in the divine court was not relevant, and so there was no obvious motivation to humility or other Christian virtues (although Mandeville did not deny private virtue or deny that it was virtue). By unmasking the real springs of virtue, and the complexity of our motivations, and by resting virtue (unlike Rochefoucauld) on a naturalistic account of the passions (as opposed to maxims or essays), Mandeville made a case, through a natural scientific analysis of the passions, that prudential goods and happiness are better brought about by private vice and lack of self-knowledge than public virtue and that Shaftesbury's attempt to reunify them in the wake of the challenges of Nicole and others was hopeless.

In the "Essay on Charity Schools" Mandeville argued, conversely, that actions that are publicly presented as virtuous often hide vicious motivations and have outcomes that are less morally good and happy-making than the ordinary natural course of the worka-day unreflective vices. The end result of these parallel arguments was that the connection between self-knowledge, moral actions and virtues, and goods was effectively severed. Vicious self-deception was more likely to result in all sorts of goods, and in happiness, than virtue. Most of what was publicly presented as virtue was in fact self-deceptive vice. And true virtue and self-knowledge might be desirable, if rare and nearly unattainable, but there was no reason to assume that they gave rise to any sort of happiness that ordinary human beings desired.

9.3. Coda: Butler, Smith, Hume, and Rousseau

How to respond to this? Butler argued that Mandeville had, like Hobbes, gotten self-love wrong by confusing it with our particular passions and by viewing it as a passion at all.[37] For Butler self-love properly understood is rational, inseparable from our general interest and demanding of a great degree of self-knowledge.[38] From the value that vicious agents place on particular passions, and from their apparent happiness in their vice, it does not follow that virtue properly understood does not give rise to greater happiness. This is true both in this life and in the next. A virtuous agent is a self-reflective agent who consults his *conscience*, which for eighteenth-century authors was coextensive with consciousness and self-reflection.[39] Although we may be, and often are, self-deceived about our present actions, consciousness as reflective knowledge of the nature of past actions and of our vices and virtues has a kind of authority that is capable of trumping proximate self-interest and offsetting particular passions in well-developed agents.

That said, three of Butler's *Sermons* were devoted to self-deception, and particularly the kind of self-deception that is exacerbated and reinforced by our credulity in believing what others say about us. As was the case for the French Moralists and for Mandeville, the lies that people tell one another to interact civilly in social contexts have adverse consequences for our self-knowledge insofar as, in conjunction with our native credulity and mental laziness, they reinforce self-deception.[40] And Butler was as suspicious as Mandeville of agents who presented themselves as guiding public morality.[41]

---

37 Joseph Butler, *Sermons Delivered at Rolls Chapel*, 2nd ed. (London: James & John Knapton, 1729), 9n.

38 Ibid., xxix.

39 See Bob Tennant, *Conscience, Consciousness and Ethics in Joseph Butler's Philosophy and Ministry* (Woodbridge: Boydell Press, 2011).

40 See particularly Butler, *Sermons*, 7.

41 Butler, Joseph. *The Analogy of Religion*, 2nd ed. (London: James, John & Paul Knapton, 1736), 465–66.

But perhaps most surprisingly, Butler recognized that our capacity for self-deception undermined our ability to apply the reasoning of our conscience to ourselves and led to our undermining of this reasoning when it served our interest. The only solution to this was to provide rigid rules for oneself and to rigorously keep to them even when it seemed acceptable to be lax. Both the criticisms of Mandeville and the muted agreement with him can be seen in Adam Smith and his account of the impartial spectator in the *Theory of Moral Sentiments*. Self-knowledge as conscience and the application of rigid rules to self were for Smith a hallmark of well-developed moral agents, as was the desire to be in agreement with what a well-informed agent takes as morally authoritative—in Smith's case the impartial spectator. But Smith was, like Butler and Mandeville, deeply suspicious of reformers presenting themselves as moral, and he recognized that self-love arising from mixed motivations and self-deception was not only a far more powerful motive than noninterested moral motivations but also gave rise to public benefits.

As mentioned in the opening of this chapter, Humean skepticism had a strong affinity with the challenges to self-knowledge through self-deception in the French Moralists. As presented in *A Treatise*,[42] natural reason and philosophy itself were prone to fundamental self-deception problems, although the solution was not recognition of a supernatural deity! Like Hobbes and Mandeville, Hume offered a sophisticated version of the mechanistic science of the passions as providing a form of self-knowledge that counterbalanced skepticism. As for Mandeville, pride and vanity were fundamental motivations. Pride was Hume's central passion, but Hume argued that it and vanity could be seen to be motivations to virtue once we accept that a virtuous action or disposition could be reinforced by a vice like vanity and need not have a sole cause in virtuous motivations. Hume also challenged

---

42 Hume, *Treatise*, I.iv.

the border between seeming to have a virtue and actually possessing the internal states and motivations associated with virtue, as well as the border between natural abilities and virtues, effectively arguing that self-knowledge was not necessary to virtue; rather one had to be evaluated and judged as virtuous.

In his four "Essays on Happiness," Hume drew a further consequence in the spirit of Montaigne and La Bruyère's *Characters* by suggesting that no standard for judging and evaluating oneself can be accessed that is not already influenced by one' preexistent character and the constituent passions that give rise to my particular conception of happiness.[43] This is true of the Skeptic and the Epicurean as much as the Platonist and the Stoic. Character is prior to self-knowledge, and the character or temperament with which one began was a contingent matter. We can know ourselves, but we know ourselves through characters that predetermine how we value this knowledge. And the reasons by which we know ourselves and others follow the passions that are given by our constitution.

Finally, Rousseau revived many of the themes of Calvin and the French Moralists but gave them a new and historical form. Our incapacity to understand ourselves was the consequence of our psychology—*amour propre*—but in conjunction with our perfectibility and a series of contingent historical changes that made us more and more estranged from ourselves. Because we are so thoroughly self-deceived in our present historical state, the Hobbesian science of the passions was no longer a means to self-knowledge. Indeed, it was a symptom of historical self-deception. Rousseau presented the history of *amour propre* in many literary forms, from thought experiments and a priori speculation on the origins of our present condition to Montaigne-like autobiographical essays, reveries, and soliloquies. This suggested a different problem, the problem of ideology and how we might know

---

43 David Hume, *Essays Moral, Political, and Literary*, ed. Eugene F. Miller (Indianapolis: Liberty Fund, 1985), I.XV.n.

ourselves through it or in spite of it, and an alternative response to the problem of self-deceit.

Acknowledgment

This chapter is dedicated to the memories of Bob Tennant and Raymond Frey.

CHAPTER TEN

Kant's Ideal of Self-Knowledge

Dina Emundts

In a passage from the *Metaphysics of Morals* Kant says:

On the First Command of All Duties to Oneself, §14: This command is "know (scrutinize, fathom) *yourself,*" not in terms of your natural perfection ... but rather in terms of your moral perfection in relation to your duty. That is, know your heart—whether it is good or evil, whether the source of your actions is pure or impure, and what can be imputed to you as belonging originally to the *substance* of a human being or as derived (acquired or developed) and belonging to your moral *condition.*[1]

---

1 Immanuel Kant, *The Metaphysics of Morals*, trans. and ed. Mary Gregor (Cambridge: Cambridge University Press, 1997), 191. Cf. Immanuel Kant, *Gesammelte Schriften*, ed. Preussische Akademie der Wissenschaften et al. (Berlin: Verlag Georg Reimer, 1900), 6:441.

With this statement, Kant gives the *Socratic ideal* of self-knowledge a significance that is remarkable in several respects.

First, Kant relates the ideal of self-knowledge to moral self-knowledge. More precisely, what is addressed here are our motives for moral actions and our moral character.

Second, Kant talks about duty. Not only is self-knowledge something we should strive for and thus, in this sense, an *ideal* that we do not have to claim to be capable of fully realizing, but Kant also claims that we have a duty to strive for practical self-knowledge.

Third, Kant understands the notion of "knowing oneself" to mean that one actively and systematically looks for something. He does not mean that we should be careful (not to step beyond our human boundaries) or that we should be aware (of the fact that we know nothing). Rather, he takes it to be an imperative that we act based on the resulting knowledge concerning our character and motives.

The first section of this chapter will deal with the first point, namely Kant's understanding of the ideal of self-knowledge as it relates to moral self-knowledge. The other two points—namely the theses that self-knowledge is a duty and that it is an active process—will be clarified in sections 10.2 and 10.3, which focus, respectively, on questions concerning character and questions concerning motives.

10.1. The Ideal of Self-Knowledge

The following discussion will focus on various forms of self-relation in Kant's philosophy that could be called self-knowledge and on the question of whether self-knowledge can be seen as a duty.

One could have a very broad concept of self-knowledge, according to which it simply refers to the knowledge one has about oneself. Then, as a part of this, there could be self-knowledge in the sense of knowledge of ourselves as rational human beings. This kind of anthropological knowledge is possible, in Kant's view. But for him this is, strictly speaking, not a kind of *self*-knowledge because it is the result of observing human beings and therefore not dependent on any special self-relation.[2] Moreover, a lot of what is going on in Kant's philosophy amounts to a kind of *philosophical self-knowledge*. What we learn about the boundaries of our theoretical knowledge can be understood as a kind of Socratic insight into the finitude of human beings.[3] This knowledge is also about human beings as such, and in this sense it is anthropological. However, it is not learned exclusively by observing human beings, but rather also requires as a source of the knowledge the special relation we have to ourselves. This kind of insight could indeed also be understood as an ideal. Because philosophical knowledge can help us avoid various mistakes concerning our standards and rights, there is a sense in which we should strive for philosophical self-knowledge. Maybe one could additionally say that, in Kant's view, this knowledge is reached in the course of the history of philosophy and is something that everyone ought to realize. We would thereby give the ideal a meaning within an historical context.[4]

There is another form of theoretical self-knowledge that Kant discusses. This is knowledge about ourselves as individual persons that we obtain through introspection. But Kant does not want to understand this kind of self-knowledge as something we should strive for. First of all, Kant is skeptical that we can really attain self-knowledge by means of introspection. He thinks that we lack sufficient means for knowing

---

2 Cf. Immanuel Kant, *Gesammelte Schriften*, 7:120. Cf. Immanuel Kant, *Anthropology from a Pragmatic Point of View*, trans. and ed. Robert B. Louden (New York: Cambridge University Press, 2006), 4.

3 Stephen Engstrom, "Self-Consciousness and the Unity of Knowledge," in *International Yearbook of German Idealism*, vol. 11, ed. Dina Emundts and Sally Sedgwick (Berlin: Walter de Gruyter, forthcoming), interprets, in a convincing manner, Kant's first Critique as a kind of Socratic project that can be understood as (nontheoretical) self-knowledge.

4 Hegel picks up these elements in his discussion of self-knowledge, according to which history is the fulfillment of the Socratic imperative: "Know thyself." Georg W. F. Hegel, *Enzyklopädie der philosophischen Wissenschaften im Grundrisse (1830)*, ed. Wolfgang Bonsiepen and Hans-Christian Lucas (Hamburg: Felix Meiner Verlag, 1992), sec. 377; and Georg W. F. Hegel, *Hegel's Philosophy of Mind*, trans. (from the 1830 edition, together with the *Zusätze*) William Wallace and Arthur V. Miller, with revisions and commentary by Michael J. Inwood (New York: Oxford University Press, 2007), 4.

inner states when we focus only on them and not also on the outside world.[5] Kant makes this point in the context of issues concerning theoretical knowledge, but, as we will see later on, he makes a similar point regarding introspection and self-knowledge in a practical context. However, concerning "theoretical" self-knowledge, this is not his only doubt. Kant also seems to think that the extensive examination of one's own feelings and ideas hinders a natural and social manner of action. It can potentially lead to a kind of selfishness. For this reason, "theoretical" self-knowledge is nothing we should aim for. This is why in a famous passage in the *Anthropology* Kant warns us that too much self-reflection can lead to a pathological state.[6] That might seem like a very simple thesis, but even so, it must be stated that, for Kant, there is at least no reason to consider this kind of self-knowledge to be something worth striving for. Thus, concerning knowledge about ourselves as individual creatures, Kant restricts the ideal of self-knowledge to morally relevant self-knowledge.

In practical philosophy, finally, the insight expressed by the categorical imperative seems also to offer an important kind of self-knowledge insofar as the explication of the categorical imperative offers an explication of how we act rationally. Nevertheless, Kant seems to take knowledge of the categorical imperative to be a case of philosophical knowledge and *not* a kind of self-knowledge. This could mean that it is the result of pure analysis on the part of rational beings that does not require any special self-relation. However, it also seems plausible to say that our understanding of ourselves as beings for whom the law of reason is valid does require a special self-relation that is distinct from pure introspection and is therefore another kind of self-knowledge. Could we then say that insight regarding the nature of

---

5 Cf. Immanuel Kant, *Kritik der reinen Vernunft*, ed. Jens Timmermann (Hamburg: Felix Meiner Verlag, 1998), B 293f. Cf. Immanuel Kant, *Critique of Pure Reason*, trans. and ed. Paul Guyer and Allen W. Wood (Cambridge: Cambridge University Press, 1998), 336f.

6 Cf. Immanuel Kant, *Gesammelte Schriften*, 7:133f. Cf. Kant, *Anthropology from a Pragmatic Point of View*, 22.

the categorical imperative is an ideal we should strive for? We need to take into account here the fact that this kind of knowledge is a knowledge that we somehow always already have.[7] Maybe we can say that we should strive for a better understanding of the categorical imperative. But even the knowledge of the categorical imperative as such does not seem to be a good candidate for an ideal or a duty. What we can strive for is not a clarification of the categorical imperative, but rather a clarification of our moral character and the role that the imperative plays for us. This is a case of self-knowledge, and it is part of the ideal of knowledge about our character that the next section of this chapter focuses on.

In addition to this sort of philosophical analysis, there exists a possible kind of self-relation that is closely linked to this philosophical analysis: the awareness of oneself as a thinker and as an agent and, furthermore, the awareness of the principles according to which one thinks or acts. The philosophical analysis would not be possible without this self-awareness, because it is at least partly an analysis of this awareness. However, the philosophical analysis is not the same thing as the self-awareness, and the self-awareness is itself not, strictly speaking, knowledge, but rather only very important for knowledge. At least terminologically it seems to be clear that Kant would not call this self-awareness self-knowledge. Thus, I will call it self-*consciousness*. In any case, it is not something we could claim is a duty or an ideal, because it is a substantial element of who we are and not something we can lose, or gain, or strive for.

To summarize: Kant seems to regard the philosophical insights provided by theoretical philosophy as a kind of self-knowledge but, in general, and with this exception aside, wants to restrict the ideal of self-knowledge to morally relevant practical knowledge on account

---

7 Cf. Kant, *Gesammelte Schriften*, 4:403, 412 and 5:91. Cf. Immanuel Kant, *Groundwork of the Metaphysics of Morals*, trans. and ed. Mary Gregor and Jens Timmermann (New York: Cambridge University Press, 2012), 18f and 26. Cf. Immanuel Kant, *Critique of Practical Reason*, trans. and ed. Mary Gregor (New York: Cambridge University Press, 1997), 77.

of his suspicion of all sorts of selfishness. In practical philosophy, the knowledge of the categorical imperative itself seems not to be a case of self-knowledge, but knowledge about our relation to the categorical imperative can count as self-knowledge in the form of knowledge of our character. As I already mentioned, the relevant cases of moral self-knowledge concern knowledge about character and motives, and I will discuss each of these two aspects in the following sections.

10.2. The Idea of Knowledge of One's Own Character

In what follows after the passage that I quoted from the *Metaphysics of Morals*, Kant explains that practical self-knowledge is the beginning of wisdom, which consists in the agreement between the will and the end in itself. He then goes on to maintain that this form of self-knowledge would mean both that we acknowledge the value of human beings and that we judge ourselves impartially.

We have to take into account the fact that the *Metaphysics of Morals* is from 1797, about ten years after the *Groundwork* and the *Critique of Practical Reason*. In general, the later Kant focuses more on the idea of character and its dispositions for good or evil than on the principle of morally good actions. This does not necessarily mean that he changed his views, and can rather mean that he simply concentrates on other aspects, namely on character and the general conditions for being moral. In this later focus, self-knowledge seems to be of value because we can discover our original disposition to act in accordance with the categorical imperative. But why is this valuable? The passage in which Kant says that this kind of self-knowledge leads to an insight into the value of human beings seems to imply that this value lies in our original disposition. However, self-knowledge is also itself of moral value, because this insight can strengthen our intention to follow the categorical imperative. Although we do not have to learn that the categorical imperative is rational, we can attain knowledge about our relation to the categorical imperative. Self-knowledge can lead us to acknowledge that we are indeed rational and can thereby motivate us to act according to the categorical imperative. And, according to Kant in the *Metaphysics of Morals*, this knowledge is something we should strive for. What is meant here by self-knowledge? It could mean the knowledge about ourselves that is implicit in the philosophical analyses of morality. Moreover, it can mean something that we learn about ourselves when we attend to what is going on inside ourselves, for example, by becoming aware of our moral feelings. These feelings can help us better understand our original moral disposition. In this latter case—which I take to be the relevant one—self-knowledge does imply that we have a special self-relation, and therefore the concept of "self-knowledge" really does seem justified.

However, according to Kant, we not only recognize our original disposition when we attain self-knowledge. We also become aware of the fact that we, in our real lives, are often misguided in our actions because we do not follow our original disposition. We could discover that our motives were not purely guided by the categorical imperative, and we could thereby discover our weakness and the tendency to simply prefer our own desires to the categorical imperative.[8] What interests me here is that, in this case, even in the context of questions concerning character, self-knowledge is to be understood as knowledge about the motives for our actions.[9] For this kind of self-knowledge, we have to ask questions like these: What was my real motive? According to which principle did I really act? Although Kant does not elaborate on these questions in the passage from the *Metaphysics of Morals*, it seems clear that he thinks that it is a duty to strive for this kind of

8 Cf. Immanuel Kant, *Religion within the Boundaries of Mere Reason and Other Writings*, trans. and ed. Allen Wood and George di Giovanni (Cambridge: Cambridge University Press, 1998), 45ff. and 75ff. Cf. Kant, *Gesammelte Schriften*, 6:19ff. and 57ff.

9 Kant does not have to claim that we need self-knowledge in order to form our character, for the idea is that the effect of the categorical imperative itself helps us to form our character. Cf. Kant, *Gesammelte Schriften*, 4:410f. and 5:85. Cf. Kant, *Groundwork*, 24f. Cf. Kant, *Critique of Practical Reason*, 73.

self-knowledge and therefore that this self-knowledge is possible—not in the sense of full self-knowledge, but at least in terms of having an established duty to strive for it.

10.3. The Idea of Knowledge of One's Own Motives

Paragraph 9 of the *Metaphysics of Morals* offers an answer to the question of why we should consider self-knowledge a duty. Following Kant's discussion there, we have a duty to tell ourselves the truth because we are rational autonomous beings and ought to treat ourselves as such. Self-deception is a form of not telling the truth, and therefore it should be morally condemned. Thus, self-deception is not to be condemned because we could harm other people, but rather because we are not permitted to treat ourselves in this way. Kant talks (in the following sections) about two kinds of self-deception: intentional and nonintentional self-deception. Intentional self-deception means that I somehow hide something about myself from myself. I take something about myself (or something that is connected to things I believe about myself) to be true, although, at the same time, I do not take this thing to be very likely, or I even think it is not true. Kant confesses that it is mysterious how this is even possible. Nonintentional self-deception means that I take something about myself to be the case although I am able to know better. In this case, it does not come to my mind that what I believe is not really the case. However, for some reason, I have a fear or a wish that prevents me from taking a closer look, and it would be possible for me to do better. I would come to a better result if I were to check more carefully. Kant thinks that both kinds of self-deception are in contradiction with treating oneself as a rational autonomous person. Thus, both variants are to be condemned, and we have a duty to strive for self-knowledge and to act against possible self-deception. Kant picks up on this idea again in paragraphs 14 and 15 when he talks about the ideal of self-knowledge. And this is one of the reasons why

Kant understands self-knowledge to be an activity. In order to avoid self-deception we must constantly examine and study ourselves with respect to our motives. This is Kant's justification for the duty of striving for self-knowledge. Is there also a need for self-knowledge that is more directly motivated by the specific setup of Kant's moral philosophy?

In the *Groundwork*, in the first section, Kant introduces a distinction that is crucial for his theory of morality: there are actions from duty and actions that are in accordance with duty. An action is an action from duty when the thought of duty is the only, or at least the substantial reason for acting the way we do. In the second part of the *Groundwork* Kant then introduces the categorical imperative as the principle of moral actions. The categorical imperative is the principle that determines whether an action is of *moral value* and whether it is *right* (this distinction is in accordance with the distinction between *from duty* and in conformity *with duty*). If the principle is the *ground* for the action, then the action is morally valuable; if the action is in accordance with the principle, then it is an action that is morally right. This explains what moral actions are and in what sense they can be right or valuable. Such an explication seems to be an important task for the metaphysics of morality. However, in addition to this, we can, according to Kant, use this principle in the moral doings of everyday life. Here we can use it as a *principium executionis*. Namely, we can use it to answer the question of what we ought to do. We only have to ask whether the maxim of our action can be universalized. Is self-knowledge necessarily involved in this process? We must recognize our maxims and we must know the moral principle. Both could count as self-knowledge, but Kant does not pick this out as a central theme. The knowledge of the categorical imperative was already a topic in the previous section of this chapter: knowledge of the categorical imperative as such is not self-knowledge, but rather simply knowledge of the rational principle of actions. The knowledge of one's own maxims seems to be unproblematic for Kant. This is so because an intentional action implies knowledge of one's maxims, and this knowledge is not part of an extra consideration or act.

Yet there is another function that the categorical imperative is supposed to have in the moral doings of everyday life. It can inform us whether an action was morally right or valuable. Thus, the categorical imperative can serve as a tool to judge past actions, that is, as a *principium diiudicationis*. Only an action that was done because of the categorical imperative has a moral value. However, the difference between an action motivated solely by the categorical imperative and an action in conformity with it can only be established from a first-person perspective. No external observation of the action itself can tell us whether an action is motivated by the categorical imperative, and no other person can really judge here. The judgment about an action being morally valuable can thus only be made from a first-person perspective. If this judgment is assumed to be possible, we must be able to know whether we acted because of the categorical imperative or not. Thus, we must be able to know our motives. In my eyes, it is essential for a philosophy of morality that it also give us a criterion for evaluating actions that have been committed. Thus, Kant has to claim that self-knowledge in the sense of knowledge about our own motives is possible. In the *Metaphysics of Morals* Kant obviously really thinks that such self-knowledge is possible. Given this and given the consideration thus far, it is surprising to read in the *Groundwork*:

> In fact we can never, even by the most strenuous examination, get entirely behind our covert incentives, because when moral worth is at issue what counts is not the actions, which one sees, but their inner principles, which one does not see.[10]

---

10 Kant, *Groundwork*, 22. Cf. Kant, *Gesammelte Schriften*, 4:407 and 6:392.

In order to deal with this passage, we should answer three questions: (1) How does Kant think self-knowledge works with respect to one's own motives? (2) Why is Kant skeptical that such knowledge is possible? (3) Is this skepticism disastrous for Kant's moral philosophy on account of the fact that he needs to leave room for the possibility of self-knowledge?

(1) The question of how we can obtain knowledge of the motives that have been responsible for our actions reaches deep into Kant's moral philosophy. One can ask whether and how it is at all possible for human beings like us to recognize determination by a law of reason. The idea of self-consciousness that I brought up earlier is of some importance for this question. I think that, according to Kant, we have, both from a theoretical and from a practical perspective, a consciousness of ourselves as thinkers and agents, and also a consciousness of the principles that guide us. One could therefore say that thinking and acting are conscious and self-conscious activities. After all, Kant explicitly says that we have to be aware of the law of reason (or the categorical imperative) in order to act morally.[11] However, all this does not yet answer the question of how we can obtain self-knowledge, for this consciousness is not knowledge, nor does it automatically lead to knowledge. Concerning moral actions, despite such a consciousness, we cannot say that we know that we acted because of the categorical imperative.

Kant seems to agree on this point. He namely thinks that in order to have knowledge of our motives we have to question and examine ourselves. Thus, we need additional criteria in order to judge. One could say that one's own action was guided by the categorical imperative in cases where there has been no inclination to do the action at all. This is what Kant is actually doing at the beginning of his *Groundwork*:[12] he identifies actions that are done out of duty by constructing cases where

11 Cf. Kant, *Gesammelte Schriften*, 4:403. Cf. Kant, *Groundwork*, 18f.

12 Cf. Kant, *Groundwork*, 12f.

all inclinations speak against the action. However, following this line, one can only account for the obvious cases. Kant's further answer to the question of how we know that we really have been determined by the categorical imperative lies in his theory of moral feelings.[13] The moral law causes in us a feeling of respect. We can therefore refer to this feeling of respect when we evaluate whether we acted because of the moral law, that is, the categorical imperative. If we feel respect but also have other inclinations to act in this way, one has to ask: would I also have acted in the same way without these inclinations? Furthermore, other feelings can play a suggestive role. In the context of self-knowledge, a good or bad conscience is an interesting feeling. Maybe in some special cases a bad conscience could also exist if we act according to the categorical imperative but not because of it. If this were possible, a bad conscience would be a criterion for judging our motives.

(2) The reason for Kant's skepticism concerning knowledge of one's own motives lies in Kant's estimation of the strength of the knowledge of something that is only present in what Kant calls "inner sense." Something that is only given in inner sense cannot be held fast, and there is no possibility to repeat it or to examine it intersubjectively. Self-knowledge in the sense of knowledge of something given in inner sense is thus even less secure than knowledge about the world. It might always be that I do not remember correctly, and all indicators that I can take into account—like the presence of certain feelings—are part of the memory of the first-person perspective. An error of memory, however, becomes more likely the farther in the past an action lies, whereas

---

13 The idea that the feeling of respect tells us something about our motives is worked out by Sven Bernecker, "Kant zur moralischen Selbsterkenntnis," *Kant-Studien* 97 (2006): 182. I agree with a lot of what he says, though he takes Kant to be more optimistic than I would take him to be with respect to our privileged epistemic access to our inner states. Thomas Höwing, *Praktische Lust: Kant über das Verhältnis von Fühlen, Begehren und praktischer Vernunft* (Boston: de Gruyter, 2013), 189 and 219, also defends the thesis that moral feelings are an "indirect consciousness of our motives." For a discussion of the development of these feelings cf. Paul Guyer, "Moral Feelings in the *Metaphysics of Morals*," in *Moral Feelings in the Metaphysics of Morals*, ed. Lara Denis (New York: Cambridge University Press, 2010), 130–51.

it is not very likely when the action has just taken place a moment ago. So this error is possible, but this does not seem entirely disastrous for the possibility of having knowledge of one's past motives. However, there is another source of error. This source is the tendency to deceive oneself. It could be that in the previous moment it was in fact not the categorical imperative but self-love or vanity that was responsible for my doing the action that stands in accordance with the categorical imperative. The very moment after having done the action I could wrongly describe the action on account of not wanting to believe that vanity was my motive, and I would thereby prevent that understanding. The same is possible when I come to the conclusion that it was vanity: it could be that I in fact committed the act from duty, but that I have a tendentious view of myself. The problem here is not memory, but rather a suppression or a strong wish that leads to a sort of ignorance or self-deception. There is then no outer control to exclude this kind of error. Such a case is what Kant has in mind when he says:

> For at times it is indeed the case that with the acutest self-examination we find nothing whatsoever that—besides the moral ground of duty—could have been powerful enough to move us to this or that good action . . . ; but from this it cannot be inferred with certainty that the real determining cause of the will was not actually a covert impulse of self-love under the mere pretense of that idea.[14]

Self-deception poses the main danger for self-knowledge.

(3) The previous quotation sounds as if the danger of self-deception is so serious that we are better off when we do not depend at all on our own judgments of our motives. If this were true, the criterion for the evaluation of past actions could not be taken seriously. Kant is indeed right to see problems with respect to self-knowledge. Also, he is right in

---

14 Kant, *Groundwork*, 22. Cf. Kant, *Gesammelte Schriften*, 4:407.

making explicit the possibility of self-deception. Nobody is ever infallible in judging her or his motives, and there are cases where it really does not make sense to trust one's own judgment. But this is not a good reason to doubt in general the possibilities for self-knowledge of one's own motives. Thus I think that Kant's drastic remarks concerning self-deception are rhetorically misguided, for doubts about the secureness of knowledge need not destroy the possibility of knowledge in general.

There are cases in which I do know that my motive was vanity, even though all other people might think that it was an action done out of duty. And there are also cases where, aside from a strong feeling of respect for the moral law, I had no inclination to do the action. In these cases I can say that I know that I acted because of the categorical imperative. The knowledge is not infallible, but the indices are strong enough. There can also be cases where I do not know exactly whether I acted because of the categorical imperative or because of my inclination, but I can still know that I had the feeling of respect. If I hesitate in these cases to count them as part of my great merit, that is correct, and there is no problem in leaving this open. However, it will not completely change the picture I have of myself, for even if this action was not of moral value, I have had respect for the categorical imperative. Thus, in similar situations in which there is no positive inclination for the action, I will probably act as a result of the categorical imperative. And it is much less likely that I am wrong about having had a feeling of respect than that I am overlooking a last-minute change in my motives. We can say the same with regard to the cases Kant offers in which I think I acted due to inclinations, but in fact acted out of insight into my duty: there are probably cases that are quite clear and others that are not clear. There is no reason to question the possibility of self-knowledge on the grounds that there are unclear cases or that no case is without possibility of error. We can take the clear cases to be cases of (fallible) knowledge. Meanwhile, the fairly clear ones can tell us a lot about ourselves, and they can also help us to decide about our motives in future cases. Namely, it becomes understandable here that the examination of my character by looking at my motives can indeed help me to consider my motives in other cases where my motives are less clear. Thus, self-knowledge can play a crucial role in moral reflection even though we do not have to think of self-knowledge as particularly secure. Kant's conception of how we evaluate past actions can still be viable, even though he himself sometimes sounds as if this is not the case. Kant then stresses the danger of self-deception and the impossibility of complete self-knowledge so much that one can get the false impression that we have to deny self-knowledge in general.

Yet it also becomes clear why Kant rightly saw self-deception as posing a danger to his conception of moral philosophy. Even if the criterion can still work, it is less secure than we might wish it to be. We can think of Kant's idea concerning the highest good in the *Critique of Practical Reason* as standing in the context of these considerations. If I cannot fully trust my own judgment and if other people cannot judge my motives, then this seems to be a good reason to think of God as an authority that judges me correctly, and to take this as the yardstick for justice. In analogy to how we understand the highest good, we can also make sense of what Kant says about self-knowledge in the *Metaphysics of Morals*. In the *Groundwork*, the idea that we have a *duty* to examine ourselves does not come up. But it should be apparent by now that there is a clear motivation for this duty. Namely, we want to be able to *better* trust our own judgments about our motives. And therefore we have an interest in reducing the possibility of self-deception. This is the reason why, in the passage from the *Metaphysics of Morals*, Kant points out that self-knowledge is active: it is an active and even suspicious examination of oneself. This examination of oneself is a duty because it helps to exclude the self-deception that gets in the way of real self-knowledge. If we attain a picture of ourselves by examining rather clear cases of our motives, then we can better judge ourselves in the less clear cases. In the *Metaphysics of Morals* Kant also says that we become impartial judges as a result of this sort of self-examination in which we evaluate our motives. We can understand this now as the claim that we learn to avoid self-deception by means of improved self-knowledge. Improved self-knowledge provides us with more criteria by which to decide which motive was the relevant one. Because everyone can only judge the value of her actions herself, everyone also ought to strive to make this self-knowledge as reliable as possible. Although it is possible to know one's own motives, we also know that self-deception is a danger for this kind of self-knowledge.[15] This is where the ideal of self-knowledge becomes relevant for Kant. Self-examination is meant to lead to a situation in which I still can judge my motives only from a first-person perspective—that must be so—but as if I were impartial and therefore not very easily self-deceived.

Acknowledgments

Many thanks to Rolf-Peter Horstmann for his comments and Marcus Lampert for his careful reading. Thanks are also due to all participants of the workshop in Konstanz, and especially to Ursula Renz.

---

15 This skepticism has some parallels to what Aaron Garret pointed out about moralists in this volume. The skepticism is not without alternatives. For Hegel, Kant's mistake lies in the fact that although he is skeptical about purely inner self-knowledge, he still thinks that there is a true story to discover in the agent, and it is only hidden from the person insofar as she judges. Hegel rejects this picture in its entirety.

Reflection II

SHELLEY AND THE LIMIT OF SELF-KNOWLEDGE

Laura Quinney

For the author of any kind of fiction, the failure of self-knowledge is an irresistible subject, inherently fascinating, widely variable, and ripe for either comic or tragic exploitation. Within the literature of modern Europe, the psychology of self-deception has been plentifully examined, and has led to innovations in narrative and dramatic form, from the soliloquizing protagonists of Shakespeare to Austen heroines, shown in free indirect discourse to be subtly practicing upon themselves, and on into the unreliable narrators of modernist and postmodernist experimentation. To study such narrative explorations might seem the obvious choice for this reflection on literature and self-knowledge, but I am going to begin in a different place, with the Romantic treatment of self-consciousness and its investigation of the limit of self-knowledge. Countering the Delphic oracle, Shelley in particular asks: Is self-knowledge really effective? What can it not do?

In the meditative and autobiographical strain of their poetry, the British Romantics explore the inner drama of the subject in confrontation with itself, seeking to locate, define, and understand its own nature. Responding to their education in Lockean and Kantian epistemology, a number of these poets—Wordsworth

and Coleridge in particular—represent this as a hard struggle
with a fundamentally elusive aim. In his poem "Self-Knowledge,"
Coleridge concludes that the self cannot be known, because what is
within is merely "Dark fluxion, all unfixable by thought."[1] Shelley,
however, took "Know thyself" as "his motto," according to his
biographer Anne Wroe.[2] He invokes this injunction respectfully,
many times, in his poetry and criticism. (The goal of tragedy is to
teach "self-knowledge and self-respect."[3]) Yet, by the time he wrote
his last poem, *The Triumph of Life*, left unfinished at his early death,
he seems to have lost confidence in the project of self-knowledge.
He had reached the pessimistic conclusion, not that self-knowledge
is impossible (as Coleridge had said), but that it is inefficacious.
The fortunes of the character Rousseau exemplify the failure of
self-knowledge, and Shelley must have chosen him for this role, in
part, because like Shelley himself Rousseau had taken the Delphic
injunction as a motto.

In *The Triumph of Life*, Shelley presents a hierarchy in degrees of
self-knowledge. The anonymous masses follow the Chariot of Life
blindly:

All hastening onward, yet none seemed to know
Whither he went, or whence he came, or why
He made one of the multitude.[4]

The more distinguished captives are "The Wise, / The great, the
unforgotten," whom the narrator's guide, Rousseau, dismisses
with lofty contempt. Bishops, kings, generals, and those who wore

---

1 Samuel Taylor Coleridge, *The Major Works*, ed. H. J. Jackson (Oxford: Oxford University Press, 2009), 1.7.

2 Anne Wroe, *Being Shelley: The Poet's Search for Himself* (London: Vintage, 2008), 313.

3 Ibid., 520.

4 Percy Shelley, *Shelley's Poetry and Prose*, ed. Donald H. Reiman and Neil Fraistat, 2nd ed. (New York: Norton, 2002), ll. 47–49.

"wreaths of light / Signs of thought's empire over thought," all were
wise in an inessential way:

> their lore
>
> Taught them not this—to know themselves; their might
> Could not repress the mutiny within,
> And for the morn of truth they feigned, deep night
>
> Caught them ere evening.[5]

When he comes to describe his own defeat, Rousseau insists he was
different:

> I was overcome
> By my own heart alone, which neither age
>
> Nor tears nor infamy nor now the tomb
> Could temper to its object.[6]

While implicitly claiming he had greater self-knowledge, Rousseau
makes a strange distinction: whereas the rest were "conquered" by
Life, he was "conquered / By [his] own heart alone." Perhaps he
boasts emptily—it's open to question—yet we are also meant to
think about what this distinction might mean. In the case of "The
Wise, the great, the unforgotten," experience and thought failed
to create self-knowledge, and that failure of self-knowledge led to
a fatal "mutiny within." The word "mutiny" points to radical self-
conflict, specifically the revolt of something dormant or suppressed
in the self, which at length demands expression and precipitates an
incoherence of aims. Shelley indicates the nature and consequences
of such a "mutiny" a few lines later when, beholding Napoleon,
chief Romantic emblem of self-betrayal, chained to the car, the

5 Ibid., ll. 211–15.
6 Ibid., ll. 240–43.

narrator "grieve[s] to think how power and will / In opposition
rule our mortal day—And why God made irreconcilable / Good
and the means of good." The failure to understand one's own
motives and desires leads to outright self-deception, the perversion
of the will and, in turn, to bad faith and moral or political error.

But Shelley's Rousseau insists this was not his problem; he
contrasts himself specifically with other major figures from the
enlightenment who exemplify the treachery of the will. To be
"overcome / By [his] own heart alone" was to suffer self-conflict,
yes, but, Rousseau maintains, his self-conflict did not entail self-
deception. He remained faithful to his passion, his ideal—better
to say, his high Platonic Love—and never accepted any of the
world's poor substitutes. His legacy was a disaster, he confesses, but
the real defeat was internal. His proper passion cohabited with its
corruption, and his self-knowledge remained lucid but impotent.

He has appeared before the narrator as a grotesque figure—looking
like "an old root," with "thin discoloured hair" and "holes" that "had
been eyes." When the narrator asks him who he is, he introduces
himself as an imprisoned spirit vainly decrying its erosion:

> And if the spark with which Heaven lit my spirit
> Earth had with purer nutriment supplied
>
> Corruption would not now thus much inherit
> Of what was once Rousseau—nor this disguise
> Stain that within which still disdains to wear it.[7]

Rousseau sees what is happening to him, but cannot stop it. Time
brings on the erosion of the spirit, whatever faithfulness to Love
persists, and self-knowledge cannot counteract this failure. Love
doubles back upon itself to become self-loathing. In Napoleon and
his ilk the will was treacherous because they did not perceive its

---

7 Ibid., ll. 201–5.

changes; in their lack of self-knowledge, they did not see through its "disguise." Rousseau beheld his own deterioration, he saw his powers metastasize, and his very bitterness and outrage made him an enemy to himself. He was overcome by his own heart alone. In this model, self-conflict does not require self-deception, nor, conversely, does self-conflict yield to self-knowledge. Later in the poem, Rousseau admits that he does not, in fact, fully comprehend his origin, his purpose, and his destiny. At least, in good Socratic fashion, he knows that he does not know, but for Shelley, the distinction becomes irrelevant.

Here we reach the crucial redaction in Shelley's thought: degrees of difference in self-knowledge do not issue in significant practical effects. All are swept up alike in a momentum that forestalls deliberation, in the "hurry" of the conqueror. The conqueror is Time, our element and true adversary:

> From every form the beauty slowly waned,
>
> From every firmest limb and fairest face
> The strength and freshness fell like dust, and left
> The action and the shape without the grace
>
> Of life[8]

Shelley has incisively captured the paradox of living in time: its breathless "hurry" causes "slow" and gradual erosion. Hurtled forward, rushing toward but never reaching the clear summit of reflection, Rousseau is meanwhile, moment by moment, being sapped by the precipitation itself; eventually it takes its toll. Self-knowledge turns out to be a weak instrument with which to contend against time: in fact self-knowledge may be the origin of our experience of the temporality that precludes its fulfillment.

---

8 Ibid., ll. 519–23.

Self-awareness never catches up because consciousness itself dawns only belatedly, and reflection, dispersed over the moments, cannot gather itself into a force. Thus, Rousseau awakens in bewilderment in the "oblivious valley," and he cannot summon his "spirit" to combat his erosion. His experience of temporal momentum allows him only to identify and experience the failure of self-coincidence.

Post-Cartesian literature can—and likes to—tell this story. I say "post-Cartesian" because the literature of selfhood booms after Descartes, and I say "literature," as opposed to philosophy, because literature is, sometimes, a storytelling mode. Many works of literature portray willful self-deception, but some concentrate on the way in which temporality, aided by self-deception, inhibits the development of self-knowledge. Events occur too rapidly for understanding to catch up with them; understanding what you were about or felt comes too late; different ages bring different, partial forms of understanding that do not accumulate into clarity; memory is misleading; experience fails to teach. Any number of nineteenth- and twentieth-century authors depict self-knowledge falling beneath the confounding or corrosive effects of time: Tennyson in "Ulysses," Eliot in *Middlemarch*; Dostoevsky in *The Brothers Karamasov*, Chekhov in *The Three Sisters*; Woolf in *To the Lighthouse*; Roth in *Sabbath's Theater*; Ashbery in "Self-Portrait in a Convex Mirror"; Proust, *passim*. Delayed recognition is a characteristic theme for Henry James; in *The Aspern Papers*, for example, the narrator realizes too late that he loves the woman he has rejected. Beckett, in turn, fixes on the way that temporality limits us to fragmentary self-knowledge: in *Krapp's Last Tape*, also a story of lost love, Krapp listens to the accounts of himself that he has given over the years, each benighted with respect to the other, but all involved in his folly, while *Waiting for Godot* renders perfectly what it is be lost in time. In *The Triumph of Life*, Shelley gives form to a common intuition: something in the psyche interferes with the goal of self-knowledge, but so does something in the temporal structure of self-knowledge, with the result that its means and its end are irreconcilable.

CHAPTER ELEVEN

Self-Knowledge in Kierkegaard

John Lippitt

Throughout his authorship, Kierkegaard shows an intense fascination with Socrates and Socratic self-knowledge. This chapter will trace, in roughly chronological order, (1) the young Kierkegaard's autobiographical reflections on self-knowledge, when first coming to understand his task as an author; (2) Socrates as a negative figure in *The Concept of Irony*—where self-knowledge is understood in terms of separation from others and the surrounding society—and the contrast with the *Concluding Unscientific Postscript*'s treatment of Socrates as an exemplary "subjective thinker"; (3) in *Either/Or*, the connection between self-knowledge and self-transparency, and the link between self-knowledge and "choosing oneself," understood as willing receptivity; (4) in writings such as *The Concept of Anxiety* and *The Sickness unto Death*, the importance of sin and our utter dependence upon God for the question of whether self-knowledge is ever really possible; and (5) in

Judge for Yourself! and related journal entries, a more precise specification of what Christian self-knowledge might amount to. I shall show that, in his account of self-knowledge as much as elsewhere, treatments of Kierkegaard as a proto-existentialist risk misleadingly downplaying the deeply and explicitly Christian nature of his thought.

11.1. YOUTHFUL REFLECTIONS

Kierkegaard raises the importance of "knowing oneself" very early on. In a letter to a student friend written at the age of twenty-two, he admits that he has enjoyed the limelight and attention of fellow students when in Copenhagen, something he considered a weakness in himself. He admires the "strength" of those fish able to remain in the depths of the sea out of view, rather than feeling the need, like the sunfish, "to display one's silvery light on the surface."[1] He reports that his summer trip to the small northern village of Gilleleje (from which the letter is written) is enabling him "to focus upon my inner self, it spurs me on to comprehend myself, my own self, to hold it fast in the infinite variety of life, to direct towards myself that concave mirror with which I have attempted until now to comprehend life around me."[2] Socratic inwardness is starting to bite. A month later, still in Gilleleje, Kierkegaard wrote one of his most famous journal entries, which is about self-knowledge in the sense of finding "*the idea for which I am willing to live and die.*"[3] This entry is often cited (somewhat misleadingly) as one of the founding texts of existentialism. It indirectly introduces tropes, such as "truth as subjectivity," that will later feature so strongly in some of the best-known (and most commonly

---

1 Letter to P. E. Lind, 6 July 1835. Søren Kierkegaard, *Letters and Documents* (*LD*), trans. Henrik Rosenmeier (Princeton, NJ: Princeton University Press, 1978), 48.

3 Søren Kierkegaard, *Søren Kierkegaards Skrifter* (*SKS*), vol. 17, ed. Niels Jørgen Cappelørn et al. (Copenhagen: Gad, 1997–2013), AA:12; Søren Kierkegaard, *Kierkegaard's Journals and Notebooks* (*KJN*), vol. 1, ed. Niels Jørgen Cappelørn et al. (Princeton, NJ: Princeton University Press, 2007–), AA:12.

misunderstood) aspects of Kierkegaard's authorship. Here the young Kierkegaard downgrades the importance of any theorizing in which the subject is not himself passionately engaged.[4] It is in this sense that we should understand his assertion that "one must first learn to know oneself before knowing anything else. Only when the person has inwardly understood *himself*, and then seen the way forward on his path, does his life acquire repose and meaning."[5]

11.2. SOCRATES AND SELF-KNOWLEDGE IN *THE CONCEPT OF IRONY*—AND LATER

Few readers of Kierkegaard could fail to notice his admiration for Socrates, the "wise old man of antiquity," as he tends to call him. In the pseudonym Johannes Climacus' *Concluding Unscientific Postscript* (1846), Socrates is presented as an exemplar not only of "indirect communication" but also of the valorized figure labeled the "subjective thinker." Socrates' approach to self-knowledge is key here, in that Climacus focuses on how Socrates "was occupied solely with himself."[6] What he means by this can be seen in Socrates' discussion of whether the soul is immortal: what impresses Climacus is that Socrates "stakes his whole life on this 'if' ";[7] he is continually concerned with making the abstract question of whether the soul is immortal concrete ("the relation of the existing person, in his very existence, to what is said").[8] But there are important shifts in the views of Socrates presented in different parts of the Kierkegaard corpus, and the concomitant relation to the question of self-knowledge.

---

4 "And what use would it be . . . if I were to discover a so-called objective truth, or if I worked my way through the philosophers' systems and were able to call them all to account on request, point out inconsistencies in every single circle? . . . What use would it be to be able to propound the meaning of Christianity . . . if it had no deeper meaning *for myself* and *my life*?" (*KJN*, 1:AA:12; *SKS*, 17:AA:12).

5 *KJN*, 1:AA:12; *SKS*, 17:AA:12.

6 Søren Kierkegaard, *Concluding Unscientific Postscript* (*CUP*), trans. Howard V. Hong and Edna H. Hong (Princeton, NJ: Princeton University Press, 1992), 147n; SKS, 7:137n.

7 *CUP*, 201; *SKS*, 7:185.

8 *CUP*, 202–3; *SKS*, 7:185–86.

In his postgraduate dissertation *The Concept of Irony* (1841), Kierkegaard notes how customary it is to characterize Socrates' position with "the well-known phrase" "Know thyself."[9] But his position in that text is that Socrates is a purely *negative* figure. Kierkegaard complains that the phrase "Know thyself" is "often torn completely out of the complex of ideas to which it belongs and for some time now has been vagabonding in literature unchallenged."[10] Rather than the phrase being about "subjectivity in its fullness, inwardness in its utterly infinite wealth," for Socrates it has a starker meaning: "Separate yourself from the other."[11] This connects with Kierkegaard's ostensibly audacious claim that the self did not exist prior to Socrates.[12] How so?

First, on the question of Socrates' private daemon, Kierkegaard sides with Plato's view that the daemon only warns Socrates *against* doing certain things, as opposed to Xenophon's view that the daemon also urged him to *positive* actions. Ultimately Socrates' negativity inheres in his characteristic irony ("infinite absolute negativity," to borrow Hegel's phrase). Socrates is a figure who justifiably uses his chief weapon— irony—against both the unreflective acceptance of conservative morality and the Sophists' trickery. But from the state's perspective, this is as dangerous as his trial judged it to be; Socrates is a negative figure who has turned away from his society's traditional beliefs and values. In his discussion of Hegel's view of Socrates, Kierkegaard associates "knowing oneself" precisely with having taken oneself out of the "substantial ethic" of the surrounding Greek culture.[13] And this is contagious: as a

---

9 Kierkegaard returns numerous times to passage 229c–30a in Plato's *Phaedrus*: see for instance *Fear and Trembling and Repetition*, trans. Howard V. and Edna H. Hong (Princeton, NJ: Princeton University Press, 1983), 100n, 162–63; SKS, 4:190n, 37 and *Philosophical Fragments*, trans. Howard V. and Edna H. Hong (Princeton, NJ: Princeton University Press, 1985), 39, 47; SKS, 4:244, 251–52.

10 Søren Kierkegaard, *The Concept of Irony* (*CI*), trans. Howard V. Hong and Edna H. Hong (Princeton, NJ: Princeton University Press, 1989), 177; *SKS*, 1:224.

11 *CI*, 177; *SKS*, 1:224.

12 *CI*, 177; *SKS*, 1:224.

13 *CI*, 228; *SKS*, 1:270.

result of Socratic questioning, each individual becomes alienated from others and the wider society, and simply left to find the truth within himself.

So the claim that the self does not exist prior to Socrates refers to a radical dependence of each individual upon himself. But also relevant here is Reidar Thomte's suggestion that Kierkegaard's method in *The Concept of Anxiety* (1844)—"keyed to the principle *unum noris omnes*" (If you know one, you know all)—expresses "the same as the Socratic 'know yourself.'" As Thomte glosses this, "Every human being possesses, or is within himself, a complete expression of humanness, whose essential meaning cannot be gained from scientific studies."[14] What is common to all human beings is available to each of us through self-reflection—but not of a purely abstract kind. The view is that neither speculative philosophy nor natural science can disclose to me my essential nature. Rather, "Self-knowledge is attained by man in existing; that is, self-knowledge is coordinate with the actualizing of one's potentiality to become oneself."[15] Perhaps, among other things, this betokens a shift from the early view of Socrates as pure negativity to what has seemed to several commentators as a significantly different Socrates in the Climacus writings (*Fragments* and *Postscript*), in which, as Paul Muench puts it, Socrates' ethically engaged "philosophical activity is not a mere precursor to something else but [is] itself the human ideal (the best ethical and religious life available outside of Christianity)."[16]

---

14 Reidar Thomte, "Historical Introduction," in *The Concept of Anxiety*, trans. Reidar Thomte (Princeton, NJ: Princeton University Press, 1980), xv.

15 Ibid.

16 Paul Muench, "Kierkegaard's Socratic Point of View," in *Kierkegaard Research: Sources, Reception and Resources*, vol. 2, *Kierkegaard and the Greek World*, tome 1: *Socrates and Plato*, ed. Jon Stewart and Katalin Nun (London: Ashgate, 2010), 18–19; cf. John Lippitt, *Humour and Irony in Kierkegaard's Thought* (Basingstoke: Palgrave, 2000).

11.3. SELF-KNOWLEDGE AND SELF-TRANSPARENCY

Another theme worth noting in *The Concept of Irony* is Kierkegaard's view of what "living poetically" truly means. Against the Romantics, Kierkegaard stresses being "absolutely transparent to [one]self." He claims: "Living poetically is not the same as being in the dark about oneself . . . but it means becoming *clear and transparent* to oneself, not in finite and egotistical self-satisfaction but in one's absolute and eternal validity."[17]

Both self-transparency and grasping oneself in one's "eternal validity" are significant themes in his first major post-dissertation work, *Either/Or* (1843). In his second letter to the aesthete "A" in the second part of that work, the ethicist Judge William asserts that "to become conscious in one's eternal validity is a moment that is more significant than everything else in the world."[18] This is what it means to recognize what one is and is meant to be ("before God"); precisely that which A is trying to hide from himself. Grasping oneself in one's "eternal validity" is presented as being the way in which one can unify the temporal and eternal aspects of the self, and possibility and necessity.[19] Choosing oneself "in freedom" (possibility and particularity) and yet "in repentance" requires one continually to realize this freedom in action: "He who has chosen himself on this basis is *eo ipso* one who acts."[20]

In that same letter, the judge presents self-knowledge as key to the difference between the "aesthetic" and "ethical" modes of life. The ethical individual's being transparent to himself "encompasses everything":

---

17 *CI*, 298; *SKS*, 1:332 (my emphasis).

18 Søren Kierkegaard, *Either/Or* (*EO*), vol. 2, trans. Howard V. Hong and Edna H. Hong (Princeton, NJ: Princeton University Press, 1987), 206; *SKS*, 3:198.

19 *EO*, 2:231–22; *SKS*, 3:221–22. Compare here the 1840 journal entry in which Kierkegaard glosses "eternal validity" in terms of both my "divine necessity" and my "accidental finitude" (being born as a specific individual in a particular land at a particular time). *Søren Kierkegaard's Journals and Papers* (*JP*), vol. 2, ed. and trans. Howard V. Hong and Edna H. Hong (Bloomington: Indiana University Press, 1967–78), 1587 (Pap. III A 1).

20 *EO*, 2:232; *SKS*, 3:222.

The person who lives ethically has seen himself, knows himself, penetrates his whole concretion with his consciousness, does not allow vague thoughts to rustle around inside him or let tempting possibilities distract him with their juggling; he is not like a "magic" picture that shifts from one thing to another, all depending upon how one shifts and turns it. He knows himself. The phrase know yourself is a stock phrase, and in it has been perceived the goal of all a person's striving. And this is entirely proper, but yet it is just as certain that it cannot be the goal if it is not also the beginning. The ethical individual knows himself, but this knowing is not simply contemplation, for then the individual comes to be defined according to his necessity. It is a collecting of oneself, which itself is an action, and this is why I have with aforethought used the expression "to choose oneself" instead of "to know oneself."[21]

So what matters most about self-knowledge is that it is a crucial precursor to the development of an "authentic" individual. But it is important to note here that by "choosing oneself" Judge William has in mind something very different from radical choice à la Sartre. Elsewhere he qualifies this by replacing talk of "choosing" oneself with "receiving" oneself[22]—that is, willing receptivity; recognizing what are, and are not, serious possibilities for you. Here the active striving will is complemented—indeed, to some extent replaced—by a more passive recognition of value that breaks through, requiring our acknowledgment.[23] In working out the implications of this, there is an important interplay between possibility and necessity, and between first- and third-person perspectives that we shall need to explore in more detail.

---

21 *EO*, 2:258; *SKS*, 3:246.

22 *EO*, 2:17; *SKS*, 3:172.

23 Edward F. Mooney, *Selves in Discord and Resolve* (New York: Routledge, 1996), 17–19, talks here of *willingness* rather than *willfulness*.

11.4. SELF-KNOWLEDGE: FIRST OR THIRD PERSONAL? THE PROBLEM OF SIN AND DEPENDENCE UPON GOD

Is "Socratic" self-knowledge essentially first personal, or does third-personal knowledge of human properties also count? I shall argue that for Kierkegaard, we need both: despite his association with slogans such as "Truth is subjectivity," it is not just the former. Later, I shall suggest how he tries to hold both together, in such a way that there is also a crucial second-person aspect in how we are to relate to God.

Kierkegaard tackles this question obliquely in *The Concept of Anxiety*. His pseudonym Vigilius Haufniensis criticizes the "German" view of self-knowledge as being about "pure self-consciousness, the airiness of idealism."[24] The target here is typically taken to be Danish Hegelians who had imported Hegel's idea that self-knowledge is not about my particular character, capacities, flaws, and so on, but rather universal knowledge of spirit as it expresses itself in human history and the state.[25] For Kierkegaard, self-knowledge cannot be *only* a third-personal matter, and we might see the portrayal of A in *Either/Or* as a critique of the attempt to take a disinterested, purely third-personal stance toward oneself.[26] Haufniensis adds: "It is about time to seek to understand it [self-knowledge] in the Greek way, and then again as the Greeks would have understood it if they had possessed Christian presuppositions."[27] The chief such presupposition appears to be sin, the topic that frames Kierkegaard's discussion of anxiety. We'll shortly see in more detail the importance of sin—and its forgiveness—for Kierkegaard's view of self-knowledge.

All this takes us beyond the "ethical" stage to the "religious." In this territory, Kierkegaard puts a greater emphasis on our ultimate

---

24 *CA*, 79; *SKS*, 4:382.

25 See the editorial note at *CA*, 240.

26 Cf. Daniel Watts, "Kierkegaard and the Search for Self-Knowledge," *European Journal of Philosophy* 21.4 (2013): 530.

27 CA, 79; SKS, 4:382.

dependence upon the mercy of God, insisting that full self-knowledge is not possible. In *Christian Discourses* (1848), he asks:

> Alas, who does know himself? Is it not exactly this to which the earnest and honest self-examination finally leads as its last and truest, this humble confession: "Who knows his errors? From my hidden faults cleanse thou me" (Psalms 19: 12). And when a person examines his relation to Christ, who then is the human being who completely knows his faithlessness, who the human being who would dare to think that in his very self-examination there could not be faithlessness? Therefore you do not find rest this way. So, then, rest; then seek rest for your soul in the blessed comfort that, even if we are faithless, he still is faithful.[28]

Elsewhere, however, our "absolute need of God" is presented as a prerequisite for self-knowledge (or whatever self-knowledge we may have).[29] We might relate this emphasis on God-dependence to the famous formula of *The Sickness unto Death* (1848), Kierkegaard's major discussion of despair: "The formula that describes the condition of the self when despair is completely rooted out is this: *in relating itself to itself and in willing to be itself, the self rests transparently in the power that established it.*"[30] This "resting transparently" is a manifestation of self-knowledge insofar as the self knows what it owes to God, but experiences this not as guilt and debt but gratitude for the forgiveness of sins.[31] Here we start to see the importance of a second-person relationship with God, or "God-relationship."

---

28 Søren Kierkegaard, *Christian Discourses*, trans. Howard V. Hong and Edna H. Hong (Princeton, NJ: Princeton University Press, 1987), 287–88; *SKS*, 10:308.

29 *JP*, 1:53 (Pap. V B 196).

30 Søren Kierkegaard, *The Sickness unto Death (SUD)*, trans. Howard V. Hong and Edna H. Hong (Princeton, NJ: Princeton University Press, 1980), 14; *SKS*, 11:130 (my emphasis).

31 *Sickness* describes the forgiveness of sins as the crucial difference between Christianity and paganism (*SUD*, 117; *SKS*, 11:228).

Sickness is indeed a text that highlights the difficulty of self-knowledge. The varieties of despair that the author Anti-Climacus portrays are often forms of self-deception in which we willfully resist the self-transparency Judge William emphasized. Anti-Climacus makes the striking claim that despair is a *universal* human phenomenon.[32] He anticipates that this claim is likely to seem overblown, and suggests that the reason for this is our tendency to overlook that "not being conscious of being in despair, is precisely a form of despair."[33] Just as the physician knows that there can be purely imaginary forms of health as well as of sickness, so the "physician of the soul" recognizes this is also true of spiritual ill-health. In other words, many of us are in despair without realizing it. It is thus precisely a failure of self-knowledge that can hide from me what I most need to grasp.

Sickness also highlights the important link between self-knowledge and knowledge in the abstract. Sometimes Kierkegaard seems to hold that knowledge per se is only of instrumental value; what really matters is what Climacus, in the *Postscript*, calls "essential" (that is, ethical and religious) knowledge: "essential" in its value for the task of living.[34] It is also in this mode—its connection with living ethically and religiously—that self-knowledge is considered indispensable in passages such as that slightly later in *Sickness*, where knowing is presented in its "fantastic" mode. Some background is necessary here. Anti-Climacus defines the fantastic (*Det Phantastiske*) as follows:

> The fantastic is generally that which leads a person out into the infinite in such a way that it only leads him away from himself and thereby prevents him from coming back to himself.[35]

---

32 *SUD*, 22–28; *SKS*, 11:138–44.

33 *SUD*, 23; *SKS*, 11:139.

34 In this sense, for Kierkegaard, ethical and religious knowledge has a particular claim to be called self-knowledge (cf. Watts, "Self-Knowledge," 538).

35 *SUD*, 31; *SKS*, 11:147.

Anti-Climacus then briefly illustrates this through three such forms of the fantastic—feeling, knowing, and willing—through each of which the self becomes weakened or "volatilized" (*forflygtiges*) and thus "lost." *Fantastic feeling* replaces a genuine concern for a concrete other with "a kind of abstract sentimentality that inhumanly belongs to no human being."[36] Fantastic willing fails to ally its lofty ambitions with the small part of its grand task that can be accomplished "this very day, this very hour, this very moment."[37] What then of fantastic knowing? Here Anti-Climacus claims:

> The law for the development of the self with respect to knowing, insofar as it is the case that the self becomes itself, is that the increase of knowledge corresponds to the increase of self-knowledge, that the more the self knows, the more it knows itself. If this does not happen, the more knowledge increases, the more it becomes a kind of inhuman knowledge, in the obtaining of which a person's self is squandered, much the way men were squandered on building pyramids.[38]

In other words, Anti-Climacus is warning against the valorization of knowledge abstracted from the concrete concerns of living that Kierkegaard often associates with speculative philosophy. Down that route lies a kind of comical self-forgetfulness to which Kierkegaard seems to think the intellectual is particularly prone. Behind his various satires about losing oneself is a familiar question. What shall it profit a man, he effectively asks, if he shall gain the whole world— of knowledge—and yet lose his own soul?[39] Here as elsewhere,

---

36 *SUD*, 31; *SKS*, 11:147.

37 *SUD*, 32; *SKS*, 11:148.

38 *SUD*, 31; *SKS*, 11:147.

39 Cf. Mark 8:36. I discuss the philosophical purpose of some of the *Postscript*'s satire in Lippitt, *Humour and Irony*, especially chapter 2.

Kierkegaard privileges "essential" knowledge. A major concern in *Sickness* is the loss of the self in abstraction that Anti-Climacus considers to be a variety of despair.[40] Yet such a loss of the self—or failure to rise to the task of *becoming* a self—is presented there as entirely normal:

> A self is the last thing the world cares about and the most dangerous thing of all for a person to show signs of having. The greatest hazard of all, losing the self, can occur very quietly in the world, as if it were nothing at all. No other loss can occur so quietly; any other loss—an arm, a leg, five dollars, a wife, etc.—is sure to be noticed.[41]

Passages such as this have been used in support of reading Kierkegaard as a proto-existentialist, concerned about the inauthenticity of *das Man* (Kierkegaard's roughly equivalent term for which is the "public").[42] And yet there is a specifically Christian dimension to this, as we shall shortly see.

Anti-Climacus briefly returns to the question of self-knowledge a little later, in the guise of the importance of having (in an echo of the judge) "clarity about oneself."[43] He defers to later discussion an important question, namely whether it is possible simultaneously to have such self-clarity and yet still be in despair. In doing so, he also defers discussion of the possibility that such clarity of self-knowledge might "simply wrench a person out of despair, make him so afraid of himself that he would stop being in despair."[44] In other words, could self-knowledge be a *cure* for despair? Frustratingly, this refers to a section D, contemplated but never written.[45] But we can get some idea of

---

40 *SUD*, 32; *SKS*, 11:148.

41 *SUD*, 32–33; *SKS*, 11:148.

42 See especially Søren Kierkegaard, *Two Ages*, trans. Howard V. Hong and Edna H. Hong (Princeton, NJ: Princeton University Press, 1978), 90–96; *SKS*, 8:86–91.

43 *SUD*, 47; *SKS*, 11:162.

44 *SUD*, 47; *SKS*, 11:162.

45 See the supplement to *SUD*, 177 n. 53.

what Kierkegaard's answer to this question would likely have been in two ways. First, a little later, echoing Kierkegaard's view in *Christian Discourses*, Anti-Climacus hints that a fully realized ideal of self-knowledge is not possible for us. Rather, we are typically dimly aware of being in despair in much the same way as is the person with a physical illness who "does not want to acknowledge forthrightly the real nature of the illness."[46] Second, he presents the opposite of despair as being not self-knowledge but *faith*, in line with the argument of the second part of the book, that despair is *sin*, for which faith is the only cure.

11.5. Self-Knowledge "before God"—and Action

These themes are continued in *Judge for Yourself!* (1851), where Kierkegaard offers a more precise specification of what *Christian* self-knowledge amounts to. In the first section, Kierkegaard defines "becoming sober" thus: '*to come to oneself in self-knowledge and before God as nothing before him, yet infinitely, unconditionally engaged*.'[47]

Christianity and the "purely human point of view" can agree that self-ignorance and self-misunderstanding are like forms of intoxication.[48] But they *disagree* on what it means "to come to oneself in *self-knowledge*."[49] Kierkegaard compares the "objective knowing" at which speculative philosophy aims to spiritual dizziness. As in the *Postscript*, objective knowing is presented as occasioning a self-forgetfulness that is the very opposite of the self-knowledge that sobriety requires.

For Kierkegaard, only the self-knowledge that leads to knowing oneself "before God" is self-knowledge of the right sort. Extending the earlier references to self-transparency, the claim is now explicitly

---

46 *SUD*, 48; *SKS*, 11, 163.

47 Søren Kierkegaard, *Judge for Yourself!* (*JY*), trans. Howard V. Hong and Edna H. Hong (Princeton, NJ: Princeton University Press, 1987), 104; *SKS*, 16:160.

48 *JY*, 104; *SKS*, 16:161.

49 *JY*, 104; *SKS*, 16:161.

that the transparency of sobriety is only possible before God. In the same way as the expert lash of the royal coachman brings his horse up short, forcing a realization of who is boss, so God, without whom I am nothing, brings home to me "the unconditioned" (*det Ubetingede*)— and this realization is what makes me sober.[50] In this condition, one comes to oneself "as nothing," and realizes one's absolute dependence upon God.[51]

Is this paralyzing? No, apparently, because although one becomes "as nothing," one does so in a way that is "infinitely, unconditionally engaged,"[52] such that "all one's understanding becomes action."[53] As Kierkegaard is famous for saying, life must be lived forwards. To *do* what one understands is an effort, and so we tend to focus all our attention on understanding or knowing, pretending that this is where the difficulty lies. This is precisely the ethico-religious evasion about which Kierkegaard so often warns. But whereas mere knowing can leave one's life untouched,[54] "My action changes my life,"[55] and "the truly simple exposition of Christianity is—to do it,"[56] and "immediately."[57] This is true sobriety.

An associated journal entry from 1851 gives one of Kierkegaard's clearest statements on how he understands the ideal of self-knowledge.

---

50 *JY*, 107–9; *SKS*, 16:163–65.

51 In their introduction to their collection of Kierkegaard's writings from the last two years of his life, the Hongs suggest that ultimately for Kierkegaard "Self-knowledge comes through imitating [Christ], and spiritual progress becomes retrogression in the light of the ideal requirement" (Howard V. Hong and Edna H. Hong, "Historical Introduction," in Søren Kierkegaard, *The Moment and Late Writings*, trans. Howard V. Hong and Edna H. Hong [Princeton, NJ: Princeton University Press 1998], M xii.). This is in line with the idea expressed as early as the sermon at the end of *Either/Or*, that in relation to God we are always "in the wrong." But it means, controversially, that there is a kind of self-knowledge that is only available to the Christian.

52 *JY*, 106; *SKS*, 16:160.

53 *JY*, 115; *SKS*, 16:170.

54 I assume the warning here is about "fantastic" knowing, as discussed above.

55 *JY*, 116; *SKS*, 16:171.

56 *JY*, 116; *SKS*, 16:171.

57 *JY*, 120; *SKS*, 16:175.

The topic is "What is Required in Order to Look at Oneself with True Blessing in the Mirror of the Word."[58] Here he suggests that a certain degree of self-knowledge is necessary in order for the self-recognition here discussed to be possible at all. But in what follows, the above claims are crystallized in a particularly succinct way:

> Paganism required: Know yourself. Christianity declares: No, that is provisional—know yourself—and then look at yourself in the Mirror of the Word in order to know yourself properly. No true self-knowledge without God-knowledge or [without standing] before God. To stand before the Mirror means to stand before God.[59]

Only "before God" can I truly see myself—the mirror provides a continual "Thou art the man"[60]—and any self-knowledge that falls short of this revelation is a "fraud."[61]

To clarify: the primary meaning of "the Word" here means *scripture* (not God qua Logos),[62] while "God knowledge" means not "objective" third-person knowledge of the divine, but an essentially two-way second-person "God-relationship" in which God loves his creatures, who in turn stand "before God" in faith. The focus is more on "knowing God" in a *relational* sense than on knowing *about* God.

---

58 *JP*, 4, 3902 (Pap. X4 A 412). For an insightful study of Kierkegaard's use of mirror imagery, see Patrick Stokes, *Kierkegaard's Mirrors* (Basingstoke: Palgrave, 2010).

59 *JP*, 4:3902 (Pap. X4 A 412).

60 *JY*, 35–40; *SKS*, 13:62–66.

61 *JP*, 4:3902 (Pap. X4 A 412). However, Kierkegaard thinks the recognition one can find in the Mirror of the Word is already there in embryonic form in Socrates. In his later writings on the Greek thinker, Kierkegaard takes Socrates to draw a key distinction between human and divine wisdom, and "to ground claims of human wisdom in an individual's ability to remain aware of that distinction" (Muench, "Kierkegaard's Socratic," 20). Thus he claims: "Socrates' ignorance was a kind of fear and worship of God, . . . the Greek version of the Jewish saying: The fear of the Lord is the beginning of wisdom" (*SUD*, 99; *SKS*, 11:211).

62 See especially *JY*, 25; *SKS*, 13:53–54. Kierkegaard's discourse on this topic (*JY*, 7–51; *SKS*, 13:39–76) is a reflection on James 1:22–27, which is about putting one's faith into action.

We should also note how Kierkegaard cashes out the need for this ruthless self-examination. Although he concludes the journal entry by emphasizing the importance of "an implacable hatred for the self that the mirror shows as being that to which one should die,"[63] we should not miss the preceding passage, in which two kinds of error are stressed. In wanting only the truth, one should "neither vainly wish to be flattered nor self-tormentingly want to be made a pure devil." This second error is just as important as the first: for all his focus on sin, Kierkegaard is at least as concerned with the *forgiveness* of sins and its link to self-forgiveness,[64] a topic with which he wrestled, on a deeply personal level, for most of his life. That the God before whom we stand is a God of love who forgives our sins is for Kierkegaard the ultimate good news. There is a dialectic at work in self-knowledge analogous to that in self-love, Kierkegaard being concerned to tease out the difference between proper and improper forms of the latter. Just as I must come in a certain sense to hate myself in order to be able to love the version of myself I *should* love, so I need to recognize the limits of what I can naturally know about myself in order that true self-knowledge may (at least to an extent) be possible: by looking at myself in the Mirror of the Word.

This allows us finally to return to the question of whether we should understand self-knowledge in first- or third-personal terms—and how this also involves a second-person element. We are now better placed to see how Kierkegaard is trying to combine these factors.[65] While rejecting the third person ("German") view, it is misleading to see him as committed to the single, isolated subject being the sole defining locus of selfhood. There are plenty of instances where Kierkegaard *sounds* like he has signed up to this picture (not least in the slogan

---

63 *JP*, 4:3902 (Pap. X4 A 412).

64 See John Lippitt, *Kierkegaard and the Problem of Self-Love* (Cambridge: Cambridge University Press, 2013), ch. 8.

65 See also Watts, "Self-Knowledge."

"Truth is subjectivity"), but it is now increasingly recognized that he intends for this to serve as a corrective to a *misapplied* objectivity of the kind associated with speculative philosophy: a rescuing of the particular from the universal; of individual being from thought.[66] The subjective thinker's task is to understand himself—including (though not limited to) the sheer givenness of such "universal" aspects as his creatureliness—in his concrete, particular existence. "No true self-knowledge without God-knowledge": the journal passage is one of many in which Kierkegaard seeks to combine first-, second-, and third-personal aspects as outlined above. This is, then, also how we should understand his remark that self-knowledge should be understood "in the Greek way, and then again as the Greeks would have understood it if they had possessed Christian presuppositions."[67] As we have seen, the concept the Greeks lacked is sin. I need to understand sin as an objective property in which all humanity is implicated,[68] but to relate to this on a first-person, subjective level as something that applies *to me*. Standing "before God" (in second-person relation) is what brings this home. The focus on the phenomenology of feelings and moods that Kierkegaard undertakes in his works on anxiety and despair highlights this subjective dimension (and there is a lengthy discussion of "subjective anxiety"), but these are meant to be universal claims about the human condition.[69] One of the uses of anxiety, it emerges in the final chapter of *The Concept of Anxiety*, is the insight it gives us into our own guilt. Haufniensis' claim that "if a man is guilty, he is infinitely guilty"[70] means that no guilty person can make himself once again

---

66 See *CA*, 78n; *SKS*, 4:381.

67 *CA*, 79; *SKS*, 4:382.

68 See Gregory R. Beabout, *Freedom and Its Misuses: Kierkegaard on Anxiety and Despair* (Milwaukee: Marquette University Press, 1996), 53–54.

69 Early on, Haufniensis distinguishes between "dogmatics" and "psychology" and claims to be engaged in the latter. But Beabout plausibly suggests that what he means by "psychology" is closer to philosophical anthropology: he is concerned with the "study, description and explanation" of what is essential to being human (ibid., 36).

70 *CA*, 161; *SKS*, 4:460.

innocent. What this highlights is the need for an external forgiver of sins: the ability to forgive sins is a "chasmal qualitative abyss" between God and man.[71] I need to know—third-personally—that sins can be forgiven, but also to grasp—first-personally—that this applies *to me*. As Kierkegaard seems to have experienced firsthand, this move is far from automatic, but—he thinks—it is a gift of grace.[72] Ultimately, then, from Kierkegaard's Christian point of view, a key part of self-knowledge is to experience myself as a sinner whose sins have been forgiven. What Climacus would call "old-fashioned orthodoxy" is for Kierkegaard both the deepest form of self-knowledge and the most valuable gift of grace.

---

71 *SUD*, 122; *SKS*, 11:233.

72 Indeed, he claims that only God can grant not only forgiveness, but the condition that enables the believer to believe in it (Søren Kierkegaard, *Works of Love*, trans. Howard V. and Edna H. Hong [Princeton, NJ: Princeton University Press, 1995], 379–80; *SKS*, 9:372–73).

CHAPTER TWELVE

Self-Knowledge as Freedom in Schopenhauer and Freud

Bernard Reginster

12.1. THE ELUSIVENESS AND SIGNIFICANCE OF SELF-KNOWLEDGE

I propose to examine together the views on self-knowledge developed by Schopenhauer and Freud because they display some broad, if superficial, similarities. They both reject the Cartesian notion that self-knowledge—specifically, the knowledge of one's own mental states—is immediate and indubitable. The existence of mental states of which their subject remains unconscious is a Freudian commonplace, but Schopenhauer already notes the difficulty of knowing oneself: "The intellect remains so much excluded from the real resolutions and secret decisions of its own will that sometimes it can only get to know them, like those of a stranger, by spying out and taking unawares."[1]

---

1 Arthur Schopenhauer, *The World as Will and Representation*, trans. E. F. J. Payne, 2 vols. (New York: Dover Publications, 1969), 2:xix, 209. Hereafter cited as *WWR*. Cf. *Arthur Schopenhauer's*

Self-knowledge therefore represents a genuine achievement, which requires a commitment of time and effort.

At the same time, these philosophers accept the broadly Socratic idea that self-knowledge is an ethical imperative, insofar as it is necessary to achieve a desirable existential state, which they both describe as a kind of freedom. The notion that self-knowledge is a necessary condition of freedom is also commonplace: by making me aware of the existence of forces operating within me, it gives me the opportunity to control their influence. In contrast with this commonplace, Schopenhauer and Freud both argue that self-knowledge is not just a necessary means for achieving freedom, but also in some sense *constitutive* of it. To know oneself is already, in a sense, to *be* free. Finally, both take self-knowledge to be constitutive of freedom only if it is *living* self-knowledge.

12.2. SCHOPENHAUER, SELF-KNOWLEDGE, AND DELIVERANCE

Asking what we mean when we call a thing "good," Schopenhauer answers that "we call everything good that is just as we want it to be."[2] A thing is good by virtue of satisfying some desire. We gain a deeper understanding of what it is for a thing to be good by examining what satisfying desires actually does. Schopenhauer denies that anything in the world has intrinsic value. The satisfaction of our desires can therefore not acquaint us with the intrinsic worth of their objects. We might then suppose that such satisfaction is a source of *pleasure*. But pleasure, in Schopenhauer's view, is nothing more than the experience of the

---

sämtliche Werke (Munich: R. Piper Verlag, 1911–42), 2:235. Hereafter cited as *GW*. All references to Schopenhauer's work are to the English translations of particular works (sections or chapters and pages) and to the relevant volume and page of the original German edition.

2 *WWR*, 1:360, sec. 65. Cf. *GW*, 1:427.

removal or absence of pain, of which the arousal of desire is either a cause or a consequence. Satisfaction thus amounts to the "quieting" of desires and the production of "peace of mind."

Happiness, understood as *fulfillment* (a condition that satisfies all our desires once and for all), is therefore regarded as the "highest good" not because it constitutes the secured possession of intrinsically good objects, but because it brings peace of mind. Schopenhauer's famous pessimism is the claim that happiness so conceived is impossible: "Everything in life proclaims that happiness on earth is destined to be frustrated or recognized as an illusion. The grounds for this lie deep in the very nature of things."[3] The knowledge required to grasp this fact is, in large part, self-knowledge.

Self-knowledge comes in different varieties. Sometimes it designates knowledge of *one's own self or nature*, and sometimes it designates knowledge of *one's own mental states*. Schopenhauer has the first in mind when he argues that we know our own self as *will*: "Thus the known within us as such is not the knower, but the willer, the subject of willing, the will. . . . When we look inside ourselves, we always find ourselves as willing."[4] This concept designates the whole of our volitional and affective nature, "willing and not-willing, being contented and not contented, with all the modifications of the thing called feelings, emotions, and passions."[5] Such self-knowledge reveals that the will is the "essence" or "kernel" of our self because Schopenhauer argues that our being will is a necessary condition of self-knowledge. If we were "pure intelligence," our consciousness would be absorbed by the world it "mirrors" or "illuminates," and would be never be induced to turn back on itself.[6] It is in virtue of

---

3 *WWR*, 2:xlvi, 573. Cf. *GW*, 2:656.

4 *GW* 3:252, sec. 42; trans. Reginster.

5 *WWR*, 2:xix, 239. Cf. *GW*, 2:271. See also Schopenhauer, *Essay on the Freedom of the Will* (New York: Liberal Arts Press, 1960), 11. Cf. *GW*, 3:482.

6 Cf. *WWR*, 2:xix, 201–2. Cf. *GW*, 2:226–27.

having desires that we become conscious of an opposition between our self as subject of those desires and the world in which those desires may or may not find satisfaction.

We learn that fulfillment is impossible not simply by learning that our "real self" is will, but also by recognizing that this will is "a vain striving, an inward conflict, and a continual suffering."[7] This further self-knowledge is achieved not through the sort of transcendental argument sketched out above, but by way of a decidedly empirical investigation in the vicissitudes of desire, which involves self-knowledge understood as knowledge of our own mental states. Thus, the "inward conflict" may be taken to refer to the presence of two kinds of desires in our volitional makeup: not just first-order desires for objects such as wealth, fame, love, subsistence, and the like, the frustration of which causes pain, but also a second-order desire to desire, the presence of which is required to account for our very susceptibility to boredom. In the absence of intrinsic goods, the satisfaction of desires of the first kind entails the frustration of desires of the second kind, and vice versa. Hence, "Life swings like a pendulum to and fro between pain and boredom."[8] There is always something left to be desired; fulfillment is impossible.[9]

However, fulfillment is not the only "path" to peace of mind; through *detachment (Erlösung)*, "the peace, always sought but always escaping us on that first path of willing, comes to us of its own accord, and all is well with us."[10] The peace of mind we sought through the satisfaction of our desires can actually be achieved through their renunciation. In fact, such "will-lessness" is "the only radical cure for the disease against

---

7 *WWR*, 1:379, sec. 68. Cf. *GW*, 1:449.

8 *WWR*, 1:312, sec. 57. Cf. *GW*, 1:369.

9 For a detailed discussion of this argument, cf. Bernard Reginster, *The Affirmation of Life* (Cambridge, MA: Harvard University Press, 2006), 107–23.

10 *WWR*, 1:196, sec. 38. Cf. *GW*, 1:232.

which all other good things, such as fulfilled wishes . . . , are only palliatives, anodynes."[11]

Detachment comes in two main forms—aesthetic contemplation and complete resignation—and in both cases it is brought about by knowledge. But there are significant differences with respect both to the character of the detachment and to the manner in which it is achieved. Aesthetic contemplation of things produces detachment not in virtue of what it reveals about its *content* but in virtue of the *stance* it takes upon it. For those who possess intellectual capacity in excess of what is required for the service of the will, the beauty or sublimity of certain objects may so captivate their mind that it raises it to a state of "pure" or "disinterested" contemplation, a condition in which they are, if only for a moment, free from the agitations of emotion and desire.[12] Detachment is achieved here through a kind of *distraction*, a turning of the attention away from the attachments characteristic of our ordinary experience of the world. Detachment may be achieved through the aesthetic contemplation of our self, or our own mental states,[13] but it need not, and so it is not necessarily linked to *self*-knowledge.

Perhaps because it rests on mere distraction, the detachment produced by aesthetic contemplation is fleeting. A more lasting detachment is made possible by reflective self-knowledge when the person attends to its *content*. Grasping this content causes "the complete self-effacement and denial of the will," the achievement of a condition of "will-lessness" Schopenhauer calls "complete resignation." Complete resignation differs from ordinary resignation (which Schopenhauer tends to associate with Stoicism)[14] in that it consists in renouncing not the *pursuit* of desires, but the *desires* themselves.[15]

---

11 *WWR*, 1:362, sec. 65. Cf. *GW*, 1:429.

12 Cf. *WWR*, vol. 1, secs. 38–39. Cf. *GW*, vol. 1, secs. 38–39.

13 *WWR*, 2:xxx, 372. Cf. *GW*, 2:424.

14 Cf. *WWR*, vol. 1, sec. 16. Cf. *GW*, vol. 1, sec. 16.

15 Cf. *WWR*, 1:253, sec. 51. Cf. *GW*, 1:300.

Such resignation "comes from knowledge." However, it is not "arrived at by intention or design, but comes from the innermost relation of knowing and willing in man; hence it comes suddenly, as if flying in from without."[16] In other words, the insight into the impossibility of fulfillment we gain from self-knowledge operates not as a premise in a deliberation that issues in an intention to resign, but as a *direct* factor of resignation, "a *quieter* of the will."[17] Self-knowledge has this quieting effect by virtue of acquainting us with the *necessity* of suffering, and therefore the impossibility of fulfillment:

> We are not usually distressed at evils that are inescapably necessary and quite universal . . . . It is rather a consideration of the accidental nature of the circumstances that have brought suffering precisely on us which gives this suffering its sting. Now we have recognized that pain as such is inevitable and essential to life . . . . If such a reflection were to become a living conviction, it might . . . greatly reduce our anxious concern about our own welfare.[18]

The mechanism whereby self-knowledge produces resignation rests on "the innermost relation of knowing and willing in man." Schopenhauer refers here to relation between the susceptibility to pleasure or pain and "expectation," or *modal* belief. He observes that a deprivation believed to be unavoidable "relatively" (to our accidental circumstances) causes less pain than one believed to be avoidable, and a deprivation believed to be unavoidable "absolutely" (given our nature and the nature of the world in which we live) may cause no pain at all.[19] Knowledge of the absolute impossibility of fulfillment might thus leave us indifferent to

---

16 *WWR*, 1:404, sec. 70. *GW*, 1:479.

17 *WWR*, 1:404, sec. 70. *GW*, 1:479.

18 *WWR*, 1:315, sec. 57. Cf. *GW*, 1:373. Cf. sec. 55, pp. 306–7. Cf. pp. 362–63.

19 Cf. *WWR*, vol. 1, sec. 16. Cf. *GW*, vol. 1, sec. 16.

it, and therein lies the key to complete resignation: "All suffering results from the want of proportion between what we demand and expect and what comes to us. But this want of proportion is to be found only in knowledge, and through better insight it could be wholly abolished."[20] This indifference amounts to will-lessness: "The good things that must of necessity remain denied to it are treated with indifference, and in consequence of this human characteristic every wish soon dies and so can beget no more pain."[21] To desire something essentially is *not being indifferent* to it. If the deprivation of something that one desires is believed to be absolutely unavoidable, it is treated with indifference. This implies that the desire for it has "died."

Schopenhauer notes that the insight into the necessity of suffering has this effect only if it becomes a "living conviction." Presumably, this is meant to address the objection that a person can believe—perhaps because she is persuaded by Schopenhauer's arguments—that pain is "inescapably necessary," and yet continue to be distressed by it. We might therefore suppose that knowledge is "living" when it is "firsthand" or *experiential,* rather than "secondhand" or *merely intellectual* knowledge—"the suffering personally felt" as opposed to "the suffering merely known."[22] But Schopenhauer maintains that resignation may proceed from either kind of knowledge. They constitute two possible "paths" to resignation.[23]

A conviction may be "living" in another sense. Schopenhauer argues that gaining the knowledge necessary for resignation requires a "withdrawal into reflection."[24] This may refer to disinterestedness, which Schopenhauer often presents as a condition of epistemic correctness: "A purely objective, and therefore correct, apprehension of things

20 *WWR,* 1:88, sec. 16. Cf. *GW,* 1:105–6.

21 *WWR,* 1:87, sec. 16. Cf. *GW,* 1:105.

22 *WWR,* 1:392, sec. 68. Cf. *GW,* 1:464.

23 Cf. *WWR,* 1:397, sec. 68. Cf. *GW,* 1:471.

24 *WWR,* 1:85, sec. 16. Cf. *GW,* 1:103.

is possible only when we consider them without any personal participation in them, and thus under the complete silence of the will. ...
This state is conditioned from outside by our remaining wholly foreign
to, and detached from, the scene to be contemplated, and not being at
all actively involved in it."[25] If knowledge of the necessity of suffering
leaves us personally uninvolved, it is hard to see how it could affect us
in the manner required to produce complete resignation. In order to
produce resignation, knowledge would have to be "living" in the sense
of being *interesting* to us, by somehow bringing the inescapable necessity of suffering "terribly near to us."[26]

This creates a problem for the very possibility of complete resignation: it requires correct and interested knowledge, but knowledge cannot be both. We can avert this problem with two observations. First,
our interests do not necessarily cause cognitive distortion; they can
also produce cognitive enhancement: "The understanding of the stu-
pidest person becomes keen when it is a question of objects that closely
concern his willing."[27] Second, "withdrawal into reflection" arguably
refers only to the *abstraction* necessary to achieve modal knowledge,
and not to *disinterestedness*. Resignation is prompted by knowledge of
the necessity of suffering, and such knowledge requires only abstraction from "what is present and actual,"[28] not disinterestedness.

The following observation suggests a more promising understanding
of "living" knowledge:

> Even in the case of the individual who approaches [knowledge of the
> necessity of suffering], the tolerable condition of his own person,
> the flattery of the moment, the allurement of hope, and the satisfac-
> tion of the will offering itself again and again, i.e., the satisfaction

---

25 *WWR*, 2:xxx, 373. Cf. *GW*, 2:425.

26 *WWR*, 1:254–55, sec. 51. Cf. *GW*, 1:301–2.

27 *WWR*, 2:xix, 221. Cf. *GW*, 2:249.

28 *WWR*, 1:84, sec. 16. Cf. *GW*, 1:101.

of desire, are almost invariably a constant obstacle to the denial of the will, and a constant temptation to a renewed affirmation of it.[29]

A person with "mere" knowledge of the necessity of suffering might simultaneously enjoy a "tolerable condition in his own person" and the frequent satisfaction of his desires, which make him susceptible to the "flattery of the moment, the allurement of hope." As a consequence, he only "approaches," but does not fully achieve, the knowledge of the necessity of suffering; or, having achieved this knowledge, he is induced to suppress it. In any event, he is unable to attend to this knowledge and its implications and keep them "live" in his mind in the way required for producing resignation. To achieve resignation, he must therefore take measures to ensure that this insight becomes a "living conviction."[30]

12.3. FREUD, SELF-KNOWLEDGE, AND AUTONOMY

Freud's typical patient is one who has seemingly well-defined ideals and values, but whose realization of them is impeded by peculiar obsessions or compulsions that are puzzling and unintelligible even to him. Freud's fundamental conjecture is that these obsessions or compulsions express *unconscious* mental states, such as desires that have been repressed, or patterns of affective response that were formed under conditions of vulnerability and are then defensively transferred to situations that might no longer warrant them.

The freedom under threat has often been conceived in either of two ways. In one view, the unconscious mental states are alien forces, external to the patient's will, and their interference poses a threat to his *freedom of action*, or his ability to conduct himself in accordance with his

---

29 *WWR*, 1:392, sec. 68. Cf. *GW*, 1:465.

30 This may be the proper role of ascetic practices (*WWR*, vol. 1, sec. 68; *GW*, vol. 1, sec. 68)—to remove impediments to this knowledge becoming a "living conviction." A person accustomed to deprivation is less susceptible to the allurements of desire.

will.[31] Identifying those unconscious states restores this freedom by allowing him to develop more effective strategies to control them. In another view, these unconscious mental states are seen as parts of the agent's true self, which have been repressed, for example, because they conflict with social expectations.[32] Since the effectiveness of their repression depends in part on its success in removing them from the agent's awareness, self-knowledge is a necessary first step in their liberation.

Freud, however, takes the self-knowledge produced by psychoanalytic therapy to have a different effect. It does not consist, in the first place, in enhancing the control professed values (typically moral values) have over the repressed impulses: "You must not conclude from this that we influence them in favor of conventional morality."[33] Neither does it consist in giving free rein to the repressed (typically sexual) impulses:

> Thus you cannot explain the therapeutic effect of psychoanalysis by its permitting a full sexual life. . . . By carrying what is unconscious into what is conscious, we lift the repressions, we remove the preconditions for the formation of symptoms, we transform the pathogenic conflict into a normal one for which it must be possible somehow to find a solution. All that we bring about in a patient is this single psychical change.[34]

---

31 This view is implicit in the characterization of the typical Freudian patient in Stephen Mitchell, *Hope and Dread in Psychoanalysis* (New York: Basic Books, 1993) and explicit in others. Cf. Bela Szabados, "Freud, Self-Knowledge and Psychoanalysis," *Canadian Journal of Philosophy* 12.4 (1982): 696.

32 This is a frequent theme in mid-twentieth-century psychoanalytic theory. Cf. Jacques Lacan, *Écrits: A Selection*, trans. Alan Sheridan (New York: Norton, 1977) and Ronald Laing, *The Divided Self* (Baltimore: Penguin, 1965).

33 Sigmund Freud, *The Standard Edition of the Complete Psychological Works of Sigmund Freud*, trans. and ed. James Strachey in collaboration with Anna Freud, assisted by Alix Strachey and Alan Tyson, 24 vols. (London: Hogarth Press, 1956–74), 16:434. Hereafter cited as *SE*. Cf. *Gesammelte Werke* (London: Imago, 1991), 11:450. Hereafter cited as *GW*. All references to Freud's work are to the relevant volume and page of the *Standard Edition* and to the relevant volume and page of the *Gesammelte Werke*, respectively.

34 *SE*, 16:435. Cf. *GW*, 11:451.

The objective of psychotherapy is not to *resolve* the conflict between professed values and repressed impulses, as if the ones were expressions of the patient's true self and the others alien forces threatening his autonomy. It is a matter of transforming "a pathogenic conflict into a normal one." A conflict is pathogenic when it causes repression. Such repression removes the conflict from the reach of the agent's autonomous deliberation, thus preventing him from finding a genuine "solution" to it. In other words, it affects not just the agent's ability to govern his actions in accordance with his will—his self-control—but his will itself. Accordingly, the objective of psychotherapy is not simply to enhance the agent's freedom of action, but to make possible his freedom of will: "There is nothing we would rather bring about than that the patient should make his decisions for himself."[35]

Freedom of will understood in a minimal negative sense is the condition in which no mental state is barred from deliberative consideration—from having a role in the determination of what is to be done or valued. If deliberation proceeds in ignorance of some of the agent's existing attitudes, such as beliefs, desires, or feelings, it is bound not to express his standpoint adequately. The purpose of substituting what is conscious for what is unconscious is to ensure that deliberation adequately expresses the agent's standpoint. It does not replace the process of deliberation, but it enables it. Suppose my sexual desires stand in conflict with the socially prevailing moral norms. Resolving this conflict through the repression of the sexual desires poses a threat to my freedom: unable to consider the claims of these desires, my deliberations do not adequately reflect my standpoint as an agent; moreover, the repressed desires might disrupt my deliberations in ways I cannot monitor. Lifting the repression enables me to consider the claims of my sexual desires and thus reconsider the claims of the moral norms I have internalized, and make up my own mind. I might still decide to eschew

---

35 Ibid., *SE*, 16:433. Cf. *GW*, 11:450.

the gratification of my sexual desires, but in this case, my decision will be an autonomous act.

Freud argues that, in order to have therapeutic value, self-knowledge must be of a certain sort. He distinguishes between two kinds of self-knowledge: "Knowledge is not always the same as knowledge: there are different sorts of knowledge, which are far from equivalent psychologically. . . . The doctor's knowledge is not the same as the patient's and cannot produce the same effects."[36] The first kind of self-knowledge is the knowledge the doctor acquires of his patient's mind. It is akin to what contemporary philosophers call *third-person* self-knowledge insofar as it consists in knowing one's mental states in precisely the same way one would know the mental states of another:

> It could be pointed out, incidentally, that this was only treating one's own mental life as one had always treated other people's. One did not hesitate to ascribe mental processes to other people, although one had no immediate consciousness of them and could only infer them from their words and actions. But what held good of other people must be applicable to oneself.[37]

In other words, self-knowledge consists in examining the evidence of one's own words and actions and inferring to the mental states that constitute the best explanation of it.

This self-knowledge is a difficult achievement:

> Experience shows that we understand very well how to interpret in other people (that is, how to fit into their chain of mental events) the same acts which we refuse to acknowledge as being mental in ourselves. Here some special hindrance evidently deflects our

---

36 Ibid., *SE*, 16:281. Cf. *GW*, 11:290–91.

37 *SE*, 20:32. Cf. *GW*, 14:57.

investigations from our own self and prevents our obtaining a true knowledge of it.[38]

In this regard, Freud is more alive than Schopenhauer to the complex nature of the obstacles faced by self-knowledge. Schopenhauer was content to evoke an "excess of intellect" to account for its possibility. Freud, by contrast, believes that self-knowledge requires the recourse to special techniques, such as free association, or even the presence of another person—the analyst—who allows transference to unfold within the controlled confines of the therapeutic situation.[39]

The difficulty of achieving the required form of self-knowledge becomes more evident when we consider that for a patient to hear and accept the doctor's interpretation of his mental states is not sufficient to have therapeutic effects on him. Such self-knowledge may not succeed in substituting "something conscious for something unconscious"—in other words, it does not necessarily lift *repression*. Consider how Freud contrasts unconscious from conscious states:

> On superficial consideration this would seem to show that conscious and unconscious ideas are different and topographically separated records of the same content. But a moment's reflection shows that the identity of the information given to the patient with his own repressed memory is only apparent. To have heard something and to have lived something are psychologically two different things, even though the content of each be the same.[40]

Lifting repression is not simply a matter of moving some content from one area of the mind (the unconscious) to another (the conscious). Even

---

38 *SE*, 14:169–170. Cf. *GW*, 10:268.
39 Cf. *SE*, vol. 11, Lecture 19. Cf. *GW*, vol. 11, Vorlesung 19.
40 *SE*, 14:176. Cf. *GW*, 10:275.

when available to the agent's conscious awareness, this content may in turn be the object of two different kinds of consciousness—"having heard" (*das Gehörthaben*) and "having lived" (*das Gelebthaben*). The same content will have different "effects" on the patient's psychological economy depending on whether it is the object of one or the other form of consciousness. The mode of "having heard" presumably refers to the sort of knowledge of his own states the patient may have learned from his doctor's interpretations. But lifting repression requires self-knowledge in the mode of "having lived." This latter form of self-knowledge involves more than the purely intellectual recognition that, say, sexual attraction toward another person is the best explanation of my otherwise puzzling behavior toward her. It requires me to "live" this attraction. What does this mean?

Suppose I recognize that the presence of an unacknowledged sexual desire is the best explanation of some peculiarly obsessive behavior of mine. I accept, on the basis of that evidence, the claim that "I am agitated by such-and-such sexual desire." Presumably, that sexual desire was repressed because it caused a conflict, for example, with the social norms internalized in my superego. The mere awareness of my sexual desire may not fundamentally alter its psychological status; on the contrary, it might induce me to become more ruthlessly effective in its suppression. Under the pressure of my superego, I continue to treat it as an alien entity, with no presumptive claim to my deliberative attention. I may *know* of it, but I do not *recognize* it in the sense of seeing it as entitled to my deliberative consideration.

The contrast at work here has evoked to some the contemporary distinction between (third-person) *reporting* on a state and (first-person) *avowing* that state.[41] This is misleading: the self-knowledge Freud takes to have therapeutic value is a genuine and difficult achievement. But the self-knowledge involved in avowals is not a cognitive achievement

---

41 On this distinction and its application to Freud, cf. Richard Moran, *Authority and Estrangement: An Essay in Self-Knowledge* (Princeton, NJ: Princeton University Press, 2001), 89–94.

at all; arguably, it is in the very nature of the objects of avowals that they are self-known to the agent.[42] Freud's call for "living" self-knowledge is therefore more plausibly understood as highlighting the special difficulty of achieving therapeutically effective self-knowledge.

Freud sometimes characterizes as "living" awareness of a mental state one that involves an experience of the full affective charge characteristic of it. I can recognize that the sexual attraction I feel for a person is the best explanation of my peculiar behavior toward her, and yet feel none of the affective charge characteristic of such attraction. Yet, in one respect, coming to experience the characteristic affective charge of an attitude I discover in myself does not necessarily make this discovery more therapeutically efficacious. I can continue to experience it as an alien feeling that "comes over me," and not see it as meriting my deliberative consideration.

The "living" knowledge of my own states suggests a special kind of appropriation of them. In "Remembering, Repeating, and Working Through,"[43] Freud distinguishes two stages in the achievement of therapeutic self-knowledge. This important paper on technique focuses on the case of transference. Transference is evident in the pathological "repetition" of past experiences (for example, past relationships) in the present. "Remembering" is a first stage in self-knowledge: it consists in recognizing past experiences *as past* (and therefore not necessarily applicable to present experience) and in gaining awareness of the (repressed) disposition to interpret the present in terms of them.

However, remembering alone does not suffice to undo repression. A second stage of self-knowledge is required, which Freud describes as "working through":

The first step in overcoming the resistances is made, as we know, by the analyst's uncovering the resistance, which is never recognized by

---

42 Avowals are endorsements or commitments, and these cannot be unconscious. On this point, cf. Akeel Bilgrami, *Self-Knowledge and Resentment* (Cambridge, MA: Harvard University Press, 2006), appendix 1, who uses the terminology of *dispositions* and *commitments* to characterize the objects of reports and avowals respectively with particular attention to Freud.

43 Cf. *SE*, 12:147–56. Cf. *GW*, 10:126–36.

the patient, and acquainting him with it. Now it seems that begin-
ners in analytical practice are inclined to look on this introductory
step as constituting the whole of their work. I have often been asked
to advise upon cases in which the doctor complained that he had
pointed out his resistance to the patient and that nevertheless no
change had set in. . . . The analyst had merely forgotten that giving
the resistance a name could not result in its immediate cessation.
One must allow the patient time to become more conversant with
this with which he has now become acquainted, to *work through* it,
to overcome it. . . . Only when the resistance is at its height can the
analyst, working in common with the patient, discover the repressed
instinctual impulses which are feeding the resistance; and it is this
kind of lived experience (*Erleben*) which convinces the patient of
the existence and power of such impulses.[44]

By virtue of being *motivated* ignorance, repression opposes resistance
to its overcoming. It is a matter of knowing something the patient
in some sense does not want to know. Once the resistance has been
named, it seems as though the patient now knows what he wanted not
to know. But the resistance does not thereby cease, for several related
reasons. First, given the resistance opposed by the forces that repressed
it, this knowledge is difficult to keep "alive" in the mind: thus, while
I may recognize both that I have repressed sexual desires and that they
have a legitimate claim to my deliberative consideration, I may still
resist taking this claim into consideration as I deliberate about what to
do in a situation in which they have practical relevance. Second, recognizing that I have repressed desires is not yet understanding the forces
that *caused* their repression in the first place ("the repressed instinctual
impulses which are feeding the resistance"): without this understanding, I am less likely to know when, or even whether, repression is taking

---

44 *SE*, 12:155. Cf. *GW*, 10:135–36.

place.[45] Third, the full extent of the influence of repressed desires (their "power")—for example, the variety of circumstances in which their influence might be at work—is not revealed by the mere recognition that I have them: it takes a protracted, engaged experience of them to appreciate the scope and depth of their influence.

"Living" self-knowledge is therefore not *privileged* (first-person) self-knowledge. It remains a knowledge that could, in principle at least, be achieved by someone else. Freud calls it "lived" because it requires the direct or *lived* experience of the states that are its objects: for example, in the unfolding of transference (though only in a controlled analytic setting, to allow for the reflection required for "remembering" and "working through"). It is therefore more likely to be achieved by the agent whose states they are than by someone else, in part because the necessary, high level of protracted engagement with her mental states would be very hard for anyone other than the agent herself to sustain.

Self-knowledge is therapeutically effective if it allows mental states such as desires to be available to the agent's deliberative consideration. Her repressed desires are once again available to her consideration only if the knowledge she achieves of them is *living* knowledge. Once this self-knowledge is achieved, the agent *is* free in the sense that mental states that were once barred from her deliberative consideration are now available to it.[46]

---

45 Focus on resistance is distinctive of an important offshoot of classical Freudian theory, known as *ego psychology*. Cf., e.g., Anna Freud, *The Ego and the Mechanisms of Defense* (London: Hogarth Press, 1966).

46 At times, Freud suggests that self-knowledge only affords the patient some freedom from his pathological proclivities but does not altogether eliminate them: "Analysis does not set out to make pathological reactions impossible, but to give the patient's ego *freedom* to decide one way or the other" (*SE*, 19:50n; cf. *GW*, 13:279n). At other times, he suggests that successful analytic treatment achieves deeper and more permanent effects: "An analytic treatment demands from both doctor and patient the accomplishment of serious work, which is employed in lifting internal resistances. Through the overcoming of these resistances the patient's mental life is permanently changed, is raised to a high level of development and remains protected against fresh possibilities of falling ill" (*SE*, 16:451; cf. *GW* 11:469). For more on the theme of "development" in connection with the translation of something unconscious into something conscious, cf. Jonathan Lear, *Freud* (New York: Routledge 2005), ch. 1.

CHAPTER THIRTEEN

Husserl's Phenomenology and the Project of Transcendental Self-Knowledge

Dermot Moran

The Delphic motto, "Know thyself!" has gained a new signification. Positive science is a science lost in the world (*Wissenschaft in der Weltverlorenheit*). I must lose the world by *epoché*, in order to regain it by a universal self-examination (*in universaler Selbstbesinnung*). "*Noli foras ire*," says Augustine, "*in te redit in interiore homine habitat veritas.*"

EDMUND HUSSERL, *Cartesian Meditations*[1]

For Edmund Husserl, philosophy is first and foremost a science of subjectivity, or specifically, of subjectivity understood as "sense constituting" (meaning forming),[2] rather than what he characterizes as "the science of objective subjectivity, the subjectivity of men and other animals, a subjectivity that is part of the world."[3] For the mature Husserl, however, knowing what subjectivity is yields not just knowledge but

---

1 Trans. Dorion Cairns (Hague: Nijhoff, 1950), sec. 65, 157. Quotations from English translations are followed by section number and page number as well as by references to the critical edition of Husserl's works, *Husserliana: Gesammelte Werke* (Dordrecht: Springer, 1956–). Hereafter cited as *Hua*. Thus the reference here is *Cartesian Meditations*, sec. 64, 157. Hereafter cited as *CM*. Cf. *Hua*, 1:183.

2 According to Husserl, conscious life knits (synthesizes) itself into a coherent unity and intentionally invests with meaning and designates as some kind of being all its objects, including giving sense to the overall context ("horizon") of its world. For Husserl's discussions of *Abbau* and *Rekonstruktion*, cf. *Hua*, 8:356.

3 *CM*, sec. 13, 30. Cf. *Hua*, 1:68.

self-knowledge in a very special sense. Self-knowledge, thus, is the central goal of Husserl's phenomenology, although interpreted in his own peculiar way. Self-knowledge, for Husserl, is not to be conceived in terms of the subject's direct, immediate, noninferential awareness of his or her own mental states, as in most versions of contemporary analytic philosophy of mind. It means, at the very least, to know that one *is* a self, to know what kind of developmental and temporal being a self is (and how the self spans its temporality), and, crucially, to know the a priori conditions governing the meaning-constitution of all there is, including the self itself, other selves, and the intersubjective objective world as a whole.

Thus Husserl regards self-knowledge as an imperative, for both theoretical insight and practical wisdom. On the theoretical side, it is vital to recognize that true knowledge of the self cannot be attained in the natural attitude, but demands a very particular *transcendental* approach. As he writes in the first draft (1927) of his *Encyclopaedia Britannica* article on phenomenology:

> Through the transcendental reduction, *absolute* subjectivity, which functions everywhere in hiddenness, is brought to light along with its whole transcendental life, in whose intentional syntheses all real and ideal objects, with their positive existential validity, are constituted.[4]

Phenomenological self-knowledge, in the Husserlian conception, first and foremost involves gaining a detached intellectual appreciation (purified of all naturalistic presuppositions) of the self and its constituting activities; but knowing oneself in such a radical way is also *transformative* for any life. That's why transcendental self-knowledge may be seen as offering an *ethical* vision for human life. Self-knowledge

---

4 Edmund Husserl, "Phenomenology [Draft A]," in *Psychological and Transcendental Phenomenology and the Confrontation with Heidegger (1927–31)*, trans. Thomas Sheehan and Richard E. Palmer, *Collected Works*, vol. 6 (Dordrecht: Kluwer Academic Publishers, 1997), 98. Cf. *Hua*, 9:250.

is necessary for ethical "self-renewal," as Husserl puts it in his *Kaizo* articles titled "Renewal" written in 1923–24.[5] Self-knowledge enables humans to free themselves from the prejudices of daily living and allows them to be motivated by grounded rational motives, realizing the ideal of what Husserl calls "genuine humanity" (*echtes Menschentum*).[6]

As a result of this self-knowledge, Husserl believes, one can live a fully rational life since one's motives have been clarified and one has come to adopt the most rational of motives. I become self-responsible in the deepest and most radical sense, not just responsible *for* myself but responsible or answerable *to* myself. For Husserl, living with self-knowledge is living a "life of ultimate responsibility,"[7] since it is only through self-knowledge that we learn to explicate the true sense of our culture, its guiding values and norms.

In what follows I shall discuss Husserl's views on self-knowledge in three steps. First I offer a brief exposition of the Socratic and, what amounts to the same thing, the Cartesian heritage underlying his phenomenology. I shall then give an overview of Husserl's philosophical development. In particular, I shall focus on two peculiarities. Considering the conception of the "self" or "ego," I shall discuss the increasing attention Husserl pays to the function of the I in the constitution of all meaning. Second, I shall point out how, in his mature writing, Husserl comes to distinguishing between natural and transcendental self-reflection. Third, I shall discuss the value of Husserl's concept of epoche, that is, suspension of belief commitments, for self-knowledge. Generally, one can say that, for Husserl, it is due to the insight gained by the exercise of the epoche that phenomenology

---

5 Cf. *Hua* 27:23. Husserl wrote several articles for a Japanese journal called *Kaizo*. Only the first article, "Renewal as an Individual-Ethical Problem," was published. Cf. Edmund Husserl, *Shorter Works*, trans. and ed. Frederick Elliston and Peter McCormick (Notre Dame, IN: University of Notre Dame Press, 1981), 326–34. Cf. *Hua*, 27:3–13.

6 Edmund Husserl, *Formal and Transcendental Logic*, trans. Dorion Cairns (The Hague: Nijhoff, 1969), 5. Hereafter cited as *FTL*. Cf. *Hua*, 17:9.

7 *FTL*, 5. Cf. *Hua*, 17:9.

can be understood as a particular way of acquiring philosophical self-knowledge or of obeying the imperative to know oneself.

13.1. THE SOCRATIC AND CARTESIAN HERITAGE OF HUSSERL'S PHENOMENOLOGY

Husserl regards his form of self-knowledge as the most ultimate that can be gained in philosophy. It will raise life to a new level. He praises Socrates for having made the original breakthrough to self-aware, transcendental life. Socrates proposed a reform of life, away from blind, absorbed living in unclarity[8] and toward a life of reflective self-evidencing, a genuine life of reason.[9] Husserl allied this Socratic breakthrough to Descartes' return to selfhood. Husserl often describes phenomenology as a "new Cartesianism": "We can say also that a radical and universal continuation of Cartesian meditations, or (equivalently) a universal self-knowledge, is philosophy itself and encompasses all self-accountable science."[10]

For Husserl, the Cartesian cogito is the anchor point of the whole of phenomenology. He accepts the basic truth of the cogito—I have the direct, immediate, incorrigible, apodictic, necessary truth that "I exist." This truth cannot be canceled out; it is *undurchstreichbar*.[11] I experience my "living present"; I cannot doubt that I exist—I cannot even imagine myself not existing because the imagined self that does not exist will not be I but another.

While Husserl credits both Socrates and Descartes with developing philosophy's interest in self-knowledge, he himself claims to be the first to have methodically uncovered and explored an infinite domain of self-experience. He is even willing to call his philosophy a kind of

---

8 Cf. *Hua*, 7:10.
9 Cf. *Hua*, 7:12.
10 *CM*, sec. 64, 156 (translation modified by Dermot Moran). Cf. *Hua*, 1:182–83.
11 *Hua*, 14:152.

universal egology[12] although, in his mature writings, he writes that transcendental subjectivity always implies or is involved in a "nexus" of transcendental intersubjectivity, and hence that one can be oneself only in relation to "being-with-others" (*Mitsein, Miteinandersein*).[13]

Self-knowledge requires minimally that one's mental states or lived experiences can be reflectively apprehended. Husserl maintains it is an essential law that every mental experience can be brought to reflective apprehension.[14] Husserl furthermore lays heavy emphasis on the apodictic character of one's immediate direct presence of oneself, although he believes there is much more to be apprehended here.

Phenomenology, for Husserl, is preeminently a systematic science of first-personal experience, although he rarely uses the precise terminology of the "first person." The first person also participates in second- and third-personal stances; the self is in part constituted through intersubjective involvements with others (the "I-you relation"). There is also a first-person plural, and, as we shall see, Husserl thinks that the Cartesian *ego cogito* should strictly speaking by interpreted as a "we think."[15]

Once one recognizes the necessary truth of the cogito, one enters immediately and without warning into a new domain of experience— "transcendental self-experience,"[16] an "infinite realm of being of a new kind,"[17] a domain that can be intuitively explicated once one adopts the correct approach. I begin from the apodictic experience of the "I am" in the flowing present and also apprehend the intentional structure of the "I think" as an I-thinking-a-thought, *ego-cogitatio-cogitatum*. Around this immediate core of intuitive givenness are clustered "horizonal" experiences, of the past and future, possibility and actuality, of

---

12 Cf. *CM*, sec. 13, 30. Cf. *Hua*, 1:69, sec. 21, 53; 1:89.

13 Cf. *Hua*, 6:260, 15:267.

14 Cf. Edmund Husserl, *Ideas for a Pure Phenomenology and Phenomenological Philosophy. First Book: General Introduction to Pure Phenomenology*, trans. Daniel O. Dahlstrom (Indianapolis: Hackett, 2014), sec. 38, 66. Hereafter cited as *Ideas I*. Cf. *Hua*, 1:67.

15 *Hua*, 8:316.

16 *CM*, sec. 9, 22. Cf. *Hua*, 1:62.

17 *CM*, sec. 12, 27. Cf. *Hua*, 1:66.

"intentional implication" that are, Husserl maintains, also "apodicti-cally experienceable."[18] The manner in which the self structures its temporal presence can be explored and likewise its manner of giving something the value of actuality, possibility, and so on.

Husserl is quite aware that the cogito is a performative act that dis-closes the I in its self-presence. Furthermore, this I or ego needs to be de-constructed carefully in a reflection that goes beyond natural reflec-tion, which is, for Husserl, always inhibited by a commitment to "belief in being," *Seinsglaube*. The exploration of the true nature of the ego requires "transcendental reflection" so that its horizons, syntheses, pas-sivities, habitualities, and lawful essential structure can be understood.

Natural reflection, for Husserl, is trapped in a kind of innate "natu-ralism"; it remains very much human reflection saturated with anthro-pological and psychological prejudices. It is hard therefore to access the conscious egoic life of the self in its original purity. Borrowing a technique from the ancient skeptics and modifying Descartes' radical doubt, Husserl proposes a new method of transcendental epoche—bracketing of belief in being, abstaining from all belief commitments—adopting the standpoint of what Husserl will call the "disinterested" or "detached" transcendental spectator. He says in his Amsterdam Lectures of 1929:

A mere reflection on consciousness does not yet yield the mental in purity and in its own essentiality. Rather, we must in addition abstain from that believing in being (*Seins-Glaubens*) by virtue of which we accept the world in the natural life of consciousness and our reflecting on it; as phenomenologists, we are not permitted to go along with this (and in further consequence, indeed, we must abstain from every position-taking of any kind toward the world naively accepted by us). As phenomenologists we must be as it were

18 *CM*, sec. 12, 28. Cf. *Hua*, 1:67.

non-participating onlookers at the life of consciousness, which can only in this way become the pure theme of our experiencing."[19]

In his works, Husserl takes it for granted that transcendental self-knowledge is a necessary, vital acquisition of humankind, but to show that this is so, he will have to go beyond the mere essential description of transcendental life and show why it must be carried out by those seeking to live rational lives. Husserl's entire philosophical focus, therefore, may be said to be on the practice of "self-awareness," "self-apperception,"[20] or "self-knowledge,"[21] and the living of a life of rational "self-responsibility"[22] (*Selbstverantwortlichkeit*).[23] But how this is to be understood changes between his earlier and later works.

13.2. THE DEVELOPMENT OF HUSSERL'S PHENOMENOLOGY OF EGO AND SELFHOOD

While Husserl was always interested in conscious subjectivity and its sense-making, he initially was not interested in the "I" or ego-self as such. He originally identified phenomenology with descriptive psychology (with its practice of "inner perception"), as developed by his former teacher Franz Brentano (1838–1917) both in *Psychology from the Empirical Standpoint* (1874)[24] and in his lectures *Descriptive Psychology* (1887–91).[25] Brentano conceived his descriptive psychology ("psychognosy") as a

---

19 Edmund Husserl, "Amsterdam Lectures," in *Psychological and Transcendental Phenomenology*, 222. Cf. *Hua*, 9:307.

20 *CM*, sec. 45, 99. Cf. *Hua*, 1:130.

21 Ibid., sec. 64, 156. Cf. *Hua*, 1:182.

22 Edmund Husserl, *The Crisis of European Sciences and Transcendental Phenomenology: An Introduction to Phenomenological Philosophy*, trans. David Carr (Evanston, IL: Northwestern University Press, 1970). Hereafter cited as *Crisis*.

23 *Hua*, 6:272.

24 Franz Brentano, *Psychology from the Empirical Standpoint*, trans. Antos C. Rancurello, D. B. Terrell, and Linda McAlister (London: Routledge, 1995). Cf. Franz Brentano, *Psychologie vom empirischen Standpunkt*, 2 vols, ed. Oskar Kraus (Hamburg: Felix Meiner Verlag, 2013).

25 Franz Brentano, *Descriptive Psychology*, trans. Benito Müller (London: Routledge, 1995). Cf. Franz Brentano, *Deskriptive Psychologie*, ed. Roderick M. Chisholm and W. Baumgartner (Hamburg: Meiner, 1982).

science that "acquaints us with the objects of our own self."[26] Insofar as descriptive psychology was concerned with self-knowledge, Brentano was satisfied simply with the immediate evident truth that was gained in inner perception of one's psychic states. The aim was to describe the essential makeup of conscious experiences, excluding attention to the ego.

According to the mature Husserl, despite his recognition of intentionality, Brentano never came to grasp it as a "complex of performances,"[27] achievements of "sense-giving" subjectivity. Everything and every person—including the very idea of an objective reality called "nature" and indeed even God—is "for me what he is, in consequence of my own achievement of consciousness."[28] Husserl claims in his *Crisis of European Sciences* to have recognized this "universal a priori of correlation between experienced object and manners of givenness"[29] already in 1898 while writing the *Logical Investigations*.

Initially, in the first edition of the *Logical Investigations*,[30] Husserl asserted (in Humean manner) that he could not find the "I" in the stream of experiences. He also rejected the neo-Kantian Paul Natorp's (1854–1924) account of "consciousness"[31] as a "primitive center of relations": "I must frankly confess, however, that I am quite unable to find this primitive, necessary centre of relations. The only thing I can take note of and therefore perceive, are the empirical ego and its empirical relations to its own experiences."[32]

At this time Husserl thought of the empirical, psychological ego more or less as an object appearing in consciousness. He writes:

Objection may be raised to our previous assertion that the ego appears to itself, enjoys a consciousness and, in particular, a

26 Brentano, *Descriptive Psychology*, 78. Cf. *Deskriptive Psychologie*, 76.

27 *FTL*, sec. 97, 245. Cf. *Hua*, 17:252.

28 *FTL*, sec. 99, 251. Cf. *Hua*, 17:258.

29 Husserl, *Crisis*, sec. 48, 166n. Cf. *Hua* 6:169 n. 1.

30 Edmund Husserl, *Logical Investigations*, trans. John Findlay, ed. Dermot Moran, 2 vols. (New York: Routledge, 2001).

31 Cf. Paul Natorp, *Einleitung in die Psychologie nach kritischer Methode* (Freiburg: Mohr, 1888).

32 *LU*, Fifth Investigation, sec. 8, II, 92. Cf. *Hua*, 19.1:374.

perception of itself. Self-perception of the empirical ego is, however, a daily business, which involves no difficulty for understanding. We perceive the ego, just as we perceive an external thing.[33]

By the time of his next major publication, *Ideas* (1913),[34] however, and the revised second edition of the *Logical Investigations* (1913), Husserl came to agree with Kant that the "I think" must accompany all experiences. He writes:

> The pure ego lives itself out in a particular sense in every current cogito, yet all background experiences belong to it as well and it belongs to them. All of them, by virtue of belonging to the one stream of experience (*Erlebnisstrom*) that is mine, must be capable of being converted into current *cogitationes* or of being included in them immanently. In Kantian language: "The 'I think' must be able to accompany all my representations."[35]

The ego belongs to every experience, but, contrary to what Natorp claimed, it can be grasped in a special way:

> It pertains in general to the essence of every cogito that a new cogito of the kind called by us "Ego-reflection" is in principle possible, one that grasps, on the basis of the earlier cogito. . . . the pure subject of that earlier cogito. It consequently pertains . . . to the essence of the pure Ego that it be able to grasp itself as what it is and in the way it functions, and thus make itself into an object. Therefore it is in no way correct to assert that the pure Ego is a subject that can never become an Object.[36]

---

33 *LU*, Fifth Investigation, sec. 8, II, 93. Cf. *Hua*, 375.

34 Husserl, *Ideas I*.

35 *Ideas I*, sec. 57, 105. Cf. *Hua*, 3.1:123.

36 Edmund Husserl, *Ideas Pertaining to a Pure Phenomenology and to a Phenomenological Philosophy, Second Book*, trans. Richard Rojcewicz and Andre Schuwer (Dordrecht: Kluwer, 1989), sec. 23, 107. Hereafter cited as *Ideas II*. Cf. *Hua*, 4:101.

From 1913 onward, Husserl adopts the neo-Kantian term "pure ego," for example, in the second edition of the *Logical Investigations*, where he speaks of "the pure ego" (*das reine Ich*),[37] which he had originally dismissed as an unnecessary postulate for the unification of consciousness.[38] But Husserl is beginning to formulate new distinctions and to claim that besides the empirical ego, there must be postulated a "pure" ego and then a transcendental ego. He thenceforth attempts to chart the contribution of the sense-constituting self to all experience.

From now on, Husserl's phenomenology is no longer a descriptive psychology of individual mental episodes as in the Brentano school,[39] but involves a specific, sustained, methodological reflection on the unified "stream of conscious life" (*Bewusstseinsstrom*), a radical "sense explication" of "self-experience." Thus the transcendental ego is the only true source of all "meaning and being."[40] The positive sciences, the sciences of the world, have lost this sense of the manner in which all meaning is constituted by human intentional activities and passivities, since they study what they regard as (to invoke Hilary Putnam's phrase) a "ready-made" world. So a return to the sources of the self is a return to the origins of meaning formation, of original sense-making.

Husserl came to regard the self as much more than just a formal "ego pole" that unifies experiences. It is capable of acquiring habits, characteristics, a "style" of its own. Husserl recognizes that ego is not fixed but has a history: "The ego constitutes itself *for itself* in, so to speak, the unity of a history."[41] The self is conditioned by psychophysical

37 Husserl, *LU*, Fifth Investigation, sec. 5 and sec. 8.

38 Cf. *LU*, Fifth Investigation, sec. 8, II, 549n. Cf. *Hua*, 19.1:374n.

39 Cf. Liliana Albertazzi, Massimo Libardi, and Roberto Poli, eds., *The School of Franz Brentano* (Dordrecht: Kluwer, 1996).

40 *CM*, sec. 41, 84. Cf. *Hua*, 1:117.

41 *CM*, sec. 37, 75. Cf. *Hua*, 109.

restrictions, but it also accumulates sedimented traits, characteristics, capacities, powers, and habits. Husserl writes:

> Habits are necessarily formed, just as much with regard to originally instinctive behavior . . . as with regard to free behavior. To yield to a drive establishes the drive to yield: habitually. Likewise, to let one-self be determined by a value-motive and to resist a drive establishes a tendency (a "drive") to let oneself be determined once again by such a value-motive . . . and to resist these drives.[42]

Coming to awareness of how our habitual selves are formed allows us to raise this process up to a more rational form of self-development.

13.3. Transcendental Phenomenological Self-Experience through the Epoche

Radical self-reflection, for the mature Husserl, involves a deliberate stepping back (for which he uses the Greek term *epoché*) from one's involvement in the ongoing flow of life, a "suspension" or "bracketing" of one's cognitive stances or "position takings," an unplugging of normal "belief in being" (*Seinsglaube*) that saturates everyday conscious life. This allows the self-meditator to scrutinize, comprehend, evaluate, and eventually embrace or discard his commitments on the basis of a transparent rationality and a deep comprehension of the workings of spirit.[43]

In his mature writings after *Ideas*, Husserl understands the aim of philosophy itself to be to seek self-knowledge in an "absolute" sense, understanding, that is, that self has an absolute ontological primacy. Once he comes to recognize the pure ego, he becomes an explorer of

---

42 *Ideas II*, sec. 59, 267 (translation modified by Dermot Moran). Cf. *Hua*, 4:255.

43 Cf. Thomas Nenon, "Freedom, Responsibility and Self-Awareness in Husserl," *New Yearbook for Phenomenology and Phenomenological Research II* (2002): 1–21.

its infinite depths.[44] He discusses not just the active, waking, thinking ego, the cogito in the full sense, but also passive states, the passive knitting together of experiences in perception (passive synthesis), as well as exploring altered or varied states of self, for example, the sleeping, fantasizing, or dreaming ego, the ego of the child, the ego of the mature adult, as well as the ego in its collective intentional engagements with other egos. But behind all these different modalities of the ego are the absolute ego and the pure ego, which led Husserl finally into alignment with the German idealist tradition (most notably Fichte, on whom he lectured in 1917).

For Husserl, the self has many layers or strata, ranging from the most primitive unity to be found in the synthesized temporal stream of experience that binds the self together, through the levels of the "ego" driven by wants, desires, and instincts, the ego of habits and capacities, right up to the fully autonomous freely acting rational agent acting as a person in a world of persons. The self is necessarily embodied in a particular time, place, and physical condition, but it also can develop into a freely acting person that cannot be simply identified with its body. Husserl writes: "The spirit, the human being as a member of the personal human world does not have a place the way things do."[45]

And later, he adds:

In original genesis, the personal Ego constitutes itself not only as a person determined by *drives*, from the very outset and incessantly driven by original "instincts" and passively submitting to them, but *also as a higher, autonomous, freely acting* Ego, in particular one guided

---

44 Husserl uses the term "the ego" (*das Ego*) or the "I" (*Ich*) both for the first-person "empirical ego" (*Logical Investigations*), or "psychological" ego (cf. *CM*, sec. 11, 25; cf. *Hua*, 1:64), which is the subject of experiences, and provides identity across experiences, and for what he terms the "pure" (cf. *Ideas I*, sec. 57, 105; *Hua*, 3.1:109; sec. 80, 154. *Hua*, 3.1:161) or the "transcendental" ego (*das transzendentale Ego*, cf. *CM*, sec. 11, 26; *Hua*, 1:65). Husserl stresses the infinity of the ego self-experience at *CM*, sec. 12, 27. Cf. *Hua*, 1:66.

45 *Ideas II*, 215. Cf. *Hua*, 4:204.

by *rational motives,* and not one that is merely dragged along and unfree.[46]

For Husserl these drives are never purely instinctual; they are configured by the attitudes we take toward them. Our drives are humanized by being adopted or rejected by the self. One is rarely just hungry for food *as such*, but hungry for a specific meal, a certain taste, a cup *of coffee*, and so on. Our drives emerge into consciousness with a certain prefigured sense configuration.

For Husserl, there is a kind of immediate prereflective awareness of any experience that is an essential element of consciousness as such. To be conscious is to be aware. This is an eidetic truth. In this sense, all consciousness is egoic or self-centered. But this self-awareness is minimal, not yet the fully conscious ego. In *Ideas II*, the posthumously published second book of *Ideas*,[47] Husserl says that the reflecting self presupposes an "unreflected consciousness."[48] In reflection, I come to know "how I 'comport' myself under different subjective circumstances" and can enter into the "intertwining of the motivations of my cogito."[49] This allows me to understand not only what motivations actually affect me and how they affect me, I come to learn about my character. I have my "peculiarities, my way of moving, of doing things, my individual evaluations, my own way of preferring, my temptations."[50]

As we have seen, Husserl's account of self-knowledge has to be understood as twofold: life is lived in both the natural and the transcendental attitudes. In his mature work, he prefers to distinguish between natural life directed to the world in the natural attitude, and the experience of the ego as a transcendental "disinterested onlooker"

---

46 *Ideas II*, sec. 59, 267. Cf. *Hua*, 255.

47 *Ideas I*.

48 *Ideas II*, sec. 58, 259. Cf. *Hua*, 4:248.

49 *Ideas II*, sec. 58, 260. Cf. *Hua*, 4:248.

50 *Ideas II*, sec. 59, 266. Cf. *Hua*, 4:254.

(*unbeteiligter Zuschauer, uninterestierter Zuschauer*)[51] on experience. Indeed, it is one of the chief contributions of Husserl's transcendental philosophy that he thinks of the transcendental domain not just as a set of a priori formal laws and structures, but as a living dynamic *life* of sense constitution that can be lived through consciously, a domain of "transcendental experience" (a conception foreign to Kant).

Husserl maintains that in everyday natural experience—which he characterizes as naive, straightforward, natural life—we are turned outward toward the world and the various objects of our interests. Natural reflection is saturated with prejudices and prejudgments—especially those from the "psychophysical domain." It is precisely natural thinking that has, for instance, confused logic with psychology. Husserl writes about self-knowledge and self-reflection in the natural attitude:

> In the course of observing something, *I* perceive it; likewise in remembering, *I* am often "pre-occupied" (*beschäftigt*) with something; in fictionalizing phantasy, *I* closely follow goings-on in the imagined world, in a quasi-observation of them. Or I reflect, I draw inferences; I retract a judgment, occasionally "refraining" from judgment altogether. I consummate a state of being pleased or displeased, I am joyful or sad, I wish, or I want and act; or I also "refrain" from the joy, the wish, the willing and action. In all such acts, I am there with them, *currently* (*aktuell*) with them. In reflecting, I construe myself as a human being with them.[52]

For Husserl, on the other hand, *transcendental* self-knowledge is knowledge gained from the standpoint of the transcendental spectator. It presumes that human consciousness has the capacity freely to alter the course or direction of its interest, indeed modify its own

---

51 Cf. *Hua*, 6:340 and 242.

52 *Ideas I*, sec. 80, 154. Cf. *Hua*, 3.1:179.

intentional directedness in natural life, split its interest, as it were, and come to contemplate its own sense-making activities.

In *Cartesian Meditations* Husserl makes clear that the way I access my "pure" ego—elsewhere called transcendental subjectivity—is through the epoche. It is in the epoche that all "human" assumptions are dropped and I experience myself as a performing and validating subject who is constituting the world in its "sense and validity" (*Sinn und Geltung*). Husserl writes:

> The epoché can also be said to be the radical and universal method by which I apprehend myself purely: as Ego, and with my own pure conscious life, in and by which the entire Objective world exists for me and is precisely as it is for me. . . . Descartes, as we know, indicated all that by the name *cogito*. The world is for me absolutely nothing else but the world existing for and accepted by me in such a conscious cogito. It gets its whole sense, universal and specific, and its acceptance as existing, exclusively from such *cogitationes*.[53]

The meditating subject can no longer consider itself as the natural ego, a being entirely caught up on the world. As Husserl insists in the *Cartesian Meditations*, this transcendental ego is not any "little butt-end of the world"[54] (*ein kleines Endchen der Welt*)[55] that has been left behind as the last item to survive the transcendental reduction. As Husserl will insist, it is only the epoche that makes possible entrance into the life of the transcendental ego: "First the transcendental *epoché* and reduction releases transcendental subjectivity from its self-concealment (*Selbstverborgenheit*) and raises it up to a new position, that of transcendental self-consciousness."[56]

---

53 *CM*, sec. 8, 21. Cf. *Hua*, 1:60.

54 *CM*, sec. 10, 24 (translation modified by Dermot Moran).

55 *Hua*, 1:63.

56 Cf. *Hua*, 34:399 (translated by Dermot Moran).

Furthermore, Husserl insists, it necessarily belongs to the transcendental ego that it should be embodied and "enworlded" (*Mundanisierung; Verweltlichung des Ichs*). There is a tendency in Husserl to think of this transcendental ego as constituting space and time through its own time consciousness. At times he speaks of the transcendental ego as timeless and living forever. But elsewhere he insists on the strict parallelism between the transcendental ego and the natural ego. One must assume therefore that events like birth and death have a *transcendental* as well as a natural significance, and indeed this is precisely how Husserl approaches the matter in his later reflections on life and death.[57]

The main kind of direct awareness one has of oneself is an experience of primal presence. When I look for myself, I always find myself and there is no gap between the ego that is looking and the ego that is apprehended in the temporal present. Other forms of self-reflection, however, for example, memory, operate with what Husserl calls a "splitting of the ego" (*Ichspaltung*) and some kind of self-distantiation. When one apprehends oneself in an act of remembering, implicit in the remembering is the recognition that the current remembering self is not the same as the earlier self that is the target of the memory. At the same time the memory includes the specific sense that remembering self and remembered self are states of the same person. This is an example of the peculiar nature of the self-alienation and self-identification that Husserl sees as central to the life of the self. The self already has within itself an openness to what is other, or "not self." He writes in *Ideas II*: "The Ego posits the non-Ego and comports itself towards it; the Ego unceasingly constitutes its 'over and against,' and in this process it is motivated and always motivated anew, and not arbitrarily but as exercising "*self-preservation*."[58]

---

57 Cf., e.g., Edmund Husserl, "Grenzprobleme der Phänomenologie. Analysen des Unbewusstseins und der Instinkte. Metaphysik. Späte Ethik. Texte aus dem Nachlass (1908–1937)," in *Hua*, vol. 42.

58 *Ideas II*, sec. 58, 265. Cf. *Hua*, 4:253.

This leads Husserl to generalize the problem of the self-knowledge: to meditate on oneself is not just to reach the "I," but to recognize what an ego is—to have essential insight into the nature of the ego and its relation to whatever is "not ego." This relies on the notion that there is a sense of an I that is always present in experience—including controversially in sleeping or unconscious states. The cogito that is present to itself can establish well-motivated connections with earlier states of itself and also with future possible states. Husserl writes in this context:

> Let us here point out only what is most important, the most general aspect of the ego's form, namely, the peculiar temporalization by which it becomes an enduring ego, constituting itself in its time-modalities: the same ego, now actually present, is in a sense, in every past that belongs to it, another—i.e., as that which was and thus is not now—and yet, in the continuity of its time it is one and the same, which is and was and has its future before it. The ego which is present now, thus temporalized, has contact with its past ego, even though the latter is precisely no longer present: it can have a dialogue with it and criticize it, as it can others.[59]

Furthermore, it belongs to the self to have the role of constituting all other egos in their subjective egoic character. For Husserl, as for Descartes, to grasp oneself is at the same time to grasp the essence of what self is, and this allows one to at least understand the possibility of other selves in what Husserl speaks of as the "open plurality" of egos. He writes:

> [The problem is] to understand how my transcendental ego, the primitive basis for everything that I accept as existent, can constitute within himself another transcendental ego, and then too an

---

59 Husserl, *Crisis*, sec. 50, 172. Cf. *Hua*, 6:175.

open plurality of other egos —"other" egos absolutely inaccessible to my ego in their original being, and yet cognizable (for me) as existing and as being thus and so.[60]

Husserl acknowledges that the manner in which my self can "recognize" other selves is problematic since it cannot be the case that I simply counterpose myself with them. But rather than leading him to give up the assumption that transcendental self-knowledge provides us with knowledge of others, his recognition of the "entwinement" between my current and past states of self as well as those between myself and others leads him to his significant concept of *Ineinandersein*, living in and through one's relations with others in a chain of mutual intentional implication that in the end is responsible for the experience of both the objective world and the cultural community.

To conclude, the classic interpretation of the Delphic injunction to know oneself is that it is a stipulation for each of us to know our own measure, our own limits, not to overreach oneself, but to remember than one is human and not immortal or a god. Moreover, it is assumed that to know oneself as limited is to know oneself as finite and fallible. Husserl, who reads the Delphic injunction as calling for a phenomenological self-inquiry, draws another conclusion. Through the practice of the epoche the radical self-investigator can break through the limitations of her empirical human nature and recover her transcendental life in which she can be motivated by reasons, subject to norms and capable of rationally evaluating evidences. She becomes free, Husserl believes, to identify and choose enduring guiding values. Husserl writes that the self can come to orient itself by choosing its values:

The I as subject of conscience is the I of the entire life as I of remaining values; values that remain meaningful for the whole of the

---

60 *FTL*, sec. 96, 239–40. Cf. *Hua*, 17:246.

further life and that are, in retrospect, considered as universally meaningful and, in some cases, as enduringly valid.[61]

When human beings come to self-knowledge, they free themselves from living along blindly in the flow of natural life, and suspend their belief commitments in order to truly identify their motivations and become self-responsible, identifying the sustaining values to live by. The greatest achievement of human self-reflection, moreover, is that it has allowed humans to assume the universal point of view and to detach themselves from specific interests. This, for Husserl, is the philosophical life, the life of second-order reasons, the life motivated by rationality and grounded evidences, what Husserl will call "life in apodicticity"[62] (*Leben in der Apodiktizität*).[63]

---

61 This citation, taken from unpublished manuscript A V 21/84b, is to be found in Hanne Jacobs, "Towards a Phenomenological Account of Personal Identity," in *Philosophy, Phenomenology, Sciences: Essays in Commemoration of Edmund Husserl*, ed. Carlo Ierna, Hanne Jacobs, and Filip Mattens (Dordrecht: Springer, 2010), 333–61.

62 Husserl, *Crisis*, sec. 73, 340.

63 Husserl, *Hua*, 6:275.

Reflection III

ROMARE BEARDEN AND A COLLAGE
OF SELF-KNOWLEDGE

Yasmine Espert

> An artist is an art lover who finds that in all the art that he sees, something is
> missing: to put there what he feels is missing becomes the center of his life's work.
>
> ROMARE BEARDEN[1]

> Knowledge of self is like life after death. . . .
> With broad brushstrokes and tales of incarceration
> You get out of jail with that knowledge of self-determination
> Stand in ovation, because you put the hue in human. . . .
>
> BLACK STAR[2]

The year is 1977. For the first time, artist Romare Bearden (1911–
1988) exhibits *A Black Odyssey* at the Cordier and Ekstrom gallery
on the Upper East Side of Manhattan. His new series includes
twenty collages of luminous land- and seascapes. Each work
pictures an arrangement of silhouetted figures bearing traces of
African art and history. Standing from afar, the images appear to
be seamlessly painted productions. A closer look, however, reveals
how the artist cut and assembled various dyed papers to create the
illusion of a three-dimensional space and its constituent parts.

---

1 Calvin Tomkins Papers, "Some Questions and Some Answers" (New York: MoMA Archive,
Queens, 1976), quoted in Robert G. O'Meally, "Romare Bearden's Black Odyssey: A Search for
Home," in *Romare Bearden: A Black Odyssey* (New York: DC Moore Gallery, 2007), 9.

2 Black Star featuring Vinia Mojica, "K.O.S. (Determination)," on the album *Mos Def & Talib Kweli
Are Black Star* (1998).

To a viewer familiar with the exhaustive practice of ancient
Greek bards, *A Black Odyssey* also exemplifies a feat of epic
proportions: Bearden translated Homer's poem, *The Odyssey*, into
vignettes of cut papers, paint, graphite, and glue. The original
text follows a male warrior on an arduous journey to Ithaca, a
"home" from which he was long separated. Notably, the story's
poetic form demonstrates how the protagonist's interior journey
intimates his search for a physical home. We learn that internal
conflict inevitably, and perhaps necessarily, lies at the horizon of
self-knowledge. It can be argued, then, that self-knowledge is not
one sure destination, but a process. It is an *odyssey* whereby meaning
emerges, even among elements of dissonance. As Bearden's series
demonstrates, numerous episodes were critical to the construction
(and destruction) of Odysseus' sense of self. Time and again,
encounters with sirens, temptation, nymphs, beasts, and deadly
waters tested his will to survive with integrity.

A Black Odyssey depicts episodes of human and otherworldly
encounters, ranging from hostile to harmonious. To facilitate
an array of narrative possibilities, Bearden designed the series
so that knowledge of Homer's ancient poem is optional. As a
visual translator, the artist replaced Odysseus (the "he"/ "I")
with silhouettes of the human form in varying hues. Cut from
plain dark papers, these silhouettes act as shadows of the human
experience. A shadow might be the curvy cut-outs made famous by
Henri Matisse. Other lingering shadows might be the *black figure*
narratives on Greek terra cotta vases (figure 1), or the Disney movie
Hercules (1997). The latter's opening scene exhibits five curvy,
brown bodies strutting out of a Greek vase as they sing the "gospel
truth" (the tragedy of Hercules). Disney's *black figure* narrative
instructs a spectator to read a cartoon's *color* and *form* as race and
gender. The idea of an arousing, feminized blackness—filtered
through the exhaustive groans of gospel music—thus serves as the
backdrop for a heroic tale of Greek masculinity.

Similarly, a spectator's knowledges, or set of assumptions and experiences, can be mapped onto each silhouette in *A Black Odyssey*. The consequence is a perspective that slips away from Odysseus' worldview. This slippage is what activates the vignette; or to use Bearden's words, it inserts "what [the spectator] feels is missing." An end is always another beginning in this multiplication of beings and scenarios. Accordingly, the process of decoding a collage mirrors the process of self-knowledge. Both exist due to a purposeful layering and juxtaposing of phenomena. Just as self-knowledge requires conflict within and around a subject, the legibility of a collage requires a reading of fragmented color, form, and content.

Consider *The Sirens' Song* (figure 2). Here the spectator arrives at the shore of an island bearing witness to a curious scene. Eight figures stand in a horizontal fashion. At the far left, a ninth figure reclines with arms bound behind its back. A crisp, white garment barely covers its torso and groin. References to ancient Greek architecture and music can be found on the fully clothed figure at left of the composition, as well; notice the accoutrements dressing its columnar form. The silhouettes appear to look out to sea, gesturing to a ship crossing the waters. Two ivory-colored birds dive into the scene, guiding the eye across registers of bold color. Blues and greens give us sky, water, and ground. Such simple color-blocking grounds the composition while accents of white paper fragment and fill the constructed space. Like the sweeping birds, frothy waves and hints of clothing seemingly function as metaphors of calm and coolness. The same could be said for the flag atop the ship as it waves in the suggestion of breeze. Assumed signifiers of coolness and harmony, however, are compromised by a figure tied to the mast of the advancing ship. An arched back and dangling limbs signal that this figure may be in distress.

Although *The Siren's Song* is based on Homer's text, our arrival on this island is a dramatic departure from the original *Odyssey*.

Bearden visualizes the story from the perspective of the island-
dwellers rather than those at sea. Homer would have the spectator's
sight situated with—or within—the bound figure, Odysseus. In a
performance of bravado, this ancient protagonist had voluntarily
hoisted himself with the intention to resist the sonic lure of lethal
sirens. Bearden moves away from a strict interpretation. He situates
the spectator of this episode with the "sirens," if we choose to read
them as such.

Several stories, or knowledges, can coexist within one frame. In
addition to reviving the epic poem, this spectacle of island and sea
dwellers conjures thoughts of the transatlantic slave trade. Notice
how the head of the fully clothed, columnar figure is positioned
near the loop of a harp-like object. Is this a musical instrument
or is it a noose? The uncanny similarity must have been striking
to an American audience in 1977, considering the popular media
that featured black figures, people of color—mocked, mutilated,
and mourned—during the Jim Crow, civil rights, and Black
Power eras. Now look to the collars on the silhouettes at the far
right. Through the filter of the transatlantic slave trade, such
accoutrements can be read as the alloy bondages used by slave
owners to punish their human chattel. The song of these "sirens"
and their captives is not a far cry from the colonial encounters
that define centuries of western history. And the body in distress
that lingers at sea? This leads to the possibility of a third narrative.
The ship's cruciform mast recalls the biblical story of Christ's
prophesied death. These transhistorical references build on one
another, allowing a spectator to see the texture of physical and
psychological torment.

The title *A Black Odyssey* is one point of entry to Bearden's cut-and-
paste method. His visual translation of Homer's *Odyssey* situates Africa
in the western canon and vice versa. Bearden riffs on a conventional
myth to present the impossible. In the artist's world of paper
architecture, Odysseus and captured Africans witness one another. It's

at this horizon of the impossible that an understanding (of history, of conflict, of self) becomes more apparent. *The Sirens' Song* meditates on the facts of slavery and its reverberations across space and time; we may think of diasporas, exiles, and the pattern of violence that surround their existence. Encountering this image, and others in *A Black Odyssey*, is a process of continuous mapping and decoding.

The fascinating quality about *The Sirens' Song* lies precisely in its ability to resonate beyond Greek myth. It's akin to the metaphorical afterlives that Black Star conjures in the presence of tragedy. Although Black Star's lyrics equate incarceration with fatality, it offers a revelatory note: "Knowledge of self is like life after death." This abstract notion of self-knowledge puts into perspective a history of encounters—internal and otherwise—contoured by affliction *and* the hope for a revelation. It is constituted by multiple configurations of *what has been* and *what could be* possible.

CHAPTER FOURTEEN

Self-Knowledge in Hermeneutic Philosophy

Charles Guignon

It seems likely that people today, on first encountering the ancient injunction to "know thyself," would see this as enjoining them to be as clear as possible about their position in society, their skill sets and limitations, their family and social connections, and matters of this sort. It also seems clear that, like people in the ancient world, we moderns would assume that following this advice should be of value in achieving the most enriched and fulfilling life available to us. Where our response might differ from that of the ancients, I suspect, is the extent to which our contemporary project of self-knowledge could be concerned with *inner* characteristics we regard as crucial to defining our identity, such factors as feelings, desires, needs, preferences, and disinclinations. What I am suggesting here is that the rise of the modern worldview over the past four hundred years or so has led to an increased preoccupation with the inner, mental life. Whatever the cause of the centrality given to inwardness, people of today cannot think of the "real me" or the "true self" without taking very seriously what lies within.

Recent hermeneutic thinkers have suggested that it is the dominance of epistemology beginning with Descartes and running through Locke and Kant that has played a major role in promoting the modern emphasis on the mental in thinking about the self. Emphasizing the mind and its contents has led to certain ontological presuppositions about our being as humans and about out relation to the world. Hermeneutic philosophers claim that it is these assumptions that mislead us in our thinking about such topics as self-knowledge, and they propose that we see our predicament in a different way, a way that is truer to our actual experience of things as it presents itself in everyday life. In the first three sections of this chapter, I will review some highlights of the recent hermeneutic critique of mainstream modern thought and sketch out the alternative picture of our situation they propose. In the final section, I will ask whether a hermeneutically revised conception of self-knowledge can provide us with a way of seeing the beneficial dimension of self-knowledge by working out the ideal of "authenticity."

14.1. LIFE AND EXPERIENCE

According to a commonly accepted story about the history of philosophy, the preoccupation with the question of knowledge we inherit from Descartes presupposes a picture of humans according to which a sharp distinction is made between an inner mental life and a world of objects of various types that are "out there," on hand for our representing and use. The task of knowing, on this epistemological model, requires that the "subject" correctly represents the object that is to be known. Self-knowledge has a privileged status among types of knowledge, on this model, because the knower in this case has a direct access to the object to be known. The knower knowing itself in introspection has knowledge that is certain insofar as it is incorrigible, at least to the extent that no one can gainsay a person's claims about what is going on inside him or her. The claim here is that one has privileged access to one's own mind and its states and activities by means of an immediate presence of the self to the self. Once this epistemology-based ontology is in place, other types of knowing may be thought of as secondary in their degree of certainty and accessibility.

Hermeneutics challenges many of the ontological assumptions built into the epistemological model by offering us an alternative way of understanding ourselves and our world. From this standpoint, the standard view of our epistemic predicament that gives self-knowledge its privileged status arises from a tendency toward what we might call "methodologism," the idea that the procedures appropriate to natural-science inquiry also provide us with the proper way of conceptualizing humans as they exist on a day-to-day basis.[1] Methodologism gives us a picture of our ordinary lives as having the same structure as the stance we adopt when making observations and forming beliefs. According to methodologism, we are initially and most basically *subjects* receiving and processing data in a condition of disengaged receptivity. Looked at in this way, our basic goal as subjects is to correctly represent what we find around us in order to manipulate it skillfully.

In the case of self-knowledge, the object to be known is also the knowing subject. The conception of both the self as knower and the knowing process is predetermined by preconceptions about the basic ontological makeup of the epistemic situation. The *self* to be known is an enduringly present "center of actions and experiences" immediately given in the knowing. We know ourselves when we turn our attention inward and make observations about what lies within. Self-knowledge is conducive to a successful life because it examines and maintains the mechanism used in any sort of knowledge.

---

1 This account of the "reifying of method" is based on Charles Taylor, "Overcoming Epistemology," in *Philosophical Arguments* (Cambridge, MA: Harvard University Press, 1995), 1–19.

Hermeneutic thinkers set out to undercut this familiar picture of knowledge by proposing an alternative picture of our lives as we actually live them under ordinary conditions. Hermeneutics suggests that, in everyday situations, we are first and foremost *agents* involved in dealings with meaning-laden contexts of equipment in hands-on, engaged ways. As Wilhelm Dilthey famously says, "No real blood flows in the veins of the knowing subject constructed by Locke, Hume and Kant, only the diluted juice of reason, a mere process of thought."[2] Seen from this standpoint, the epistemology-based sense of self is out of touch with the vitality and dynamism of actual life. In opposition to this theoretically based framework, Heidegger regards every form of knowledge, including self-knowledge, as grounded in agential interactions with a shared lifeworld.

14.2. BEING-IN-THE-WORLD

The hermeneutic critique of the traditional epistemological model leads us to see the subject/object and mind/matter dichotomies of the epistemology-based model as arising mainly because, in philosophy, we view things from the theoretical standpoint of philosophizing. The conception of reality put forward by hermeneutics, in contrast, starts from a description of human life as primarily *agency* embedded in a seamless world of interdependencies made accessible through our attuned practical activities. In Heidegger's account, which is characterized by the primacy of the practical, human beings and the contexts of activity in which they are engaged are what they are because of their place in public "worlds." What makes a familiar sort of activity possible—for example, playing a violin—is the background of practices of a specific group of people—for example, music teachers, small

---

2 Wilhelm Dilthey, *Selected Writings*, ed. R. A. Makkreel and F. Rodi, vol. 1 (Princeton, NJ: Princeton University Press, 1989), 50. Cf. Wilhelm Dilthey, *Einleitung in die Geisteswissenschaften, Gesammelte Schriften*, vol. 1 (Leipzig: Teubner, 1923), xviii.

concert groups, inherited styles and techniques, and so on. The norms and conventions sustained by communal practices are passed on and absorbed by ever new generations of practitioners. To be human, then, is to be tuned in to the "possibilities" made accessible by the surrounding social system.

Given this fundamental involvement in the practices of a group, Heidegger can say that our identity—what we typically *are* in the course of our lives—is the *they*.[3] Seen in this light, what we have knowledge of in self-knowledge is not so much information about ourselves as individuals as it is a sense of ourselves as "points of intersection for cultural systems and social organizations with which their existence is woven," in Dilthey's words.[4] From the start we exist as nodal points in webs of relationships that shape the public world we inhabit together. Our being is a "being-with" before it is an "I"—as Charles Taylor says, "We are aware of the world through a 'we' before we are through an 'I.'"[5]

To the extent that introspection assumes that the self is something that lies within and can be discovered through a special sort of inward perception, it is not at all the most trustworthy way to achieve self-knowledge. Inward-turning is notoriously prone to self-deception, especially considering how much is at stake for our self-esteem in our findings. We are subject to self-deception, wishful thinking, exaggeration, false consciousness, repression, and plain illusion. Moreover,

---

3 Martin Heidegger, *Being and Time*, trans. John Macquarrie and Edward Robinson (New York: Harper & Row, 1962), 164. Cf. Martin Heidegger, *Sein und Zeit* (Tübingen: Max Niemeyer, 1972), 126. The German word *man* is the neuter pronoun used in expressions such as "One (*Man*) does not do that around here." Thus, it can mean "anyone" as well as "one" (though using the latter can be misleading in English). I follow the English translators in using "they," but emphasize that this does not mean someone *other than* oneself, for we are all ourselves the they. To demarcate Heidegger's use of this term, I will mark it orthographically by using italics.

4 Wilhelm Dilthey, *Selected Writings*, ed. R. A. Makkreel and F. Rodi, vol. 3 (Princeton, NJ: Princeton University Press, 1989), 270. Cf. Wilhelm Dilthey, *Der Aufbau der Geschichtlichen Welt in den Geisteswissenschaften* (Frankfurt am Main: Suhrkamp, 1974), 310.

5 Charles Taylor, *Philosophy and the Human Sciences*, vol. 2. *of Philosophical Papers* (Cambridge: Cambridge University Press, 1985), 40.

there may be aspects of our lives that fill us with dread, so that we are motivated to cover up what we discover in our self-awareness.

The hermeneutic conclusion to draw from this untrustworthiness of self-inspection is that we gain insights into ourselves not so much through introspection as through catching a glimpse of what goes on in our interactions with others. Insofar as our own being is shaped and defined by the surrounding community, the *they*, self-knowledge—knowledge of our own existence (or *Dasein*, as Heidegger uses this term)[6]—is achieved by looking at our actual ways of responding together to situations on a daily basis. This "being-with" of the *they* is so pervasive that "even one's own Dasein becomes something that it can itself proximally 'come across' only when it looks away from 'experiences' (*Erlebnisse*) and the 'center of its actions,' or does not yet 'see' them at all. Dasein finds 'itself' proximally in *what* it does, uses, expects, avoids."[7] As Heidegger says, *we are what we do.*[8]

The priority of agency in the order of knowing is evident even when I try to get an accurate sense of my own true nature. For example, inward-turning in a quiet, contemplative moment might lead me to think of myself as a calm and easygoing person. But when I notice how I respond in bad traffic, I find that my initial impression was misleading, and that the explosions of my off-the-handle temper are much more typical of the "real me." Self-knowledge, I find, is acquired not in inward-turning, but in getting a feel for how I fit into the shared world in which I find myself—in my modes of attunement (*Stimmung*) to the patterns of the surrounding world. In Heidegger's words, "One's own Dasein, like the co-Dasein of others, is encountered proximally and for

---

6 "Dasein" is the term Heidegger uses, especially in *Being and Time*, to refer to the human being. The term literally means "being-there" and is generally left untranslated.

7 Heidegger, *Being and Time*, 155. Cf. Heidegger, *Sein und Zeit*, 119.

8 Martin Heidegger, *History of the Concept of Time: Prolegomena*, trans. T. Kisiel (Bloomington: University of Indiana Press, 1985), 244, 310. Cf. Martin Heidegger, "Prolegomena zur Geschichte des Zeitbegriffs," in *Gesamtausgabe*, vol. 20 (Frankfurt am Main: Vittorio Klostermann, 1979), 336, 428.

the most part in terms of the with-world."⁹ For this reason, "Knowing oneself (*Sicherkennen*) is grounded in being-with."¹⁰ It is not surprising, then, to find that many people who are close to me know me better than I know myself. Dilthey makes a similar claim when he points out the "narrow limits" of introspection in gaining self-knowledge, saying, "Only a [person's] actions and creations, his fixed expressions of life and the effect these have on others, teach man about himself."¹¹

14.3. Expression and Understanding

Dilthey shows how coming to know who we are depends on a dynamic interaction among three fundamental "structures" making up a human existence. The first of these structure is *life experience*. Life is not just a featureless flow of events with no disruptions or emphases. It is instead constantly punctuated by meaningful, intense experiences that provide the hitching posts for the events that make up the overall flow. The second structure is called *expression*. Life experiences always *press* themselves *outward* to achieve an enduring form (*Aus-druck*) in the objective world. Giving birth to a child, getting a PhD, publishing a book—these experiences exert a pressure to manifest themselves in distinctive ways, for example, by being a parent, a teacher, or a scholar. Through these expressions, enduring "objectifications of life" appear on the scene. The third structure is *understanding*, where this word is used in a somewhat technical sense. According to Dilthey, the meaning-laden continuity among creations and products of ordinary life, together with their place in the larger lifeworld, make us comprehensible to others as well as to ourselves. The intelligibility of these comportments and products of agency make possible what Dilthey

---

9 Heidegger, *Being and Time*, 163. Cf. Heidegger, *Sein und Zeit*, 124.

10 Heidegger, *Being and Time*, 161. Cf. Heidegger, *Sein und Zeit*, 124.

11 Wilhelm Dilthey, *Selected Writings*, trans. H. P. Rickman (Cambridge: Cambridge University Press, 1976), 176 (translation modified). Cf. *Der Aufbau der Geschichtlichen Welt*, 98–99.

calls "understanding" as the ability to make sense of how things hang together.

It is because our access to human being depends on our understanding of expressions that Dilthey says that a person can "learn to recognize himself only by the detour of understanding."[12] We know who and what we are not through some immediate access to what goes on within us, but through the circuitous, roundabout route of understanding the manifestations of life that make up our shared "objective mind." For this reason, our grasp of our own lives involves a "hermeneutic circle": there is a constant back-and-forth movement between an overarching anticipation of the meaning of the whole (our "understanding") and the experiences that make up and modify that constantly emerging whole.

The hermeneutic conception of the self as practically engaged sheds new light on issues about self-knowledge. We can see that knowing ourselves is not a matter of collecting correct representations of what is directly accessible by introspection. Instead, we find that what provides us with knowledge of ourselves is *know-how*, that is, a prereflective competence in doing "what one does" in familiar situations. Any mental accompaniment of our actions ends up having a fairly minor role in grasping what we are doing and who we are. Our temptation to posit a mental activity accompanying our embodied activities is less pressing when we consider actual cases of what we do. Dilthey, for example, tries to get rid of the idea that we need to see two causally connected performances, one mental and one physical, in order to make sense of what is going on with us. In a case of fright, for instance, it is wrong to suppose that the expression of fear is distinct from the feeling that sets it off. As Dilthey says, "The gesture and the terror are not two separate things but a unity."[13] Instead of thinking of this on the "mind causes bodily motion" model, it is more accurate to think of

---

12 Dilthey, *Selected Writings*, 3:168. Cf. Dilthey, *Der Aufbau der Geschichtlichen Welt*, 98–99.
13 Dilthey, *Selected Writings*, 3:229. Cf. Dilthey, *Der Aufbau der Geschichtlichen Welt*, 256.

the outward manifestation and the feeling as one: in typical cases, the scream and the terror are two dimensions of the same thing.

Charles Taylor uses the term "expressivism" to refer to this conception of the role of expression in determining what we are in our lives.[14] Applied to the linguistic realm, this view holds that the words we use are neither simply external clothing for our ideas nor mere signs that must be read backward to their mental origin in order to grasp what the speaker has "in mind." On the contrary, the words we use give a formulation to our ideas: they *define* our feelings and thoughts and thereby enable our utterances to have nuances of meaning that rebound on who we *are* as speakers. The hermeneutic perspective holds that being a human under normal conditions is a matter of mastering and incorporating the meanings and possibilities of interpretation circulating in our public world. What we *are*, then, is an aggregate of possibilities drawn from the pool of intelligibility of our shared world. This is what it means to say that we are always and inextricably instantiations of the *they*. On this basis Rudolf Makkreel can summarize Dilthey's expressivism by saying, "The way we express ourselves, whether in communication or in action, becomes a necessary intermediary for self-understanding. Understanding [of ourselves] must proceed through the interpretation of human objectifications to be reliable."[15]

14.4. HISTORICITY AND AUTHENTICITY

The view we have been considering has the consequence that self-knowledge is achieved not by so much by inward-turning as by a know-how or competence in being a participant in the *they*, where this term refers to the lifeworld into which we are *thrown*. It is from this world that we draw our possibilities and the terms in which we negotiate

---

14 Cf. Charles Taylor, *Hegel* (Cambridge: Cambridge University Press, 1975), 13n.

15 R. A. Makkreel, "Dilthey: Hermeneutics and Neo-Kantianism," in *The Routledge Companion to Hermeneutics*, ed. J. Malpas and H.-H. Gander (London: Routledge, 2015), 79.

our self-interpretations. There is no exit from this contextualization to a standpoint from which we can achieve an especially unique or privileged understanding. Seen in this light, even our venerated idea of "individuality" turns out to be a socially constructed interpretation, one way of being among others. As Heidegger says, "The Self . . . is 'only' . . . one way of being of this entity [that is, *Dasein*]."[16] The distinctive ideas of selfhood and individuality in our contemporary culture are products of a specific historical unfolding and have no binding significance for understanding what it is to be human as such.

But this outcome raises a problem for our original project of trying to show why abiding by the dictum "know thyself" is seen as so important in our modern world. For if we accept that self-knowledge under these conditions produces only transient and contingent interpretations of who we are, interpretations as rife with possible distortions as any deliverance of the *they*, it is hard to see what benefits could be derived from such an achievement. The question then becomes: If the hermeneutic perspective maintains that our "self-knowledge" at any time is merely a collocation of local and defeasible interpretations, how can hermeneutics enable us to make sense of the deep value we accord to self-knowledge? What role does such self-knowledge have in enriching our lives?

To answer this question, we need to make sense of the central idea in Heidegger's thought, the idea of *authenticity*. Although the concept of authenticity is highly debated in Heidegger commentary, it should be possible to distill out a few core ideas relevant to our particular line of questioning. The term translated as "authenticity" is the German *Eigentlichkeit*, a neologism built on the familiar word *eigentlich* (meaning "genuine" or "really"), which in turn contains the stem *eigen* (meaning "own" or "proper"). The implication of the word, then, is that there is a "true self" or "real me" we ought to be true to (and therefore need

---

16 Heidegger, *Being and Time*, 153. Cf. Heidegger, *Sein und Zeit*, 117.

to know) if we are to live the most optimally fulfilling and worthwhile life possible for us.[17] This ideal points to a conception of individuality that is richer and more cogent than the thin current notion of individualism in popular culture today.

Heidegger holds that genuine individuality is an accomplishment rather than a given. According to his account, we discover our ownmost "ability-to-be" as individuals through certain life-transforming personal events. To summarize these events: (1) In existential *anxiety*, one realizes the contingency of all socially available possibilities and judgments of worth and realizes that one is ultimately on one's own in finding value in one's life. "Anxiety individualizes Dasein and thus discloses its *solus ipse*."[18] (2) The recognition of our finitude in facing *death* makes us realize that our lives are moving forward toward their consummation and that it is up to us to give that unfolding a content and goal. We exist as "anticipatory running-forward" toward being-a-whole. And (3), in the experience of *guilt* (*Schuld*, a word that implies "debt"), we recognize that, as *they*-selves, we are coming up short of what we could be as authentic selves, with the result that we feel a pull to transform our average everyday constellation of possibilities into a self that is our own. Given these transformations, according to Heidegger, we come to approach our lives with *resoluteness*: we own up to the choices we make and thereby act in the mode of "choosing to choose," firmly taking a stand on our current "Situation" and dedicating ourselves to what shows up under these conditions as genuinely worthy of our choice.[19]

The upshot of this new insight into what we can and should be is a recognition that our lives are temporal, future-directed unfoldings in which

---

17 Cf. Charles Guignon, *On Being Authentic* (London: Routledge, 2004), ch. 1.

18 Heidegger, *Being and Time*, 233. Cf. Heidegger, *Sein und Zeit*, 188.

19 For Heidegger, the technical term *Situation* refers to worldly conditions in a way distinguished from mere "circumstances" (*Lage*). In a "Situation," the context of action is encountered as meaning-laden, making a demand for decisiveness and intensity.

our commitment to what we will be as a whole defines how we encounter what has passed. With this sense of the "thrown projection" of our lives, we have a basis for acting coherently and clear-sightedly in the present moment. This temporal "spanning" of a life course is called *historicity*. For Heidegger, human being is characterized by historicity in a double sense. First, a life is a "happening" (*Geschehen*, a word that is etymologically related to *Geschichte*, the German word for "history") in the sense that it is a constantly forward-moving project with the structure of a hermeneutic circle. We are always in motion toward the consummation of our lives. Second, "historicity" also refers to the ongoing historical unfolding of the community into which every human being is thrown. Because of this pre-given "facticity," we are indebted to a broader world-historical story that provides the meaningful background for the choices we make in being the individuals we are. We grasp our complicity and indebtedness when we understand what that history is. As Heidegger puts it, "To understand history cannot mean anything else than to understand ourselves—not in the sense that we might establish various things about ourselves, but that we experience what we *ought* to be. To appropriate a past means to come to know oneself as indebted to that past."[20]

What defines the "self," then, is our distinctive way of stitching together the events that occur and the resulting *continuity* of events (*Zusammenhang*) that constitutes a story we can make our own. Here, the identity of the self, the "being-one's-own-self" that we think of as personal identity, is accomplished by seizing on and reconfiguring the otherwise distracted and dispersed "*they*-self" into a focused, clear-sighted projection. It is what Ricoeur calls an "*ipse*-identity," a selfsameness that results from continuity of ongoing construction rather than mere sameness (*idem*-identity).[21] The self-knowledge that emerges

---

20 Martin Heidegger, *Plato's "Sophist"*, trans. R. Rojcewicz and A. Schuwer (Bloomington: University of Indiana Press, 1997), 7. Cf. Martin Heidegger, *Gesamtausgabe*, vol. 19 (Frankfurt am Main: Vittorio Klostermann, 1992), 11.

21 Cf. Paul Ricoeur, *Oneself as Another*, trans. K. Blamey (Chicago: University of Chicago Press, 1992), 3. Cf. Paul Ricoeur, *Soi-même comme un autre* (Paris: Éditions du Seuil, 1990), 13.

through becoming authentic is not a set of correct representations that can be expressed in propositions. It is less a *knowing that* than a *knowing how*—it is a mastery in what is involved in the art of living.

Self-knowledge will have two aspects corresponding to the two constitutive dimensions of a human life: (1) being-the-*they* and (2) being able to realize our potentiality-for-being an authentic self. On the one side, our embeddedness in the *they* reveals to us our finitude and our belongingness to a human community. Like all humans, we find ourselves to be mortal, vulnerable, fallible, and lacking any real certainty about the value of what we undertake. We are condemned to finding a place for ourselves in the midst of the practices made available by our culture. To fully grasp who we are, we need to know our limits and recognize our fallibility. Yet, at the same time, having a grasp of our limits opens us to a "finite freedom" that liberates us from the illusory idea that unrealistic projects are within the realm of the possible. Because *Dasein* can take over the "*powerlessness* (*Ohnmacht*) of being abandoned to itself, thereby becoming lucid about the accidents of the disclosed Situation," it can gain the "powerless superior power (*Übermacht*) which puts itself in readiness for adversities."[22]

Having the clarity of understanding one's own existence as an ongoing "happening" moving toward a consummation opens one to the recognition that not everything is possible for us and that we need to make choices that are focused, life-defining and in tune with the "heritage" of our community. Dilthey had suggested that all people come to have an overarching purpose in the course of their lives. In living, there is a tendency toward "the achieving of over-riding purposes to which all individual purposes are subordinated, that is, the realizing of a highest good."[23] Whether or not we agree that coming to have a defining project or set of projects comes naturally to everyone, it should be clear

---

22 Heidegger, *Being and Time*, 436. Cf. Heidegger, *Sein und Zeit*, 384–5.

23 Dilthey, *Selected Writings*, 3:222–3. Cf. Dilthey, *Der Aufbau der Geschichtlichen Welt*, 248.

that making commitments to ends that present themselves as genuinely worthwhile gives us a way of understanding who we are and what we are for. When one's historicity is guided by a wholehearted and lucid commitment to a fundamental project, one finds oneself with a self that is worth knowing and caring about.[24] Resoluteness can bring about changes in the way a person lives. Heidegger emphasizes the need for *simplifying* our lives by stripping away trivial or extraneous possibilities in order to organize the possibilities we embrace in a way that defines the purpose of our lives. As he says, "Only by the anticipatory running forward of [the confrontation with] death is every accidental and 'provisional' possibility driven out. Only being-free *for* death gives Dasein its goal outright and pushes existence into its finitude. Only by grasping the finitude of one's existence is one snatched back from the endless multiplicity of possibilities which offer themselves as closest to one . . . and brought into the simplicity of fate."[25]

Simplifying enables one to achieve what I would call "focus" in one's life. Heidegger thinks of this sort of focus as realized by zeroing in on what stands out as of crucial importance in one's existence. Real freedom, he says, "*is* only in the choice of *one* possibility—that is, in tolerating one's not having chosen the others and not being able to choose them."[26] A life given direction by a defining ideal "cannot *become rigid* as regards the Situation, but must understand that the resolution . . . must be *held open* and free for the current possibility. The certainty of the resolution signifies that one *holds oneself free* for the possibility of *taking it back.*"[27] It follows that *resilience* is also part of what is involved in knowing ourselves.

24 This thesis has been developed in detail by Somogy Varga, *Authenticity as an Ethical Ideal* (New York: Routledge, 2012), Part II.

25 Heidegger, *Being and Time*, 435. Cf. Heidegger, *Sein und Zeit*, 384.

26 Heidegger, *Being and Time*, 331. Cf. Heidegger, *Sein und Zeit*, 285.

27 Heidegger, *Being and Time*, 355. Cf. Heidegger, *Sein und Zeit*, 307–8.

The authentic self is something that can come to light only when one achieves the kind of authentic historicity that imparts constancy and coherence to the self. In Heidegger's words,

The self's resoluteness against the inconstancy of distraction is in itself a *steadiness which has been stretched along*—the steadiness with which Dasein as fate "incorporates" into its existence birth and death and their "between," and holds them as thus "incorporated," so that in such constancy Dasein is, in a moment of vision, for what is world-historical in its current Situation.[28]

On my interpretation of this passage, what Heidegger is saying is that authentic resoluteness enables one to grasp what one truly *is* as an ongoing happening that comports itself toward the world; it is not just a stringing together of thoughts and feelings directly present in one's mind. Authenticity is a matter of the *how* of a life, not the *what*: it is more a matter of what we *do* and how we do it than it is of a specific content expressible in propositions.

Although the exemplars of the purpose-driven life that come to mind are figures such as Martin Luther in the religious life and Vincent Van Gogh in art, purposiveness is not just a possibility for people with a strong vocational commitment. When Dilthey says that "no life is so meager that its course lacks all shape (*Gestaltung*),"[29] he implies that even ordinary people can have life-defining commitments, as is evident in the case of working-class parents who make sacrifices so that their children can have a better life than they did. The ideal expressed in the dictum "know thyself" seems to be of value to everyone, but it is especially valid for a committed philosopher. For it enjoins us to achieve a clear-sightedness, integrity, and steadfastness that lets us be motivated by something more weighty than vanity or a desire for fame. Instead,

---

28 Heidegger, *Being and Time*, 442. Cf. Heidegger, *Sein und Zeit*, 390–1.
29 Dilthey, *Selected Writings*, 3:253. Cf. *Der Aufbau der Geschichtlichen Welt*, 287.

to know who and what you are is to be self-critical about your motives and to dedicate yourself to discovering the truth. Self-knowledge contributes to making life a continually valuable undertaking while reinforcing the humility needed to be ready to take back one's commitments if necessary.

CHAPTER FIFTEEN

The First Person and Self-Knowledge in Analytic Philosophy

Sebastian Rödl

One may doubt that there is work in the tradition of analytic philosophy that relates to Socratic self-knowledge. It is true that there is an extended literature on "I"-thought, self-reference, first-person authority, and the like. But the motive of this literature does not seem to be a desire to know ourselves in the Socratic sense. Yet it is possible, I believe, to find in analytic philosophy a strand of thought that leads us into the innermost of the Socratic question.

Socrates maintains that, as long as he lacks self-knowledge, it is ridiculous to pursue any other knowledge (or, perhaps, other-knowledge).[1] This cannot be true if self-knowledge is knowledge of

---

[1] "But I have no time for such things; and the reason, my friend, is this. I am still unable, as the Delphic inscription orders, to know myself; and it really seems to be ridiculous to look into other things before I have understood that" (Plato, *Phaedrus*, in *Complete Works*, ed. John M. Cooper [Indianapolis: Hackett, 1997]), 229e–30a).

a special object, a special topic, a special content: the self. It can be true only if self-knowledge is distinguished by its manner of knowing. Socrates' question cannot rule philosophy, it cannot rule human life, if self-knowledge, as knowledge of a certain area of reality, lies alongside knowledge of other areas of reality. There are three texts that circumscribe the space within which analytic thought on self-knowledge moves: Castañeda's "'He': A Study in the Logic of Self-Consciousness," the chapter on self-reference in Evans' *The Varieties of Reference*, and Anscombe's "The First Person."[2] These texts force upon us the question whether self-knowledge can be subsumed under a general concept of knowledge of things and how it can be thought of if it cannot. This chapter therefore shall be a reading of these texts. It is a partial reading, its partiality being dictated by the volume's topic.[3] In the end, we find analytic philosophy not to be cut off from the Socratic question. Indeed, we can represent analytic reflection on first-person thought as a struggle to restore the Socratic question to its state as the fount of philosophy.

15.1. CASTAÑEDA

In his essay "'He': A Study in the Logic of Self-Consciousness," Castañeda discusses a use of the reflexive pronoun in which it represents, in *oratio obliqua*, the first-person character of the thought or statement reported. In order to indicate that the pronoun is used in this way, he introduces a new sign, the starred pronoun: "she*".

---

2 G. E. M. Anscombe, "The First Person," in *Collected Philosophical Papers*, vol. 2, *Metaphysics and the Philosophy of Mind* (Minneapolis: University of Minnesota Press, 1981), 21–36; Hector-Neri Castañeda, "'He': A Study in the Logic of Self-Consciousness," *Ratio* 8 (1996), 130–57; Gareth Evans, *The Varieties of Reference* (Oxford: Oxford University Press, 1982).

3 The editor of Gareth Evans' *The Varieties of Reference*, John McDowell, informed me in conversation that the relevant chapter of this work has nothing to do with the Socratic question. So it is possible to read this chapter without any thought of the Socratic question. I seek to show that it is possible to read it with this question in mind. Likewise for the other texts.

The ordinary pronoun, in *oratio obliqua*, signifies that she who thinks something of someone is the same as she of whom she thinks it. It leaves open how she thinks of her. When we say, "The editor of *Soul* thinks she is a millionaire," what we say is true provided only that she whom the editor thinks is a millionaire is none other than the editor. It is true, then, if she thinks something she would express by "The person holding lottery ticket No. 17 is a millionaire," provided that person is the editor, or by "The one of whom Mary spoke yesterday is a millionaire," provided Mary spoke of the editor, and so on.

The pronoun "she*", by contrast, signifies not only that she who thinks something of someone is the same as she of whom she thinks it, but that she thinks it in a way whose expression in language requires a first-person pronoun. If we call knowledge expressed by the first-person pronoun self-knowledge, then an inquiry into the logical character of "she*" is an inquiry into the nature of self-knowledge. Thus Castañeda writes: "This use of 'he' [the one for which he introduces the sign 'he*'] . . . as a pointer to the object of someone's self-knowledge, self-belief, self-conjecture, is the main topic of this study."[4]

Castañeda notes that "she*" cannot be analyzed in any other terms. This is not surprising. But it has a consequence whose formulation Castañeda announces as "a high point of the paper."[5]

In general, Castañeda observes, it is possible to infer "p" from "X knows that p." However, if X's knowledge is represented by "she*"—if the knowledge X is reported to have is *self*-knowledge—then there is no sentence by which to express what X is said to know without introducing X as knowing it. If, for example, the editor of *Soul* knows that she* is a millionaire, we cannot express what she knows by saying "She* is a millionaire," for "she*" has no free-standing use. Nor is there any other term distinct from the first-person pronoun by which, using it

---

4 Castañeda, "He": A Study in the Logic of Self-Consciousness," 130.
5 Ibid., 131.

instead of "she*", we can state what the editor of *Soul* is said to know in "She knows that she* is a millionaire." We can bring out the significance of this finding in this way. In general, reports of knowledge conjoin a clause that specifies what is known, a term that designates her who knows it, and a verb that represents her as knowing it. And in general, we can consider what someone knows independently of the fact that she knows it. When someone knows that p, there is, on the one hand, what she knows; on the other hand, there is her knowing it. This distinction seems central to the proper conception of thought and knowledge. It finds expression in Frege's distinction of the thought, which is something that can be true or false, from the judgment, which is an act of affirming a thought. Frege's distinction is represented in the concept of a propositional attitude. A Fregean thought is a proposition, something known, the attitude, a manner in which a subject may relate to a proposition, knowing it, say. When we try thinking self-knowledge through these concepts, we are led to think that, in self-knowledge, the subject appears twice over: as knowing and in what is known. Of course, this does not distinguish self-knowledge from knowledge reported by an ordinary reflexive pronoun. When the editor of *Soul* knows something she would express by "The editor is a millionaire," then she, the editor, appears twice over: as the one of whom she knows something and as the one who knows it. In order to characterize self-knowledge, we must say more than that the subject appears twice over, as subject of the attitude and in the proposition. Now, we may hope to characterize self-knowledge by a special manner in which these two appearances of the subject are related. But Castañeda's finding shows that this is futile. When the subject self-knows, then there is no expressing what she knows in a way that does not involve the first-person pronoun and thus introduces the subject, not only as an element of what is known, but also as the one knowing it. There is no prying apart the two appearances of the subject. Which is to say that there are not two appearances, specially related, but one. In self-knowledge, there is no isolating what is known from the subject's knowing it; the distinction of thought and affirmation, proposition and attitude, does not apply.

Castañeda's reflections suggest that "self" in "self-knowledge" does not specify what is known, but the manner of knowing of it; it does not belong with the content phrase "I know SELF is F," but with the cognitive verb, "I *self*-know being F." An analogy may help bringing this contrast in view. If I possess a power to move things, I can apply this power to myself: when my right arm is paralyzed, I can move it, with my left hand, say. Here, I appear twice in the movement: as the one who moves something and as the one whom I move. Obviously, while this is movement of oneself, it is not self-movement. Moving my right arm with my left arm, I am moving my left arm; *this* is self-movement. I suppose no one would propose to define self-movement as an act of a power to move things in which she who moves not only is the same as she whom she moves, but in which, furthermore, these two roles of the subject are related in a special way. Self-movement cannot be comprehended as a special act of the power to move things. For any act of the latter power, as such, is self-movement. Hence, in self-movement, I do not appear twice, but once: moving my left arm, I self-move. "Self" in "self-movement" indicates not the thing moved, but the manner of movement.

As it is with self-movement, so it may be with self-knowledge. If I possess a power to think of things, I can apply this power to myself. I may think of Sebastian Rödl that he is F. Here the subject appears twice over: as the one who thinks of someone and as the one of whom he thinks. This is not self-thought. Our reflections on self-movement suggest that it may be wrong to try to define self-thought by a distinctive way in which, in it, the two appearances of the subject are related. Perhaps, in self-thinking, I do not apply my power to think of objects to myself. Perhaps I do not think of an object, which is I, that it is F. Perhaps, rather, I think myself to be F, or, not consonant with English grammar, but perspicuous in its logical grammar: I self-think being F. Here the subject does not appear twice, but once, and *the need to specify a relation of the two roles of the subject falls away.* So it will be, if the parallel to self-movement extends to this aspect of it: self-thought is not a special act of the power to think of objects because any act of the latter power, as such, is self-thought.

15.2. EVANS I: SELF-LOCALIZATION

Self-thinking is not thinking a distinguished content; it is a distinguished manner of thinking. We so describe the significance of Castañeda's high point by hindsight. The first response to it was different; the idea of thought as propositional attitude was so entrenched as to repel reflection. (By and large, it still is.) When we hold to the notion that self-thought, as any thought, is an attitude toward a proposition, then Castañeda will be heard to raise the question how this proposition can be specified, specifically, how the contribution of the first-person pronoun to it can be specified. For there is no form of words by which one can express what the editor knows in knowing that she* is a millionaire that isolates what she thus knows from her knowing it. A first response to *this* question was the following. The proposition known in self-knowledge does not reflect its character as self-knowledge; the first-person pronoun contributes to this proposition nothing but the object—that is, the subject knowing it—and not any manner in which she thinks of herself in knowing it. Hence with respect to the proposition known, there is no difference between the knowledge expressed by "I am a millionaire," said by a given man, and that expressed by "This man is a millionaire," referring to that same man. This is a cop-out.[6]

---

6 This response is called "neo-Russellian." The relation to Russell is of no relevance here. The neo-Russellian supplements her account with a further kind of semantic value of the sentence, its character, which is a function from an index to a proposition. The character associated with the first-person pronoun determines the speaker to figure in the proposition known in self-knowledge. This makes no difference to its being a cop-out. As this function does not figure in the speaker's thought (if it did, we would have to ask how she thinks of the relevant argument of the function: the speaker), it does nothing to explain the way in which one thinks of oneself in the first person.

The cop-out provides the background against which Gareth Evans undertook to answer the question, what does the first-person pronoun contribute to the proposition (the proposition that a presupposed theory, the theory that knowledge is a propositional attitude, postulates is known in self-knowledge)?[7] Evans' response to this question, despite himself, establishes that self-knowledge is not an application of a generic power to know of particular things to a specific such thing: oneself.

If self-knowledge is distinguished by what is known, it can and must be comprehended on the basis of a prior and independent account of what it is to know something. And if it is knowledge of a particular object, it can and must be understood on the basis of a prior account of knowledge of particular objects. This is how Evans proceeds. He lays out a general account of what it is to think of a particular object[8] in order then to explain how various forms of reference, among them self-reference, realize the given general concept of thought of a particular object.

He begins with the notion that thinking is thinking something of something: thinking something general, a concept, of something particular, an object. She who thinks understands the generality of the concept she applies. That is, she has the idea of a manifold of objects to which the concept may apply. Now, a concept does not particularize itself. Therefore, if an act of applying a concept is to be knowledge of something particular, the particular must be *given*; it is not apprehended in the concept, but *in an act distinct from the act of applying the concept*. This is the act of reference, which, from the manifold of objects the idea of which is contained in the concept, singles out a particular one. Evans identifies the first and fundamental manifold of objects with the totality of objects in space and time. Hence, in the

---

7 It is called "neo-Fregean," as it seeks to represent first-person knowledge as affirmation of a Fregean thought.

8 Cf. Evans, *The Varieties of Reference*, ch. 4.3 and ch. 4.4.

first and fundamental case, an act of reference singles out an object by representing it as distinguished from all others by its location at a given time. Moreover, as the object of reference is spread out in space and persists through time, an act of reference refers to it through its kind: the principle of its temporal and spatial unity. Evans calls the idea of an object as distinguished from all others by its kind and its location in space and time its fundamental idea; it is fundamental as any reference to an object involves the fundamental idea of this object.

According to this account, the idea of the totality of objects in space and time precedes and makes possible any reference to a particular object; it precedes and makes possible any application of a concept to such an object. This idea, being at the bottom of the fundamental level of thought, is provided by thought itself; it is active in thinking as such.

Evans proceeds to explain how demonstrative thought singles out its object.[9] Demonstrative thought is sustained by the subject's perception of its object. For, thinking demonstratively, the subject thinks of the object as the one whom she (or rather she*) is able to determine in virtue of perceiving it.[10] This is an act of reference, as perceiving the object enables the subject to locate it. She can locate the object relative to herself*, egocentrically. However, that she *locates* it means that she understands the location so specified to be one that can also be specified objectively, by reference to a relatively stable system of objects— this mountain, that tree, that river, say. In this way, perceiving the

---

9 Ibid., ch. 6.

10 The fact that perception sustaining demonstrative reference is self-conscious—that perceiving an object in this way is being conscious of perceiving it—is less than perfectly explicit in *Varieties*. Yet it is fundamental to its account. A subject's perception of an object enables her demonstratively to refer to it as her perception furnishes her with an idea that locates the object she perceives relative to herself*. In perceiving an object, then, the subject is conscious of herself*; being conscious of herself* in perceiving the object, she is conscious of herself* as perceiving it. It is irrelevant whether she knows the word "perception." The self-consciousness of perception is all but explicit in the following passage, to which I will return: "The very idea of a perceivable, objective, spatial world brings with it the idea of the subject as being in the world" (ibid., 222). This represents the idea of a perceivable world as an act of self-knowledge (the context fixes it that "the idea of the subject" is the subject's idea of herself*). This can be true only if perceiving is knowing oneself to perceive.

object, thinking of it demonstratively, the subject relates the object to its fundamental idea, distinguishing it from all others.

If we place self-thought within this account of thought, we think of self-thought as applying a concept by way of an act of reference that singles out an object from all objects in space and time. So how does someone, thinking "I", single out an object in space and time? Evans answers: egocentrically locating an object of demonstrative thought, the subject locates herself* relative to this object. She not only singles out the object of her demonstrative thought, distinguishing it from all others; she also singles out herself* from among these objects.[11]

This does *not* subsume self-thought under the given generic account of thought of particular objects. On the contrary. It shows that it cannot be so subsumed. While it is true that, thinking a demonstrative thought, the subject locates herself* relative to the object of her thought, it does not follow that there is an act of reference in which she singles herself* out from among all objects in space and time. There is such an act only if the subject's idea of this manifold *precedes* her self-thought. Only then is there the question which of these objects she thinks of in thinking of herself*, the question that an act of reference, if there were one, would answer. And this is not so. For the idea of a manifold of objects in space and time *is* an act of self-thought. This transpires in Evans in many ways, notably in a passage in which he observes that objective localization, in terms of a relatively stable system of objects, includes egocentric localization of those objects.[12] Indeed, Evans emphasizes that a subject's idea of a world of objects in

11 Evans also asserts that "we have what might be described as a general capacity to perceive our own bodies, although this can be broken down into several distinguishable capacities: our proprioceptive sense, our sense of balance, of heat and cold, of pressure" (ibid., 220). I disregard this because Evans does not say how these ways of gaining knowledge of oneself*, on their own, link up to the fundamental level of thought to provide one with an adequate idea of oneself.

12 Appendix 3 to chapter 7. Cf. ibid., 265: "In that case, the seemingly objective mode of thinking about space is, after all, contaminated by egocentricity." The editor of *Varieties* presents this as a worry of Evans', a worry, one will suppose, that he had not achieved clarity about the way in which self-thought relates to the objectivity of thought. I am elaborating this worry.

space and time is an idea of a world in which she* is located.[13] The starred pronoun, the way of thinking expressed by "I", is *inside* the idea that constitutes any act of reference as such; it is inside the idea that constitutes thinking something of something. It follows that there is no comprehending this way of thinking as a variety of reference; there is no comprehending it as an act of a power to think something of something applied to her who thinks it.

Evans is eager to assert that she of whom I think in self-thinking is a being in space and time, physical, material, sensible. (He seems to think this is important to rebut vicious philosophical tendencies, such as "Cartesianism.") But there is no need to establish as a fact that I am in space and time. We need to comprehend *how* a subject comprehends herself* to be in space and time; we need to comprehend this from an account of the way in which she thinks of herself in self-thought. So we *would*, *if* self-thought involved an act of reference that singles out, from all objects in space and time, one such object as the one of whom I think in self-thought. And this it does not. In demonstrative thought of an object she perceives, the subject locates herself*. This shows *that* a subject—anyway, one who thinks demonstrative thoughts—knows herself* to be in space and time. It does not show *how* she thinks of herself in self-thought. It shows how she does *not*: not by way of an act of reference. Thinking demonstratively of objects, she has always already distinguished herself from all objects of which she thinks demonstratively. Thinking of herself* is a single act she has always already performed in any reference, any concept, any thought. Whatever this act is, the act of thinking of oneself*, it is *not* an act of reference.

---

13 Cf. the passage partially quoted above: "Any thinker who has an idea of an objective spatial world—an idea of a world of objects and phenomena which can be perceived but which are not dependent on being perceived for their existence—must be able to think of his perception of the world as being simultaneously due to his position in the world, and to the condition of the world at that position. The very idea of a perceivable, objective, spatial world brings with it the idea of the subject being *in* the world, with the course of his perceptions being due to his changing position in the world and to the more or less stable way the world is. The idea that there is an objective world and the idea that the subject is somewhere cannot be separated, and where he is given by what he can perceive" (ibid., 222). This must be read in the first person, with stars applied accordingly.

15.3. ANSCOMBE

That "I" does not refer is asserted by Anscombe in her essay "The First Person." Evans frequently speaks of this essay and its thesis, and rejects it. But it is obvious that his response is not one of rejection, but of bafflement. He has no idea what she might be saying by these words: "I" does not refer. We are in a better position, by hindsight: Anscombe says that "self" in "self-knowledge" does not belong with the content clause, but with the cognitive verb; it does not contribute to what is known, but specifies the act of knowing. As self-movement is not an act of a power to move things, applied to oneself, so self-thought is not an act of a power to think of things, applied to oneself. For, any act of the power to move things is self-movement; in the same way, as indeed Evans shows, any act of the power to think something of something is an act of self-thought.

"I" does not refer; there is no proposition to which "I" might make a contribution. There is no such proposition because self-knowledge is not a propositional attitude. It is not predicating something of something, which something is one*self*. It is *self*-predicating something. Anscombe develops this thesis in this way: she discusses various ways in which one may refer to an object, specifically by name and demonstratively, and finds that self-thought does not involve referring to oneself in these ways. One may be tempted to respond that this does not show that "I" does not refer, but only that it does not refer in these ways. We must conclude, one might say, not that "I" does not refer, but that it refers in a different way from these. It is, in Evans' word, a different variety of reference. This response is good only if we have a general account of reference under which we can subsume self-thought. The only author of whom I am aware who not only gave the mentioned response to Anscombe, but sought to entitle himself to it by explaining self-thought within a general account of reference, is Evans. And his work bears out Anscombe's procedure. It shows that the concepts through which we think reference in general spring from

demonstrative reference: they are concepts through which we understand reference mediated by sensory affection by, and perception of,
the object to which we refer. First, Evans' account of thinking lays it
down that a concept does not particularize itself; in order for a concept to figure in particular knowledge, something particular must be
given, given in the sense that its apprehension is distinct from the act
of applying the concept. So the manifold of objects the idea of which
is contained in any concept is a totality of objects that may be given: a
totality of objects of sense experience. The idea of this totality is the
idea of the form of sense experience: the a priori character something
exhibits as an object of sense experience.[14] Moreover, as the object of
reference is given in sense experience and thus is spread out in space
and persists through time, there must be, in our thought of it, a concept through which we conceive its spatial and temporal unity, a concept of its kind, a sortal.

When Anscombe's thesis seems incomprehensible, the principle
of charity requires that we interpret it as more limited, stating not
straight out that there is no reference in self-thought, but no reference
of a certain kind. For example, one may propose that Anscombe states
merely that there is no receptive reference in self-thought, no reference
mediated by an act of receptivity, or affection.[15] Or one may say that
Anscombe holds only that in self-thought, there is no reference involving application of a sortal, as Anscombe puts it, a conception of the
object.[16] However, saying this is saying nothing at all, for there is no
concept of reference that remains intact as we subtract these features.

14 Evans introduces the idea of the manifold of objects in space and time prior to representing these
objects as objects of perception. Contrast Ernst Tugendhat, *Vorlesungen zur Einführung in eine sprachanalytische Philosophie* (Frankfurt am Main: Suhrkamp, 2010), who explains space as the form of the
perceptual relation to the object of judgment, thus conceiving the relevant totality as the totality of
objects of experience.

15 As I did. Cf. Sebastian Rödl, *Self-Consciousness* (Cambridge, MA: Harvard University Press,
2007), ch. 4.

16 Cf. Edward Harcourt, "The First Person: Problems of Sense and Reference," in *Logic, Cause and
Action: Essays in Honour of Elizabeth Anscombe*, ed. Roger Teichmann (Cambridge: Cambridge
University Press, 2000), 25–46.

15.4. EVANS II: TRANSPARENCY

Evans describes a way to determine what one believes, such that, so thinking of oneself as believing it is self-thinking: I can determine whether I believe p by considering whether p. Asking myself whether p, and reasoning that p, because, say, q, r, s, I know that I believe p, indeed, that I believe it on the ground that q, r, s. This is self-knowledge. Richard Moran, in *Authority and Estrangement*, extends this idea to desire. I can determine whether I desire X by reflecting whether X is desirable. Asking whether X is desirable, and reasoning that indeed it is because q, r, s, I come to know that I desire X, indeed, that I desire it on the ground that q, r, s. Thus I can come to know what I think by reflecting what it is right to think and why, and I can come to know what I desire by thinking about what is desirable and why.[17] This has been described by the term "transparency": a question concerning myself, namely, whether I believe p, is *transparent to* the question whether p. That the former question is transparent to the latter means: I answer the former question by considering what answer is right to the latter.

In describing this manner of gaining knowledge of oneself[18]—"transparency"—Evans calls attention to a formal character of judgment: judging that things are so is responding to the question *whether they are so or not* in the consciousness *that one is answering this question*. So judging that things are so is judging it to the exclusion of judging the contrary. Thus judging is being conscious of judging, in the manner of being conscious of judging correctly. In consequence, judging may be judging on grounds one thinks reveal one's judgment to be correct; judging on grounds in this way is being conscious of judging on these grounds.

We may designate the above-described character of judgment and the will—that judging is a consciousness of judging correctly, and thus,

---

17 Cf., e.g., Richard Moran, *Authority and Estrangement: An Essay on Self-Knowledge* (Princeton, NJ: Princeton University Press, 2001), ch. 2.6.

18 It is misleading to call this a way of *gaining* knowledge of oneself. This suggests that there is something there to be known, of which one may, or may not, come to know.

in some cases, on grounds that reveal the validity of one's judgment; that willing is a consciousness of willing well, and thus, in some cases, on grounds that reveal the goodness of so willing—by saying that judgment and will are reason. However, thinking of myself in this way, it appears that I am judgment, I am will, I am reason. The term "I" indicates the formal character of judgment, will, reason. There is no comprehension from here, it seems, of the subject as being in space and time. Evans is explicit about this. Therefore he adds that the subject, who in this way thinks of herself as believing something, must, in addition, think of herself as an object in space and time.[19] But we saw that he has no way of saying how she does so.

This difficulty remains submerged in Moran. Moran describes belief and desire as self-predicated acts. Contrary to Evans, he does not make explicit that the subject, so thought, is merely formal. Nor does he mention the necessity of conjoining his account of self-thought with an explanation of how one thinks of oneself* as in space and time. Moran asserts that what the subject knows, knowing that she believes p, is an empirical psychological fact, which as such is a proper object of empirical knowledge. But this assertion has no basis in the description Moran gives of the way in which the subject thinks of herself*. Thus he asserts the existence of two standpoints, perspectives on the same—the alleged empirical psychological fact—while providing no idea of a perspective that embraces both and thus could render comprehensible the assertion that they relate to the same.[20]

---

19 Evans, *The Varieties of Reference*, 231f.

20 In Rödl, *Self-Consciousness*, ch. 6, and in Sebastian Rödl, "Intentional Transaction," *Philosophical Explorations* 17.3 (2014): 303–16, I argue that the apprehension of *another* subject of judgment and will, which as such is apprehension of such a subject as a material and temporal reality, is not empirical.

15.5. Conclusion

"I" does not refer: this is the conclusion wrought from us by our discussion of Castañeda, Evans, and Anscombe. There is a different way in which to conceive "I": as articulating the form of reason, of judgment, of will. But we do not understand how this account of "I" can deliver an idea of the subject as in space and time, as material and sensible. Here is the Socratic question. The question expresses puzzlement: humanity is confounded by itself. Our partial survey of analytic philosophy on the topic found the wonder of humanity folded up in the very saying of "I": thinking "I", we do not know whether we think beast or god. It can be no surprise that the Socratic question lives inside the very saying of "I". The question is asked in the first person; it can only be answered in the first person. It must arise from, and its answer be locked in, "I".

Reflection IV

SELF-PORTRAITURE

Christopher S. Wood

Can self-portraiture yield self-knowledge? There would seem to be two possible ways for it to do so. The self-portraitist may come to know something about herself in the process of creating the self-portrait; or the finished self-portrait, contemplated in tranquility, may deliver special knowledge about the self. To be interesting, such knowledge would need to exceed what the person might come to know about herself through introspection alone.

Before assessing these possibilities, however, we must define self-portraiture. A portrait is an image of a human being that refers to a real person. That reference is achieved by linking a name to the image, or by creating a degree of resemblance sufficient to permit (at least some) beholders to recognize the image as a depiction of an individual. The referents of many portraits are lost, but when such depictions comply with conventions of portraiture, they may achieve an effect of reference.

Sometimes an individual who wishes to have a portrait of himself lacks the skills to make one. So he delegates the task to a painter or photographer. The sitter can continue to contribute to the project, however, by adopting a pose and so countering the will of the artist to control the meeting.

When the individual who commissions the portrait and the individual who fabricates the portrait are the same person, we speak of a self-portrait. This individual possesses a mirror and knows how to paint, or knows how to operate the timer on a camera, and so does not need to bring in a second party. The two agents behind the portrait become one. The contest of wills involved in portraiture collapses, in self-portraiture, into a feedback loop of posing and seeing through the pose. The difference between the self-portrait and the commissioned portrait is that in the latter agency is shared. The commissioned portrait can thus be understood as a special case of the self-portrait.

Can the self-portraitist come to learn something singular about himself during the process of making the self-portrait? In fixing the perception of a face, stilling it, can the self-portrait add anything to what one can already see in a mirror? Note that the topic here is self-portraiture since the fifteenth century, when effective mirrors first became available in Europe. Self-knowledge in the age of the mirror (and later the camera) aims mostly to individuate: to identify those attributes that distinguish one from others. Other traditions of self-knowledge, for example the Christian memento mori that reminds us that we are all mortal, are deindividuating.

The answer to the question "Can self-portraiture deliver individuating knowledge?" is yes. Self-scrutiny in a mirror and the effort to render the image in the mirror in paint or chalk may succeed, in a more disciplined way than introspection, in bringing the self, and the system of poses and expressions that orient the self in society, into focus. The self-portraitist, moreover, may learn to see himself from the point of view of others. Presumably the ability to see oneself in perspective is one of the paths to self-knowledge. Looking at the finished product may also yield self-knowledge because a portrait, any portrait, may deliver insights into aspects of character, personality, state of mind, hopes, fears, delusions, and so forth that are masked by social performance. Therapeutic or edifying self-knowledge may thus be achieved even when there was no sustained private learning process behind the fabrication of the image, for example, when the picture is taken inside a mechanical photo booth.

However, there are also reasons to doubt the capacity of a depiction to contribute to knowledge of a person:

First, a still, silent image reduces the many channels through which one might know a person down to a single channel. Observing a person's behavior or listening to her talk, for example, are good ways to learn something about that person, including one's self.

Second, the costume and the pose chosen by the sitter may interfere with real insight into character. That happens in life, too, and not only in portraits. It may even happen in private introspection, where vanity persuades us to pose for ourselves to protect a cherished self-image. Self-portraits nonetheless differ from self-images created in introspection, for they are likely eventually to be seen by others. Posing for a portrait, including for a self-portrait, is more like getting dressed to go out in public than it is like introspection.

Third, the medium, the technique, and the accumulated conventions that the portrait and portraitist are compelled to respect to ensure intelligibility interfere with a view onto the whole person. In particular, any pretensions that a portrait harbors to being a work of art are likely to clash with any ambitions it may have to contribute to processes of cognition, for in most—though not all—theories of art, the artwork distinguishes itself from other artifacts, texts, messages, or performances that it might resemble by failing to carry out effectively whatever nonart versions of those things are expected to do. A painting or a photograph becomes a successful work of art by supplementing, distorting, reframing, exaggerating, or otherwise obscuring a clear, rational view onto the object it represents. For Francis Bacon, the artistic, form-creating imagination was to be mistrusted as one of the "idols of the tribe" that clouds knowledge of reality. Finally, to portray an individual is also often a way of giving a person some measure of endurance, perhaps even immortality, and a portrait that is reckoned a work of art would seem to do that especially well. But self-memorialization clashes with the project of self-demystification that is central to some classic disciplines of self-knowledge.

The Dutch painter Rembrandt (1606–1669) made many self-portraits in three media, painting, drawing, and etching. An example is his depiction of himself wearing a startled expression, an etching dated 1630 and measuring 51 × 46 mm (figure 3).

He is mugging for the mirror, and this seems to drop a veil between us and any deeper knowledge about Rembrandt van Rijn. One may well wonder whether Rembrandt intended to see anything, or reveal anything, interesting about himself. Perhaps he was only using himself as a model in order to develop a convincing physiognomy for a startled figure in one of his paintings. But this is not a private study, for his own use only, for he chose the medium of etching, which publishes an image in multiple copies. He made enough etchings and paintings of himself that eventually he could count on a population of beholders who would recognize both his face and his style, and therefore recognize this image as a self-portrait. That style—the rapid lines scratched into the wax surface, mimicking the tangle of hair that is also an aspect of his stylized self; the application of expressive shadows; the focus on the face to the neglect of the body and the surroundings—is itself a dimension of the self-portrait. The artist reveals himself also through his means of depiction. Rembrandt often struck stagy poses in his self-portraits. He loved costumes. Perhaps in adopting a pose here he is admitting to himself, and revealing to us, his weakness for performance. The little image can be thought as a staging ground for self-knowledge. Yet there is no way of knowing what it meant for the artist. The feedback loop of posing and unposing is too tightly coiled.

This etching has also been prized as a work of art, and coveted by collectors and museums, for almost four centuries. A work of art is a construct of the imagination that exceeds any practical function it might also serve, including knowledge. And yet it would be incorrect to say that the art quality of this etching cancels out the cognitive value; it may add to it. Lucid appraisal of one's own finitude of the sort praised by Socrates may not be the only kind of self-knowledge. The artwork may elicit nonedifying intuitions about the self.

Can we not say the same about the so-called selfie, the self-portrait made with the cell phone camera and published on the Internet? The selfie appears at first to be nothing more than a radical democratization of self-portraiture, extending the demystification of technique initiated by the small handheld cameras of the early twentieth century, by making the procedure as simple as possible. The impulse to pose for the selfie is irresistible. The possibilities of artistic achievement in the medium are limited. And yet, remembering Rembrandt's primordial selfie, one would not wish to exclude too quickly the hypothesis that the imaginative self-styling that goes into every selfie can after all contribute to self-knowledge.

Bibliography

PRIMARY

Anonymous. *The Book of Privy Counselling*. Manuscript: British Library Harley 674 (H), fols. 92r–110v.

Anonymous. *The Cloud of Unknowing*. Manuscript: British Library Harley 674 (H), fols. 17v–31v.

Anscombe, G. E. M. "The First Person." In *Collected Philosophical Papers*, vol. 2, *Metaphysics and the Philosophy of Mind*, 21–36. Minneapolis: University of Minnesota Press, 1981.

Aristotle. *The Categories*. Translated by H. P. Cooke. Loeb Classical Library No. 325. Cambridge, MA: Harvard University Press, 1983.

Aristotle. *The Complete Works of Aristotle*. 2 vols. Edited by J. Barnes. Princeton, NJ: Princeton University Press, 1984.

Aristotle. *De anima*. Translated by D. W. Hamlyn. Oxford: Clarendon Press, 1993.

Aristotle. *Ethica Eudemia*. Edited by R. Walzer and J. Mingay. Oxford: Oxford University Press, 1991.

Aristotle. *Ethica Nicomachea*. Edited by I. Bywater. Oxford: Oxford University Press, 1963.

Aristotle. *Magna Moralia*. Edited by F. Susemihl. Leipzig: Teubner, 1883.

Augustinus. *Contra academicos, De beata vita, De ordine, De libero arbitrio*. Edited by William M. Green. Corpus Christianorum, Series Latina, 29. Turnhout: Brepols, 1970.

Augustinus, Aurelius. *Confessiones*. Edited by Martinum Skutella and Lucas Verheijen. Corpus Christianorum, Series Latina, 27. Turnhout: Brepols, 1983.

Augustinus, Aurelius. *De Trinitate*. Edited by W. J. Mountain. Corpus Christianorum, Series Latina, 50–50A. Turnhout: Brepols, 1968.

Brentano, Franz. *Descriptive Psychology*. Transl. by Benito Müller. London: Routledge, 1995.

Brentano, Franz. *Deskriptive Psychologie*. Edited by Roderick M. Chisholm and W. Baumgartner. Hamburg: Meiner, 1982.

Brentano, Franz. *Psychologie vom empirischen Standpunkt*. Edited by Oskar Kraus. Hamburg: Meiner 2013.

Brentano, Franz. *Psychology from the Empirical Standpoint*. Trans. By Antos C. Rancurello, D.B. Terrell, and Linda McAlister. London: Routledge, 1995.

Butler, Joseph. *The Analogy of Religion*. 2nd ed. London: James, John & Paul Knapton, 1736.

Butler, Joseph. *Sermons Delivered at Rolls Chapel*. 2nd ed. London: James & John Knapton, 1729.

Calvin, Jean. *Institution de la religion chrétienne*. Geneva: Philbert Hamelin, 1554.

Castañeda, Hector-Neri. "'He': A Study in the Logic of Self-Consciousness." *Ratio* 8 (1996): 130–57.

Cicero, Quintus Tullius. *De Finibus Bonorum et Malorum*. Edited by L. D. Reynolds. Oxford: Oxford University Press, 1998.

Coleridge, Samuel Taylor. *The Major Works*. Edited by H. J. Jackson. Oxford: Oxford University Press, 2009.

Descartes, René. *Oeuvres*. Edited by Charles Adam and Paul Tannery. Paris: Vrin, 1983–91.

Descartes, René. *The Philosophical Writings of Descartes*. Translated and edited by John Cottingham, Robert Stoothoff, and Dugald Murdoch (vols. 1–2), and Anthony Kenny (vol. 3). Cambridge: Cambridge University Press, 1984–91.

Dietrich of Freiberg. *Opera omnia*. Edited by K. Flasch et al. Hamburg: Meiner, 1977–85.

Dilthey, Wilhelm. *Der Aufbau der Geschichtlichen Welt in den Geisteswissenschaften*. Frankfurt am Main: Suhrkamp, 1974.

Dilthey, Wilhelm. *Einleitung in die Geisteswissenschaften. Gesammelte Schriften*, vol. 1. Leipzig: Teubner, 1923.

Dilthey, Wilhelm. *Selected Writings*. Edited by R. A. Makkreel and F. Rodi. Vol. 1. Princeton, NJ: Princeton University Press, 1989.

Dilthey, Wilhelm. *Selected Writings*. Translated by H. P. Rickman. Cambridge: Cambridge University Press, 1976.

Diogenes Laertius. "Diogenis Laertii Vitae philosophorum." In *Bibliotheca scriptorum Graecorum et Romanorum Teubneriana*, vol. 1: *Books I–X*; vol. 2: *Excerpta Byzantina*; vol. 3. Edited by Miroslav Marcovich. Stuttgart: Teubner, 1999–2002.

Eckhart, Meister. *Die deutschen und lateinischen Werke*. Stuttgart: W. Kohlhammer, 1936.

Eckhart, Meister. *The Essential Sermons, Commentaries, Treatises, and Defense*. Edited by Edmund Colledge and Bernard McGinn. Mahwah, NJ: Paulist Press, 1981.

Esprit, Jacques. *Discourses on the Deceitfulness of Humane Virtues*. Translated by William Beauvoir. London: Andrew Bell, 1706.

Esprit, Jacques. *La fausseté des vertus humaines*. Paris: Guillaume Desprez, 1678.

Evans, Gareth. *The Varieties of Reference*. Oxford: Oxford University Press, 1982.

Foucault, Michel. "L'ériture de soi." *Corps écrit* No. 5, L'Autoportrait (1983): 3–23.

Foucault, Michel. *Hermeneutics of the Subject: Lectures at the Collège de France* (1981–82). Translated by Graham Burchell. New York: Palgrave Macmillan, 2005.

Freud, Anna. *The Ego and the Mechanisms of Defense*. Translated by C. Baines. London: Hogarth Press, 1966.

Freud, Sigmund. *Gesammelte Werke*. London: Imago, 1991.

Freud, Sigmund. *The Standard Edition of the Complete Psychological Works of Sigmund Freud*. Translated and edited by James Strachey in collaboration with Anna Freud, assisted by Alix Strachey and Alan Tyson. 24 vols. London: Hogarth Press, 1956–74.

Guelincx, Arnold. *Ethics. With Samuel Beckett's Notes*. Translated by Martin Wilson, edited by Han van Ruler, Anthony Uhlmann, and Martin Wilson. Boston: Brill, 2006.

Hadewijch. *Brieven*. Edited by Jozef Van Mierlo. 2 vols. Louvain: Vlaamsch Boekenhalle, 1924–25.

Hadewijch. *The Complete Works*. Translated by Columba Hart. Mahwah, NJ: Paulist Press, 1980.

Hadewijch. *Visioenen*. Edited by Jozef Van Mierlo. 2 vols. Louvain: Vlaamsch Boekenhalle, 1924–25.

Hegel, Georg W. F. *Enzyklopädie der philosophischen Wissenschaften im Grundrisse (1830)*. Edited by Wolfgang Bonsiepen and Hans-Christian Lucas. Hamburg: Felix Meiner Verlag, 1992.

Hegel, Georg W. F. *Hegel's Philosophy of Mind*. Translated (from the 1830 edition, together with the *Zusätze*) by William Wallace and Arthur V. Miller with revisions and commentary by Michael J. Inwood. New York: Oxford University Press, 2007.

Heidegger, Martin. *Being and Time*. Translated by John Macquarrie and Edward Robinson. New York: Harper & Row, 1962.

Heidegger, Martin. *History of the Concept of Time: Prolegomena*. Translated by T. Kisiel. Bloomington: University of Indiana Press, 1985.

Heidegger, Martin. "Platon: Sophistes." In *Gesamtausgabe*, vol. 19. Frankfurt am Main: Vittorio Klostermann, 1992.

Heidegger, Martin. *Plato's "Sophist."* Translated by R. Rojcewicz and A. Schuwer Bloomington: University of Indiana Press, 1997.

Heidegger, Martin. "Prolegomena zur Geschichte des Zeitbegriffs." In *Gesamtausgabe*, vol. 15. Frankfurt am Main: Vittorio Klostermann, 1979.

Heidegger, Martin. *Sein und Zeit*. Tübingen: Max Niemeyer, 1972.

Hilton, Walter. *The Scale of Perfection*. Manuscript: Cambridge University Library MS Add. 6686, p. 284.

Hobbes, Thomas. *Leviathan*. Edited by Noel Malcolm. 3 vols. Oxford: Clarendon Press, 2012.

Hobbes, Thomas. *Leviathan*. Edited by Richard Tuck. Cambridge: Cambridge University Press, 1991.

Homer. *The Odyssey*. Translated and edited by Richard Lattimore. New York: Harper & Row, 1967.

Homeri. *Opera*. Edited by Thomas W. Allen. Oxford: Clarendon Press, 1949–51.

Hume, David. *Essays Moral, Political, and Literary*. Edited by Eugene F. Miller. Indianapolis: Liberty Fund, 1985.

Hume, David. *A Treatise of Human Nature*. 2nd ed. Edited by L. A. Selby-Bigge and revised by P. H. Nidditch. Oxford: Clarendon Press, 1978.

Husserl, Edmund. *Cartesian Meditations*. Translated by Dorion Cairns. The Hague: Nijhoff, 1967.

Husserl, Edmund. *Collected Works*. Translated by Thomas Sheehan and Richard E. Palmer. Vol. 6. Dordrecht: Kluwer Academic Publishers, 1997.

Husserl, Edmund. *The Crisis of European Sciences and Transcendental Phenomenology: An Introduction to Phenomenological Philosophy*. Translated by David Carr. Evanston, IL: Northwestern University Press, 1970.

Husserl, Edmund. "Fichte's Ideal of Humanity [Three Lectures]." Translated by James G. Hart. *Husserl Studies* 12 (1995): 111–33.

Husserl, Edmund. *Formal and Transcendental Logic*. Translated by Dorion Cairns. The Hague: Nijhoff, 1969.

Husserl, Edmund. *Husserliana: Gesammelte Werke*. Dordrecht: Springer, 1956–.

Husserl, Edmund. *Ideas for a Pure Phenomenology and Phenomenological Philosophy. First Book: General Introduction to Pure Phenomenology*. Translated by Daniel O. Dahlstrom. Indianapolis: Hackett, 2014.

Husserl, Edmund. "Ideas Pertaining to a Pure Phenomenology and to a Phenomenological Philosophy, Second Book." In *Collected Works*, vol. 3, translated by Richard Rojcewicz and Andre Schuwer. Dordrecht: Kluwer, 1989.

Husserl, Edmund. *Logical Investigations*. Translated by John N. Findlay. Edited by Dermot Moran. 2 vols. New York: Routledge, 2001.

Husserl, Edmund. *Shorter Works*. Translated and edited by Frederick Elliston and Peter McCormick. Notre Dame, IN: University of Notre Dame Press, 1981.

Jansenius, Cornelius. *Augustinus*. 3 vols. Leuven: Jacob Zegeri, 1640.

Kant, Immanuel. *Anthropology from a Pragmatic Point of View*. Translated and edited by Robert B. Louden. New York: Cambridge University Press, 2006.

Kant, Immanuel. *Critique of Practical Reason*. Translated and edited by Mary Gregor. New York: Cambridge University Press, 1997.

Kant, Immanuel. *Critique of Pure Reason*. Translated and edited by Paul Guyer and Allen W. Wood. Cambridge: Cambridge University Press, 1998.

Kant, Immanuel. *Gesammelte Schriften*. Edited by Preussische Akademie der Wissenschaften et al. Berlin: Verlag Georg Reimer, 1900–.

Kant, Immanuel. *Groundwork of the Metaphysics of Morals*. Translated and edited by Mary Gregor and Jens Timmermann. New York: Cambridge University Press, 2012.

Kant, Immanuel. *Kritik der reinen Vernunft*. Edited by Jens Timmermann. Hamburg: Felix Meiner Verlag, 1998.

Kant, Immanuel. *The Metaphysics of Morals*. Translated and edited by Mary Gregor. Cambridge: Cambridge University Press, 1997.

Kant, Immanuel. *Religion within the Boundaries of Mere Reason and Other Writings*. Translated and edited by Allen Wood and George di Giovanni. Cambridge: Cambridge University Press, 1998.

Kierkegaard, Søren. *Christian Discourses*. Translated by Howard V. Hong and Edna H. Hong. Princeton, NJ: Princeton University Press, 1987.

Kierkegaard, Søren. *The Concept of Anxiety*. Translated by Reidar Thomte. Princeton, NJ: Princeton University Press, 1980.

Kierkegaard, Søren. *The Concept of Irony*. Translated by Howard V. Hong and Edna H. Hong. Princeton, NJ: Princeton University Press, 1989.

Kierkegaard, Søren. *Concluding Unscientific Postscript*. Translated by Howard V. Hong and Edna H. Hong. Princeton, NJ: Princeton University Press, 1992.

Kierkegaard, Søren. *Either/Or*. Translated by Howard V. Hong and Edna H. Hong. 2 vols. Princeton, NJ: Princeton University Press, 1987.

Kierkegaard, Søren. *Fear and Trembling and Repetition*. Translated by Howard V. and Edna H. Hong. Princeton, NJ: Princeton University Press, 1983.

Kierkegaard, Søren. *Judge for Yourself!* Translated by Howard V. Hong and Edna H. Hong. Princeton, NJ: Princeton University Press, 1987.

Kierkegaard, Søren. *Kierkegaard's Journals and Notebooks*. Edited by Niels Jørgen Cappelørn et al. Princeton, NJ: Princeton University Press, 2007–.

Kierkegaard, Søren. *Letters and Documents*. Translated by Henrik Rosenmeier. Princeton, NJ: Princeton University Press, 1978.

Kierkegaard, Søren. *Philosophical Fragments*. Translated by Howard V. and Edna H. Hong. Princeton, NJ: Princeton University Press, 1985.

Kierkegaard, Søren. *The Sickness unto Death*. Translated by Howard V. Hong and Edna H. Hong. Princeton, NJ: Princeton University Press, 1980.

Kierkegaard, Søren. *Søren Kierkegaard's Journals and Papers*. Edited and translated by Howard V. Hong and Edna H. Hong. 7 vols. Bloomington: Indiana University Press, 1967–78.

Kierkegaard, Søren. *Søren Kierkegaards Skrifter*. Edited by Niels Jørgen Cappelørn et al. Vols. 1–28 and K1–28. Copenhagen: Gad, 1997.

Kierkegaard, Søren. *Two Ages*. Translated by Howard V. Hong and Edna H. Hong. Princeton, NJ: Princeton University Press, 1978.

Kierkegaard, Søren. *Works of Love*. Translated by Howard V. Hong and Edna H. Hong. Princeton, NJ: Princeton University Press, 1995.

Lacan, Jacques. *Écrits: A Selection*. Translated by Alan Sheridan. New York: Norton, 1977.

Mandeville, Bernard. *The Fable of the Bees*. Edited by F. B. Kaye. Oxford: Clarendon Press, 1924.

Marcus Aurelius. *Meditations*. Translated by R. Hardie. Ware: Wordsworth, 1997.

Matthew of Aquasparta. *Quaestiones de fide et cognitione*. Edited by PP. Collegii S. Bonaventurae. Quaracchi: Collegium S. Bonaventurae, 1957.

Natorp, Paul. *Einleitung in die Psychologie nach kritischer Methode*. Freiburg: Mohr, 1888.

Nicole, Pierre. *Essais de Morale*. 3 vols. Paris: Guillaume Desprez, 1701.

Nicole, Pierre. *Moral Essays, Contain'd in Several Treatises on Many Important Duties*. 4 vols. London: Printed for Samuel Manship, 1696.

Philodemus. "On the Stoics." In T. Dorandi, *Filodemo. Gli Stoici (PHerc 155 e 339)*. *Cronache Ercolanese* 12 (1982): 91–133.

Plato. *The Complete Works of Plato*. Edited by John M. Cooper and D. S. Hutchinson. Indianapolis: Hackett, 1997.

Plato. "Phaedrus." In *Complete Works*, translated by Alexander Nehamas and Paul Woodruff, edited by John M. Cooper, 506–56. Indianapolis: Hackett, 1997.

Plotinus. *Plotinus in Seven Volumes*. Translated by A. H. Armstrong. Loeb Classical Library. Cambridge, MA: Harvard University Press, 1966–88.

Plotinus *Schriften*. Translated by Richard Harder. Hamburg: Felix Meiner Verlag, 1956.

Plotinus. *Opera*. Vols. 1–3. Edited by Paul Henry and Hans-Rudolph Schwyzer. Scriptorum Classicorum Bibliotheca Oxoniensis. Oxford: Oxford University Press, 1964–83.

Porete, Marguerite. *Le Mirouer des simple ames*. Edited by Romana Guarnieri. Turnhout: Brepols, 1986.

Richard de St. Victor. *De Trinitate: texte critique avec introduction, notes et tables*. Edited by Jean Ribaillier. Paris: Vrin, 1954.

Ricoeur, Paul. *Oneself as Another*. Translated by K. Blamey. Chicago: University of Chicago Press, 1992.

Ricoeur, Paul. *Soi-même comme un Autre*. Paris: Éditions du Seuil, 1990.

Rochefoucauld, François de la. *Collected Maxims and Other Reflections*. Translated by E. H. Blackmore, A. M. Blackmore, and Francine Giguère. Oxford: Oxford University Press, 2007.

Ruusbroec, Jan. *Werken*. 2nd ed. Edited by the Ruusbroecgenootschap. 4 vols. Tielt: Uitgeverij Lannoo, 1944–48.

Ruusbroec, John. *The Spiritual Espousals and Other Works*. Edited and translated by J. A. Wiseman. Mahwah, NJ: Paulist Press, 1985.

Ryle, Gilbert. *The Concept of Mind*. Chicago: University of Chicago Press, 1949.

Schopenhauer, Arthur. *Arthur Schopenhauer's sämtliche Werke*. Edited by Paul Deussen. Munich: R. Piper Verlag, 1911–42.

Schopenhauer, Arthur. *Essay on the Freedom of the Will*. Translated by K. Kolenda. New York: Liberal Arts Press, 1960.

Schopenhauer, Arthur. *The World as Will and Representation*. Translated by E. F. J. Payne. 2 vols. New York: Dover, 1969.

Seneca. *Epistles*. 3 vols. Translated by R. M Gummere. Cambridge, MA: Harvard University Press, 1917–25.

Sextus Empiricus. *Against the Ethicists (Adversus Mathematicos XI)*. Translated by Richard Bett. Oxford: Clarendon Press, 2000.

Sextus Empiricus. *Against the Logicians*. Translated by R. G. Bury. Loeb Classical Library No. 291. Cambridge, MA: Harvard University Press, 1983.

Shaftesbury, Anthony Ashley Cooper, Third Earl of. *Characteristics of Men, Manners, Opinions, Times*. Edited by Lawrence E. Klein. Cambridge: Cambridge University Press, 1999.

Shelley, Percy. *Shelley's Poetry and Prose*. Edited by Donald H. Reiman and Neil Fraistat. 2nd ed. New York: Norton, 2002.

Spinoza, Baruch de. *The Collected Works of Spinoza*. Edited and translated by Edwin Curley. Princeton, NJ: Princeton University Press, 1985.

Thomas Aquinas. *Quaestiones disputatae de veritate*. Editio Leonina XXII. Rome: Commissio Leonina; Paris: Cerf, 1970–75.

Thomas Aquinas. *Summa theologiae*. Edited by Peter Caramello. Rome: Marietti, 1952.

Thomas Aquinas. *The Treatise on Human Nature: Summa Theologiae*. Edited and translated by Robert Pasnau. Indianapolis: Hackett, 2002.

Zinn, Grover, ed. and trans. *The Twelve Patriarchs, The Mystical Ark, and Book Three of The Trinity*. Mahwah, NJ: Paulist Press, 1979.

SECONDARY

Ackeren, Marcel van, ed. *A Companion to Marcus Aurelius*. Oxford: Blackwell, 2012.

Ackeren, Marcel van. *Die Philosophie Marc Aurels*. Vol. 1: *Textform—Stillmerkmale Selbstdialog*. Vol. 2: *Themen—Begriffe—Argumente*. Berlin: de Gruyter, 2011.

Ackeren, Marcel van, and Jan Opsomer, eds. *Meditations and Representations: The Philosopher and Emperor Marcus Aurelius in Interdisciplinary Light*. Wiesbaden: Reichert, 2012.

Allesse, Francesca. "Il tema delle affezioni nell'antropologia di Marco Aurelio." In *Antichi e moderni nella filosofia de età imperiale*, edited by Aldo Brancacci, 111–34. Naples: Bibliopolis, 2001.

Allesse, Francesca. *La Stoa e la tradizione socratica*. Naples: Bibliopolis, 2000.

Alston, William. "Varieties of Privileged Access." *American Philosophical Quarterly* 8 (1971): 223–41.

Annas, Julia. *Platonic Ethics, Old and New*. Ithaca, NY: Cornell University Press, 1999.

Annas, Julia. "Self-Knowledge in Early Plato." In *Platonic Investigations*, edited by D. J. O'Meara, 111–37. Washington, DC: Catholic University of America Press, 1985.

Asendorpf, Jens B., Veronique Warkentin, and Pierre-Marie Baudonnière. "Self-Awareness and Other-Awareness II: Mirror Self-Recognition, Social Contingency Awareness, and Synchronic Imitation." *Developmental Psychology* 32.2 (1996): 313–21.

Aubry, Gwenaëlle. "Metaphysics of Soul and Self in Plotinus." In *The Routledge Handbook of Neoplatonism*, edited by Pauliina Remes and Svetla Slaveva-Griffin, 266–72. New York: Routledge, 2014.

Barnouw, Jeffrey. "Persuasion in Hobbes's Leviathan." *Hobbes Studies* 1 (1988): 3–25.

Beabout, Gregory R. *Freedom and Its Misuses: Kierkegaard on Anxiety and Despair.* Milwaukee: Marquette University Press, 1996.

Beckwith, Sarah. *Christ's Body: Identity, Culture, and Society in Late Medieval Writings.* London: Routledge, 1993.

Beierwaltes, Werner. *Platonismus im Christentum.* Frankfurt am Main: Vittorio Klostermann Verlag, 1998.

Benson, Hugh. "A Note on Socratic Self-Knowledge in the Charmides." *Ancient Philosophy* 23 (2003): 31–47.

Bernecker, Sven. "Kant zur moralischen Selbsterkenntnis." *Kant-Studien* 97 (2006): 163–83.

Bilgrami, Akeel. *Self-Knowledge and Resentment.* Cambridge, MA: Harvard University Press, 2006.

Booth, Edward. "St. Augustine's 'notia sui' Related to Aristotle and the Early Neo-Platonists." *Augustiniana* 27 (1977): 27–29.

Borgstädt, Elvira, trans. "The 'Sister Catherine' Treatise." In *Meister Eckhart: Teacher and Preacher,* edited by Bernard McGinn, 347–388. New York: Paulist Press, 1986.

Boyle, Matthew. "Two Kinds of Self-Knowledge." *Philosophy and Phenomenological Research* 78 (2009): 133–64.

Brachtendorf, Johannes. "Augustins Begriff des menschlichen Geistes." In *Seele, Denken, Bewußtsein: Zur Geschichte der Philosophie des Geistes,* edited by U. Meixner und A. Newen, 90–123. Berlin: de Gruyter, 2003.

Brachtendorf, Johannes. *Die Struktur des menschlichen Geistes nach Augustinus: Selbstreflexion und Erkenntnis Gottes in "De Trinitate".* Hamburg: Felix Meiner, 2000.

Brachtendorf, Johannes. "Endlichkeit und Subjektivität: Zur Bedeutung des Subjekts im Denken Augustins." In *Fluchtpunkt Subjekt: Facetten und Chancen des Subjektgedankens,* edited by G. Krieger and H.-L. Ollig, 37–53. Paderborn: Schöningh, 2001.

Brachtendorf, Johannes. *Gott und sein Bild—Augustins "De Trinitate" im Spiegel gegenwärtiger Forschung.* Edited by Johannes Brachtendorf. Paderborn: Schöningh, 2000.

Brachtendorf, Johannes. "Time, Memory, and Selfhood in De Trinitate." In *Le "De Trinitate" de Saint Augustin: Exégèse, logique et noétique,* edited by E. Bermon and G. P. O'Daly, 221–33. Paris: Institut d'Études Augustiniennes, 2012.

Brennan, Tad. "Reading Plato's Mind." In *Keeling Colloquium in Ancient Philosophy,* edited by Fiona Leigh. Forthcoming.

Brennan, Tad. *The Stoic Life: Emotions, Duties, and Fate.* Oxford: Oxford University Press, 2005.

Brouwer, René. *The Stoic Sage: The Early Stoics on Wisdom, Sagehood and Socrates.* Cambridge: Cambridge University Press, 2013.

Brower-Toland, Susan. "Medieval Approaches to Consciousness: Ockham and Chatton." *Philosophers' Imprint* 12.17 (2012): 1–29.

Burge, Tyler. "Our Entitlement to Self-Knowledge." *Proceedings of the Aristotelian Society* 96 (1996): 91–116.

Burkert, Walter. *Griechische Religion der archaischen und klassischen Epoche.* Stuttgart: Kohlhammer, 2011.

Burnyeat, Myles. "Aquinas on 'Spiritual Change' in Perception." In *Ancient and Medieval Theories of Intentionality*, edited by Dominik Perler, 129–53. Leiden: Brill, 2001.

Burnyeat, Myles. "The Truth of Tripartition." *Proceedings of the Aristotelian Society* 106 (2006): 1–23.

Bynum, Caroline Walker. *Fragmentation and Redemption: Essays on Gender and the Human Body in Medieval Religion.* New York: Zone Books, 1992.

Bynum, Caroline Walker. *Holy Feast and Holy Fast: The Religious Significance of Food to Medieval Women.* Berkeley: University of California Press, 1987.

Carlo, Irena, Hanne Jacobs, and Filip Mattens, eds. *Philosophy, Phenomenology, Sciences: Essays in Commemoration of Edmund Husserl.* Dordrecht: Springer, 2010.

Carruthers, Peter. *Consciousness: Essays from a Higher-Order Perspective.* Oxford: Oxford University Press, 2005.

Carruthers, Peter. Review of Cassam's *Self-Knowledge for Humans. Notre Dame Philosophical Reviews*, 2015.04.16.

Cary, Phillip. *Augustine's Invention of the Inner Self: The Legacy of a Christian Platonist.* Oxford: Oxford University Press, 2000.

Cassam, Quassim. *Self-Knowledge for Humans.* Oxford: Oxford University Press, 2014.

Chrystal, I. "Plotinus on the Structure of Self-Intellection." *Phronesis* 43 (1998): 264–86.

Clark, Henry. *La Rochefoucauld and the Language of Unmasking in Seventeenth-Century France.* Geneva: Librairie Droz, 1994.

Cory, Therese Scarpelli. *Aquinas on Human Self-Knowledge.* Cambridge: Cambridge University Press, 2014.

Courcelle, Pierre. *"Connais-toi toi même" de Socrate à Saint Bernard.* 3 vols. Paris: Études Augustiniennes, 1974–75.

Dennett, Daniel C. "Conditions of Personhood." In *The Identity of Persons*, edited by Richard Rorty, 175–96. Berkeley: University of California Press, 1976.

Dodds, E. R. *Les sources de Plotin.* Geneva: Fondation Hardt, 1960.

Drecoll, Volker Henning. *Die Entstehung der Gnadenlehre Augustins.* Tübingen: Mohr Siebeck, 1999.

Drever, M. *Image, Identity, and the Forming of the Augustinian Soul.* Oxford: Oxford University Press, 2013.

Emilsson, E. "Plotinus on the Objects of Thought." *Archiv für Geschichte der Philosophie* 77 (1995): 21–41.

Engstrom, Stephen. "Self-Consciousness and the Unity of Knowledge." *International Yearbook of German Idealism* 11 (forthcoming).

Flasch, Kurt. *Dietrich von Freiberg. Philosophie, Theologie, Naturforschung um 1300.* Frankfurt am Main: Klostermann, 2007.

Frankfurt, Harry. "Freedom of the Will and the Concept of a Person." *Journal of Philosophy* 68 (1971): 5–20.

Friedman, Russell L., and Jean-Michel Counet, eds. *Medieval Perspectives on Aristotle's "De Anima".* Louvain: Peeters, 2013.

Gallup, G. G. "Chimpanzees: Self-Recognition." *Science* 167 (1970): 86–87.

Garrett, Aaron. "Seventeenth-Century Moral Philosophy: Self-Help, Self-Knowledge, and the Devil's Mountain." In *Oxford Handbook of the History of Ethics*, edited by Roger Crisp, 229–79. Oxford: Oxford University Press, 2012.

Gerson, Lloyd P. "Neoplatonic Epistemology." In *The Routledge Handbook of Neoplatonism*, edited by Pauliina Remes and Svetla Slaveva-Griffin, 266–72. New York: Routledge, 2014.

Gertler, Brie. "Self-Knowledge." In *The Stanford Encyclopedia of Philosophy*, edited by Edward N. Zalta. Summer 2015 ed. http://plato.stanford.edu/archives/sum2015/entries/self-knowledge/.

Gertler, Brie. *Self-Knowledge.* New York: Routledge, 2011.

Giavatto, Angelo. *Interlocutore di se stesso: La dialettica di Marco Aurelio.* Hildesheim: Olms, 2008.

Gill, Christopher. "Marcus Aurelius' Meditations: How Stoic and How Platonic?" In *Platonic Stoicism—Stoic Platonism: The Dialogue between Platonism and Stoicism in Antiquity*, edited by Mauro Bonazzi and Christoph Helmig, 189–208. Leuven: Peters, 2007.

Gill, Christopher, trans. *Marcus Aurelius Meditations: Books 1–6.* Oxford: Oxford University Press, 2013.

Gill, Christopher. *The Self in Dialogue.* Oxford: Oxford University Press, 1998.

Gill, Christopher. *The Structured Self in Hellenistic and Roman Thought.* Oxford: Oxford University Press, 2006.

Glück, J., and S. Bluck. "Laypeople's Conceptions of Wisdom and Its Development: Cognitive and Integrative Views." *Journal of Gerontology: Psychological Sciences* 66B (2011): 321–24.

Grundmann, Herbert. "Die Frauen und die Literatur im Mittelalter: Ein Beitrag zur Frage nach der Entstehung des Schrifttums in der Volkssprache." *Archiv für Kulturgeschichte* 26 (1936): 129–61.

Guignon, Charles. *On Being Authentic*. London: Routledge, 2004.

Guion, Beatrice. *Pierre Nicole moraliste*: Paris: Honoré Champion, 2002.

Guyer, Paul. "Moral Feelings in the *Metaphysics of Morals*." In *Kant's Metaphysics of Morals: A Critical Guide*, edited by Lara Denis, 130–51. New York: Cambridge University Press, 2010.

Hadot, Pierre "L'image de la trinité dans l'âme chez Marius Victorinus et chez Saint Augustin." *Studia Patristica* 6 (1962): 409–42.

Hadot, Pierre. *The Inner Citadel: The Meditations of Marcus Aurelius*. Cambridge, MA: Harvard University Press, 2001.

Hadot, Pierre. *Philosophy as a Way of Life*. Edited by Arnold I. Davidson. Translated by Michael Chase. Oxford: Blackwell, 1995.

Hager, F.-P. "Selbsterkenntnis." In *Historisches Wörterbuch der Philosophie*, edited by Joachim Ritter and Karlfried Gründer, 406–13. Basel: Schwabe, 1995.

Halfwassen, J. *Geist und Selbstbewußtsein: Studien zu Plotin und Numenios*. Mainz: Franz Steiner Verlag, 1994.

Halliwell, Stephen. *Between Ecstasy and Truth: Interpretations of Greek Poetics from Homer to Longinus*. New York: Oxford University Press, 2011.

Harcourt, Edward. "The First Person: Problems of Sense and Reference." In *Logic, Cause and Action: Essays in Honour of Elizabeth Anscombe*, edited by Roger Teichmann, 25–46. Cambridge: Cambridge University Press, 2001.

Henrich, D. "Fichtes ursprüngliche Einsicht." In *Subjektivität und Metaphysik*, edited by D. Henrich und H. Wagner, 192–95. Frankfurt am Main: Klostermann, 1966.

Hollywood, Amy. *Sensible Ecstasy: Mysticism, Sexual Difference, and the Demands of History*. Chicago: University of Chicago Press, 2002.

Hong, Howard V., and Edna H. Hong. "Historical Introduction." In *Søren Kierkegaard: The Moment and Late Writings*, translated by Howard V. Hong and Edna H. Hong, ix–xxxi. Princeton, NJ: Princeton University Press, 1998.

Horn, Christof. "Selbstbezüglichkeit des Geistes bei Plotin und Augustinus." In *Gott und sein Bild: Augustins "De Trinitate" im Spiegel gegenwärtiger Forschung*, edited by J. Brachtendorf, 81–103. Paderborn: Schöningh, 2000.

Höwing, Thomas. *Praktische Lust: Kant über das Verhältnis von Fühlen, Begehren und praktischer Vernunft*. Boston: de Gruyter, 2013.

Hughes, Aaron. *The Texture of the Divine: Imagination in Medieval Islamic and Jewish Thought*. Bloomington: Indiana University Press, 2004.

Idel, Moshe, and Bernard McGinn. *Mystical Union in Judaism, Christianity, and Islam: An Ecumenical Dialogue.* New York: Continuum, 1999.

James, E. D. *Pierre Nicole, Jansenist and Humanist: A Study of His Thought.* The Hague: Martinus Nijhoff, 1972.

Jeremiah, Edward. *The Emergence of Reflexivity in Greek Language and Thought.* Boston: Brill, 2012.

Johnston, David. *The Rhetoric of the "Leviathan": Thomas Hobbes and the Politics of Cultural Transformation.* Princeton, NJ: Princeton University Press, 1986.

Kahn, Charles. "Plato's Charmides and the Proleptic Reading of the Dialogues." *Journal of Philosophy* 85 (1988): 541–49.

Kekes, John. "Wisdom." *American Philosophical Quarterly* 20 (1983): 277–83.

Kraye, Jill. "Moral Philosophy." In *The Cambridge History of Renaissance Philosophy*, edited by Charles Schmitt and Quentin Skinner, 303–86. Cambridge: Cambridge University Press, 1984.

Laing, Ronald D. *The Divided Self.* Baltimore: Penguin, 1965.

Lear, Jonathan. *A Case for Irony.* Cambridge, MA: Harvard University Press, 2011.

Lear, Jonathan. *Freud.* New York: Routledge, 2005.

Lear, Jonathan. "Wisdom Won from Illness: The Psychoanalytic Grasp of Human Being." *International Journal of Psychoanalysis* 95 (2014): 677–93.

Leo, Friedrich. *Der Monolog im Drama: Ein Beitrag zur griechisch-römischen Poetik.* Berlin: Weidmann, 1908.

Lerner, Robert. *The Heresy of the Free Spirit in the Later Middle Ages.* Berkeley: University of California Press, 1972.

Levi, Anthony. *French Moralists: The Theory of the Passions, 1585 to 1649.* Oxford: Clarendon Press, 1964.

Lewis, David. "Attitudes *De Dicto* and *De Se.*" *Philosophical Review* 88 (1979): 513–43.

Lippitt, John. *Humour and Irony in Kierkegaard's Thought.* Basingstoke: Palgrave, 2000.

Lippitt, John. *Kierkegaard and the Problem of Self-Love.* Cambridge: Cambridge University Press, 2013.

Lochrie, Karma. *Margery Kempe and Translations of the Flesh.* Philadelphia: University of Pennsylvania Press, 1991.

Long, Anthony A. *Epictetus: A Socratic and Stoic Guide to Life.* Cambridge: Cambridge University Press, 2002.

Long, Anthony A. *Stoic Studies.* Cambridge: Cambridge University Press, 1996.

Long, Anthony A., and David N. Sedley. *The Hellenistic Philosophers.* 2 vols. Cambridge: Cambridge University Press, 1987.

Lynn-George, Michael. *Epos: Word, Narrative and the "Iliad".* London: Macmillan, 1988.

Macdonald, Scott. "The Divine Nature: Being and Goodness." In *The Cambridge Companion to Augustine*, edited by David Vincent Meconi and Eleonore Stump, 17–36. 2nd ed. Cambridge: Cambridge University Press, 2014.

Makkreel, Rudolf, A. "Dilthey: Hermeneutics and Neo-Kantianism." In *The Routledge Companion to Hermeneutics*, edited by J. Malpas and H.-H. Gander, 74–84. London: Routledge, 2015.

McCabe, M. M. "'It Goes Deep with Me': Plato's Charmides on Knowledge, Self-Knowledge, and Integrity." In *Philosophy, Ethics, and a Common Humanity: Essays in Honour of Raimond Gaita*, edited by Christopher Cordner, 161–81. New York: Routledge, 2011.

McGinn, Bernard. *The Harvest of Mysticism in Medieval Germany (1300–1500)*. Vol. 4 of *The Presence of God: A History of Western Christian Mysticism*. New York: Herder and Herder, 2005.

McKim, Richard. "Socratic Self-Knowledge and 'Knowledge of Knowledge.'" In *Plato's Charmides: Transactions of the American Philological Association* (1985): 59–77.

Mitchell, Stephen. *Hope and Dread in Psychoanalysis*. New York: Basic Books, 1993.

Mooney, Edward F. *Selves in Discord and Resolve*. New York: Routledge, 1996.

Moran, Richard. *Authority and Estrangement: An Essay on Self-Knowledge*. Princeton, NJ: Princeton University Press, 2001.

Morgan, Ben. *On Becoming God: Late Medieval Mysticism and the Modern Western Self*. New York: Fordham University Press, 2013.

Moriarty, Michael. *Disguised Vices: Theories of Virtue in Early Modern French Thought*. Oxford: Oxford University Press, 2011.

Mortley, Raoul. *Plotinus, Self, and the World*. Cambridge: Cambridge University Press, 2013.

Muench, Paul. "Kierkegaard's Socratic Point of View." In *Kierkegaard Research: Sources, Reception and Resources*, vol. 2: *Kierkegaard and the Greek World*, book 1: *Socrates and Plato*, edited by Jon Stewart and Katalin Nun, 3–25. London: Ashgate, 2010.

Nenon, Thomas. "Freedom, Responsibility and Self-Awareness in Husserl." *New Yearbook for Phenomenology and Phenomenological Research II* (2002): 1–21.

Newman, Robert J. "Cotidie meditare: Theory and Practice of the Meditation in Imperial Stoicism." *Aufstieg und Niedergang der Römischen Welt* III, 36.3 (1989): 1473–517.

Oehler, Klaus. "Aristotle on Self-Knowledge." *Proceedings of the American Philosophical Society* 118 (1974): 493–506.

Oehler, Klaus. *Subjektivität und Selbstbewußtsein in der Antike*. Würzburg: Könighausen & Neumann, 1997.

O'Brien, Lucy. *Self-Knowing Agents*. Oxford: Oxford University Press, 2007.

O'Meally, Robert G. "Romare Bearden's Black Odyssey: A Search for Home." In *Romare Bearden: "A Black Odyssey"*. New York: DC Moore Gallery, 2007.

Parke, H., and D. E. W. Wormell. *The Delphic Oracle*. 2 vols. Oxford: Blackwell, 1956.

Pasnau, Robert. *Thomas Aquinas on Human Nature: A Philosophical Study of "Summa Theologiae" Ia 75–89*. Cambridge: Cambridge University Press, 2002.

Perler, Dominik. *Theorien der Intentionalität im Mittelalter*. Frankfurt am Main: Klostermann, 2002.

Perler, Dominik, ed. "Transformations of the Soul: Aristotelian Psychology 1250–1650." Special issue of *Vivarium* 46.3 (2008).

Perler, Dominik, and Sonja, Schierbaum, eds. *Selbstbezug und Selbstwissen: Texte zu einer mittelalterlichen Debatte*. Frankfurt am Main: Klostermann, 2014.

Putallaz, François-Xavier. *La connaissance de soi au XIIIe siècle*. Paris: Vrin, 1991.

Putallaz, François-Xavier. *Le sens de la réflexion chez Thomas d'Aquin*. Paris: Vrin, 1991.

Race, William. 2014. "Phaeacian Therapy in Homer's *Odyssey*." In *Combat Trauma and the Ancient Greeks*, edited by P. Meineck and D. Konstan, 47–66. New York: Palgrave, 2014.

Radt, Stefan. *Strabons Geographika*. 10 vols. Göttingen: Vandenhoeck & Ruprecht, 2002–11.

Rappe, Sara. "Self-Knowledge and Subjectivity in the *Enneads*." In *The Cambridge Companion to Plotinus*, edited by L. P. Gerson, 250–74. Cambridge: Cambridge University Press, 1996.

Reale, Giovanni. *The Schools of the Imperial Age*. Albany: SUNY Press, 1990.

Recanati, François. "De re and de se." *Dialectica* 63 (2009): 249–69.

Reeve, C. D. C. *Socrates in the "Apology"*. Indianapolis: Hackett, 1989.

Reginster, Bernard. *The Affirmation of Life*. Cambridge, MA: Harvard University Press, 2006.

Reginster, Bernard. "Knowledge and Selflessness: Schopenhauer and the Paradox of Reflection." *European Journal of Philosophy* 16.2 (2008): 251–72.

Remes, Pauliina. *Plotinus on Self: The Philosophy of the "We"*. Cambridge: Cambridge University Press, 2007.

Remes, Pauliina. "Reason to Care: The Object and Structure of Self-Knowledge in the Alcibiades I." *Apeiron* 46.3 (2013): 270–301.

Renz, Ursula. "Self-Knowledge and Knowledge of Mankind in Hobbes' *Leviathan*." *European Journal of Philosophy*, forthcoming 2017.

Renz, Ursula. *Die Erklärbarkeit von Erfahrung: Realismus und Subjektivität in Spinozas Theorie des menschlichen Geistes*. Frankfurt am Main: Klostermann, 2010.

Renz, Ursula. "Spinoza's Epistemology." In *Cambridge Companion to Spinoza*, edited by Don Garrett. New York: Cambridge University Press, forthcoming.

Renz, Ursula. "Spinozas Erkenntnistheorie: Eine naturalisierte Epistemologie?" *Deutsche Zeitschrift für Philosophie* 57 (2009): 419–32.

Rist, John M. Augustine. *Ancient Thought Baptized*. Cambridge: Cambridge University Press, 1994.

Rödl, Sebastian. "Intentional Transaction." *Philosophical Explorations* 17.3 (2014): 303–16.

Rödl, Sebastian. *Self-Consciousness*. Cambridge, MA: Harvard University Press, 2007.

Rosen, S. H. "Thought and Touch: A Note on Aristotle's *De Anima*." *Phronesis* 6 (1961): 27–137.

Roskam, Geert. *On the Path to Virtue: The Stoic Doctrine of Moral Progress and Its Reception in (Middle-)Platonism*. Leuven: Peters, 2005.

Sandbach, F. H. "A Transposition in Aristotle, *Metaphysics* Λ c. 9 1074 b." *Mnemosyne*, 4th ser., 7 (1954): 39–43.

Schneewind, Jerome. *The Invention of Autonomy*. Cambridge: Cambridge University Press, 1998.

Sedley, David N. "The School, from Zeno to Arius Didymus." In *The Cambridge Companion to the Stoics*, edited by Brad Inwood, 7–32. Cambridge: Cambridge University Press, 2003.

Sellars, John. *The Art of Living: The Stoics on the Nature and Function of Philosophy*. Aldershot: Ashgate, 2003.

Shields, Christopher. "Intentionality and Isomorphism in Aristotle." *Proceedings of the Boston Area Colloquium in Ancient Philosophy* 11 (1995): 307–30.

Shoemaker, Sidney. "Self-Knowledge and 'Inner Sense.'" *Philosophy and Phenomenological Research* 54 (1994): 249–314.

Shoemaker, Sidney. "Self-Reference and Self-Awareness." *Journal of Philosophy* 65 (1968): 555–67.

Skinner, Quentin. *Reason and Rhetoric in the Philosophy of Hobbes*. Cambridge: Cambridge University Press, 1996.

Sorabji, Richard. "Is the True Self an Individual in the Platonist Tradition?" In *Le commentaire entre tradition et innovation*, edited by M. O. Goulet-Cazé, 293–300. Paris: Vrin, 2000.

Sorabji, Richard. *Self: Ancient and Modern Insights about Individuality, Life and Death*. Oxford: Oxford University Press, 2006.

Stokes, Patrick. *Kierkegaard's Mirrors*. Basingstoke: Palgrave, 2010.

Strayer, Brian E. *Suffering Saints: Jansenists and Convulsionnaires in France, 1640–1799*. Eastborne: Sussex Academic Press, 2008.

Szabados, Bela. "Freud, Self-Knowledge and Psychoanalysis." *Canadian Journal of Philosophy* 12.4 (1982): 691–707.

Taylor, Charles. *Hegel.* Cambridge: Cambridge University Press, 1975.

Taylor, Charles. "Overcoming Epistemology." In *Philosophical Arguments*, 1–19. Cambridge, MA: Harvard University Press, 1995.

Taylor, Charles. *Philosophy and the Human Sciences. Philosophical Papers*, vol. 2. Cambridge: Cambridge University Press, 1985.

Tennant, Bob. *Conscience, Consciousness and Ethics in Joseph Butler's Philosophy and Ministry.* Woodbridge: Boydell Press, 2011.

Teske, Roland. "Augustine's Philosophy of Memory." In *The Cambridge Companion to Augustine*, edited by Eleonore Stump and Norman Kretzmann, 148–58. Cambridge: Cambridge University Press, 2001.

Thomte, Reidar. "Historical Introduction." In *Kierkegaard, Søren: The Concept of Anxiety*, translated by Reidar Thomte, vii–xvii. Princeton, NJ: Princeton University Press, 1980.

Tiberius, Valerie. *The Reflective Life: Living Wisely with Our Limits.* Oxford: Oxford University Press, 2008.

Tomkins, Calvin. *Calvin Tomkins Papers: Some Questions and Some Answers.* New York: MoMA Archive, Queens, 1976.

Tugendhat, Ernst. *Vorlesungen zur Einführung in eine sprachanalytische Philosophie.* Frankfurt am Main: Suhrkamp, 2010.

Turner, Denys. *The Darkness of God: Negativity in Christian Mysticism.* Cambridge: Cambridge University Press, 1995.

Underhill, Evelyn. *The Essentials of Mysticism and Other Essays.* Oxford: Oneworld, 1995.

Van Fleteren, Frederick E. "Augustine's Ascent of the Soul in Book VII of the *Confessiones*: A Reconsideration." *Augustinian Studies* 5 (1974): 29–72.

Varga, Somogy. *Authenticity as an Ethical Ideal.* New York: Routledge, 2012.

Verbeke, G. "Connaissance de soi et connaissance de Dieu chez Saint Augustin." *Augustiniana* 4 (1954): 495–515.

Vernant, Jean-Paul. "A 'Beautiful Death' and the Disfigured Corpse in Homeric Epic" (originally published in 1982 as "La belle mort et la cadavre outrage"). In *Oxford Readings in Homer's Iliad*, edited by Douglas Cairns, 311–342. Oxford: Oxford University Press, 2001.

Vlastos, Gregory. "The Socratic Elenchos." *Oxford Studies in Ancient Philosophy* 1 (1983): 27–58.

Vlastos, Gregory. "The Socratic Elenchus: Method Is All." In *Socratic Studies*, edited by Myles Burnyeat, 1–37. Cambridge: Cambridge University Press, 1994.

Vogt, Katja M. *Law, Reason, and the Cosmic City*. Oxford: Oxford University Press, 2008.

Warren, Edward. "Consciousness in Plotinus." *Phronesis* 9 (1960): 83–98.

Watson, Nicholas. "Introduction." In *The Cambridge Companion to Medieval English Mysticism*, edited by Samuel Fanous and Vincent Gillespie, 1–28. Cambridge: Cambridge University Press, 2011.

Watts, Daniel. "Kierkegaard and the Search for Self-Knowledge." *European Journal of Philosophy* 21.4 (2013): 525–49.

Windeatt, Barry. *English Mystics of the Middle Ages*. Cambridge: Cambridge University Press, 1994.

Woolf, Raphael. "Socratic Authority." In *Ancient Philosophy of the Self*, edited by Pauliina Remes and Juha Sihvola, 77–107. Dordrecht: Springer, 2008.

Wright, Crispin. "Self-Knowledge: The Wittgensteinian Legacy." In *Knowing Our Own Minds*, edited Crispin Wright, Barry C. Smith, and Cynthia Macdonald, 13–45. Oxford: Clarendon Press, 1998.

Wroe, Anne. *Being Shelley: The Poet's Search for Himself*. London: Vintage, 2008.

Zahavi, Dan. "The Heidelberg School and the Limits of Reflection." In *Consciousness: From Perception to Reflection in the History of Philosophy*, edited by Sara Heinämaa, Vili Lähteenmaki, and Pauliina Remes, 267–85. Dordrecht: Springer, 2007.

Name Index

Concept Index

325